Attachment and Adult Clinical Practice

T0386438

This comprehensive volume addresses attachment theory's history as well as its integration with neurobiology, psychophysiology, theories of emotion, regulation theory, and mentalization theory. It explores how clinicians can connect with their clients so that they feel completely seen and heard.

Attachment theory speaks to one's biological drive to connect, to relate, and to feel heard. The author aims to achieve this by condensing the enormous and diverse literature of the field into a singular, manageable work that clinicians can use to foster these connections. The book traces the history of attachment theory and describes how neurobiological research has influenced the expansion of attachment theory, and how emotions and psychophysiology have become critical to our understanding of human attachment connections. It concludes with a detailed examination of how to apply these theories in clinical practice.

This practical book addresses attachment theory's take on integrating the mind, body, and emotion when striving toward well-being. It will be of great importance for psychotherapy students, beginning therapists, and experienced clinicians with an interest in attachment theory.

Toni Mandelbaum, PhD, LCSW is a clinical social worker in private practice in Philadelphia, PA, with over 25 years of experience in the field. She completed her BA in psychology at the University of Pennsylvania, her MSW at Columbia University, and her PhD in social work at Bryn Mawr College.

Attachment and Adult Clinical Practice

An Integrated Perspective on Developmental Theory, Neurobiology, and Emotional Regulation

Toni Mandelbaum

Routledge
Taylor & Francis Group

LONDON AND NEW YORK

First published 2021
by Routledge
2 Park Square, Milton Park, Abingdon, Oxon OX14 4RN

and by Routledge
52 Vanderbilt Avenue, New York, NY 10017

Routledge is an imprint of the Taylor & Francis Group, an informa business

© 2021 Toni Mandelbaum

British Library Cataloguing-in-Publication Data
A catalogue record for this book is available from the British Library

Library of Congress Cataloging-in-Publication Data
A catalog record has been requested for this book

ISBN: 9780367548544 (hbk)
ISBN: 9780367548537 (pbk)
ISBN: 9781003090878 (ebk)

Typeset in Bembo
by Taylor & Francis Books

To my mom and dad, Melanie and Martin,
who gave me everything;
And to Robbie, Ali, and Jordy, who are my everything.

Contents

Illustrations

Figures

Acknowledgments

I would like to express my deep gratitude to the many people who made this book possible. Thank you to Salman Akhtar for years of sage counsel, for uniquely wise clinical guidance, and for orchestrating this book's coming to fruition. I am forever grateful for meeting June Sroufe at the AAI training and for her constant support, help, and invaluable advice ever after. I remain indebted to Phillip Shaver, who has been a guardian angel in my study of attachment theory. I am incredibly grateful to Ting Liu who has taught me about using emotions in therapy, and to Stephen Porges, Louis Cozolino, Daniel Hill, and Howard Steele who generously offered their time to read chapters and gave much-needed feedback. Any remaining errors are my own.

Every few weeks, Sharon Baker and Diana Holquist read what I had written, gave crisp and perceptive feedback, and provided years of encouragement, for which I'm truly thankful. I offer heartfelt thanks to Mindy Lipman who painstakingly edited my entire manuscript and gave detailed and critical feedback. Thank you to Bryn Mawr College: Graduate School of Social Work and Social Research for graciously giving me full access to their libraries long after I graduated. Chloe Amen was wonderful in her responsiveness and her artistic ability to digitalize my drawings. Melanie Leitner's input on the neurobiology chapter was invaluable as were her weekly cheerleading sessions. Flora Hoodin went above and beyond with her brilliant feedback and consistent encouragement. The book happened largely because of her.

I would like to give overwhelming thanks to my dad for his nurturing of my love of books and for a lifetime of support; to my mom who was my role model and my hero; to my brother Geoff, with his heart of gold who read chapters and, in his incisive way, kept me going; to my children Ali and Jordy, who make me proud every day; and to my husband Robbie, my secure base and safe haven, for the cover design, for pushing me through my doubts, and for his utmost belief in me. Without my family, this could not have been done.

Prologue

I first fell in love with attachment theory in 2000. I was working as a clinical social worker for an agency and was tasked with developing an outcome measure, the fad of the time. To aid in this process, a colleague of mine suggested I look at measures of the relationship between clients and therapists and pointed me in the direction of attachment theory. The moment I began exploring the theory, I knew I had found what I was looking for. A whole world opened up to me, giving me an explanation of relationships that made complete sense. I had always been fascinated by human connection, but now I had a lens; an attachment lens. And so commenced (or continued) my lifelong quest to understand human relationships.

There have been three pivotal moments along my journey that deepened my understanding, inspiring me to question and explore. Shortly after I discovered attachment theory, I started a doctoral program in clinical psychology, focused on attachment theory. A professor, trying to incite me, boldly stated that clinicians (how I defined myself) did not know what they were doing. They were solely working from intuition. Researchers, he said, based everything on numbers. It was true science. I strongly disagreed with him, but did not have enough information to back up my thoughts. At that moment, I resolved to study more, to read as much as possible, and to find a way to put science into practice. Over the years, there have been many who have done just this. Little did I know that their research and ideas, as well as my own thoughts, were to be the foundation of this book.

In addition to my formal studies, I completed the certification process for the Adult Attachment Interview and began attending as many conferences as possible. It was at one of these conferences that I had a second realization. At one symposium, some argued that we must focus on emotion and attachment, while others argued strongly that our thought processes were more critical to the therapeutic process. A heated debate broke out. Their conflict challenged me to think about my beliefs, about what creates change in therapy, and in particular, what about the attachment relationship may bring about change. Do we change because of a corrective emotional experience within a relationship or because of insight that occurs within a relationship or somehow because of both? I read more and more.

There was so much happening in the attachment world, and so many divergent perspectives. As I integrated my studies into my clinical work, I was fascinated by emotion and also by cognition. This fascination was also something that fueled this book.

I then decided to pursue a doctorate in social work and continued to delve further into attachment theory. And I began teaching. During one of my first classes, a student asked if there was a comprehensive book explaining the many sides of attachment theory, from both a theoretical and clinical perspective. The readings were confusing, she said. They used different attachment terms. Some focused on emotion, while others highlighted mentalizing, or being able to think about thinking. Some emphasized the importance of moment-to-moment tracking, while other readings seemed more akin to psychodynamic thought. "How does one conceptualize a case from an attachment perspective?", she asked. "And how does all this neurobiology fit in with everything?" It was in that moment that the third and final piece fell into place and I resolved to try to write this book. And this is what I have worked towards. I have tried to give a comprehensive picture of where attachment theory is currently and how it reached this point. Though this work is far from a complete story, it is my best attempt at condensing the attachment literature into a single story. I hope I convey to the reader my enormous love for what I think of as a theory that explains the human condition.

Introduction

We live in an age where an unprecedented number of Americans are lonely and socially isolated. Newspaper articles from around the world indicate we may be confronting a loneliness epidemic (Holt-Lunstad, 2018) and researchers predict that unless we intervene, loneliness will continue to skyrocket (Holt-Lunstad, Smith, Baker, Harris, & Stephenson, 2015). It has been estimated that over a third of people, or around 42 million individuals, over age 45 feel lonely (Anderson, 2010). Furthermore, surveys document that over the last two decades, the average number of confidants of each individual has decreased by a third. Discussion networks have shrunk and the number of people reporting that they have few to no others with whom to discuss important matters has tripled (McPherson, Smith-Lovin, & Brashears, 2006). Over a quarter of individuals in this country live alone and more than half of adults are not married (Holt-Lunstad, 2018). There is a trend towards delayed marriage, an increase in single-residence households, and a decrease in intergenerational living (Holt-Lunstad, Smith, & Layton, 2010). People are more isolated than ever before.

In part, this is due to several changes in our society. The American sociologist Robert Putnam (2000) documents an alarming trend, reporting that since the late 1960s, there has been a significant decrease in social capital, or "the connections among individuals' social networks and the norms of reciprocity and trustworthiness that arise from them" (p. 19). People no longer participate as actively with religious institutions, in political organizations, or at the workplace, places they may have connected with others. Meeting attendance and club memberships have both declined dramatically. Whereas in the 1970s, two-thirds of Americans belonged to organizations with regular gatherings, such as bowling clubs, in the 1990s, that number dropped to about one-third. Now, most Americans belong to noticeably different types of clubs and organizations; those that are online, without face-to-face meetings or chances to connect in person (Goleman, 2006). Several other demographic trends contribute to our growing isolation. With increased geographic mobility, high divorce rates, smaller families, and an increasing reliance on kin instead of non-kin relationships, it seems our networks are becoming smaller and it is increasingly difficult to connect with others (McPherson et al., 2006; Umberson & Montez, 2010).

The advent of the digital age has furthered the decline in social interactions. Sitting in front of a screen now consumes large portions of our time. Studies show that 41% of American toddlers watch TV for more than two hours a day (Certain & Kahn, 2002), while the average American adult spends over ten hours per day on a screen (Hinckley, 2014). During this time, no face-to-face interaction is occurring. Twenge (2017) documents that on an typical day, high schoolers of the iGen generation, those born after 1995, spend close to six hours a day of their leisure time on a screen. The breakdown is as follows: an average of two and a quarter hours texting, one and a half hours on electronic gaming, two hours on the Internet, and close to a half hour video chatting. Middle schoolers are on new media for close to five hours a day. Given that the average adolescent spends 17 hours a day sleeping, in school, doing homework and school-related activities, it appears that most of teens' free time is spent on the screen. Research confirms that adolescents are spending fewer hours a week socializing in person. Considering that much of our social learning occurs through in-person interactions, time spent online is presumably time lost from learning how to relate.

Twenge (2017) cogently argues that increased screen time usage has had a significant negative effect on the mental health of American teenagers due to the social isolation that results from engaging with new media. Statistics show there has been a considerable increase in loneliness, where close to a third more adolescents felt lonely in 2015 as compared to 2011. Furthermore, rates of teen depression have risen dramatically since 2012, increasing by 21% for boys and by 50% for girls. And suicidality has increased significantly too, where, between 2009 and 2015, the number of high school girls who considered suicide rose by 34%, and the number who actually attempted suicide rose by 43%. Twenge (2017) suggests that these trends are intricately related to the increasing disconnection from in-person relationships, stating that those who spend more time on new media are less likely to be happy, while adolescents who spend more time on activities without a screen are more likely to be happy. Supporting this, a recent study of Facebook users found that taking a break from Facebook increased life satisfaction and promoted positive emotion (Tromholt, 2016). The type of interaction that one experiences online may not be in any way as rewarding as face-to-face interaction. Yet another study (Sherman, Michikyan, & Greenfield, 2013) examined pairs of women engaging in four types of conversations: in-person, video chat, audio chat, and instant messaging. Participants reported feeling much more connected during in-person interactions and significantly less bonded during instant messaging. Thus, it seems in-person interactions are more meaningful than the interactions that occur with digital communication.

Loneliness and social isolation can take an enormous toll on the human body. People with less social connection have been shown to have disrupted sleep patterns, increased blood pressure, more inflammation, cancer, and higher levels of stress hormones (Umberson & Montez, 2010). Studies have found that loneliness can affect the production of white blood cells, which can then impair the immune system's ability to fight infections and recent research suggests that loneliness may be a risk factor for cognitive decline and dementia (Cacioppo, Capitanio, & Cacioppo, 2014). Not only does loneliness negatively affect our physical well-being, but it is related to increased rates of mortality (Holt-Lunstad et al., 2015). Feeling alone is associated with death. In fact, loneliness and social isolation rival well-known risk factors for mortality such as obesity, substance abuse, injury and violence, and mental health issues (Holt-Lunstad et al., 2015).

The emotional ramifications of loneliness and social isolation can be staggering. When Emily Dickinson writes that loneliness is "The Horror not to be surveyed," she speaks to the devastation of feeling alone. Loneliness is linked to anxiety and to emotional stress. Additionally, it is related to and is a risk factor for depression (Cacioppo, Hughes, Waite, Hawkley, & Thisted, 2006) and feeling lonely is related to more negative and less positive affect (Pressman et al., 2005). Social isolation is potentially physically and emotionally damaging to people.

While feeling lonely and experiencing isolation are negative to our well-being, researchers posit the contrapositive, that social connection is vital to our well-being. Not only is it critical to our health, but it may be a biological need (Holt-Lunstad, 2018). There is evidence to suggest that, in fact, the motivation for social connection resulting from isolation is biologically driven. A recent study report that there may be a neural substrate representing feelings of loneliness. A cluster of cells, located in a region near the back of the brain known as the dorsal raphe nucleus (DRN), show increased activity with social contact following periods of social isolation. Mice who were housed together had DRN neurons that weren't very active. However, the animals that were isolated had DRN activity surges when they eventually encountered other mice (Matthews et al., 2016). This seems to indicate that our bodies may be programmed for social contact. We are literally wired to connect.

All in all, social isolation and loneliness are hazardous to our psychological and physical well-being. It is imperative that we combat the growing disconnection in our society. Research confirms the buffering effect of social connection. For instance, results from a meta-analysis (Holt-Lunstad, Smith, & Layton, 2010) suggest that those who are more socially connected have a 50% reduced risk of early death. Relatedly, social support is documented as reducing physiological responses to stressors. Studies find that those who are married are less likely to experience cardiovascular disease in comparison to those with ruptured marriages (Umberson & Montez, 2010). Ultimately, it seems, social connection is what combats loneliness. It follows then that we must understand what connection is, how to engender it, how to enhance relationships, and how to make social connections grow.

This is where attachment theory comes in. It is a theory that is all about social connection. It speaks to our biological drive to connect, to relate, and to feel heard. It is a theory that proposes that relationships are key to our survival. According to this theory, we are programmed to connect. We are wired to be in relation to and with other human beings. Without such a secure connection, our living can be severely compromised.

Organization of the book

This book is written to facilitate the journey into learning about attachment theory. With it, I aim to condense the enormous and diverse literature of the field into a singular, manageable work. I have written the book with a particular focus on how to utilize this theory clinically, to help foster intimate connections and ultimately, to combat loneliness. The first chapter addresses the history of the beginnings of attachment theory, with a focus on John Bowlby, the originator of the theory. The second chapter concerns Mary Ainsworth, the co-founder of attachment theory, who developed the Strange Situation, a way of *measuring* attachment, but only attachment *behaviors* in infants. The third chapter describes the work of Mary Main, who devised the Adult Attachment Interview, a measure of adult states of mind with respect to attachment. This instrument moved the study of attachment from behaviors to mental *representations* of attachment patterns. In the fourth chapter, the history of attachment and romantic relationships is explicated from the perspective of social psychologists, while the fifth chapter concerns infant research and the developmental pathways of attachment. In the sixth chapter, this book describes the neurobiology of attachment, detailing the structures of the brain and its inner workings and the seventh chapter is about psychophysiology, with an emphasis on stress and attachment. In the eight chapter, the study of emotions is explored, with a particular emphasis on emotions and attachment. The ninth chapter defines and explores affect regulation, while the tenth chapter describes the developmental trajectory of affect regulation within the context of the attachment relationship. The chapter delves into the construct of mentalization and compares regulation therapy with mentalization therapy. The eleventh chapter focuses on the client in therapy from an attachment perspective and the last chapter of this book describes the clinician in therapy from an attachment perspective. It explores how we, as clinicians can create change in our clients using attachment theory as a guideline for therapy.

Chapter 1

Attachment theory

History

Attachment theory came into being at another point in history where the harmful consequences of loneliness and socioemotional deprivation were beginning to be understood. In the early 1900s, institutionalized infants were dying at an alarming rate. In fact, in some foundling institutions in the United States, the mortality rate reached as high as 100% (British Medical Journal, 1942). Similarly, hospitalized infants slept less, tended to lose weight, and developed more infections than infants at home. They appeared listless and unhappy. "Hospitalism," or "a vitiated condition of the body due to long confinement in a hospital, or the morbid condition of the atmosphere of a hospital" (Spitz, 1945, p. 53), was first ascribed to malnutrition. Later, those who failed to thrive were diagnosed with nasopharyngitis, or cross-infection (British Medical Journal, 1942). Hospital policies often limited visitation by parents and it was not uncommon for parents to go a year without seeing their children because of the fear of cross-contamination (Karen, 1994). Infants were placed in small cubicles and masked nurses and doctors gingerly tiptoed around, careful not to agitate any bacteria that may have been present. Physical touch was strictly discouraged (Bakwin, 1942). Yet, even with all these safeguards, infants continued to deteriorate in their pristine cubicles and mysteriously recover upon return to their homes.

In the 1940s, researchers began exploring the reasons behind the negative effects of hospitalization on children. Bakwin, a noted pediatrician, questioned existing policy, stating "It is … reasonable to ask whether the measures used to prevent infection may not be harmful to the child" (1942, p. 31). He suggested that human contact may be critical to a baby's well-being, novel thinking for the time. Based on this, new policies were implemented at his place of work, Bellevue Hospital in New York City, encouraging nurses and parents to interact with hospitalized children, to cuddle them, and to visit more often. Not surprisingly, the mortality rate for infants under a year decreased dramatically from 30–35% to under 10% (Van der Host & Van der Veer, 2008). The editors at the *British Medical Journal* concluded that "in infancy the loneliness involved in separation from home may be not only undesirable but lethal" (British Medical Journal, 1942, p. 345).

During this same time period, policies around adoption also dismissed the importance of human contact. Prevailing wisdom dictated that infants remain in institutions until their intellectual abilities and personalities unfolded. This way, adoptive parents could be assured of a fitting match, choosing a child based on what they saw. If the characters of these babies were found wanting, it was assumed that it was because they were the progeny of immoral women who had given birth out of wedlock. The fact that these institutionalized children tended to be sickly was viewed as further evidence of their inferior origins (Emde, 1992). Attachments were discouraged until a child was placed permanently in a home and people went so far as to move a child from home to home to prevent such attachments from forming (Karen, 1994). Spitz challenged these notions, suggesting that the institutionalized babies were perhaps suffering from depression due to socioemotional deprivation. Though his ideas were criticized, Spitz continued his research, documenting what he termed anaclitic depression in infants placed in foundling homes and advocating for increased maternal care, love, and interaction (Spitz, 1945; Spitz, 1946).

These researchers were among the few to challenge existing paradigms. They paved the way for the originator of attachment theory, John Bowlby (1907–1990). Bowlby overturned ideas that were held as irrefutable at the time. He was the first to systematically research and document the devastating impact of maternal separation as well as the incredible importance of a secure bond between caregiver and child.[1] He was an observer of behavior and a broad theoretician capable of thinking outside the box. Drawing from ethology, control theory, psychoanalytic and object relations theory, and Darwinian theories of evolution, he brilliantly challenged and conceptualized divergent thinking, and integrated this into a coherent model of human connection: attachment theory. His theory of love and loss explained why all humans need relationships. In fact, he stated, this need is universal. Bowlby felt that, ultimately, the attachment bond is essential to human survival.

Stages in Bowlby's thinking

Timeline

- 1897 – Freud recanted his trauma theory
- 1907 – John Bowlby born
- 1925 – Entered Trinity College as a medical student
- 1926 – Melanie Klein emigrated from Berlin to London
- 1928 – Volunteered at Priory Gate School, a school for maladjusted children
- 1929 – Continued medical studies at University College Hospital Medical School, began analytic training, including his own analysis with Joan Riviere
- 1933 – Qualified as a doctor, began training in psychiatry
- 1936 – Appointed to the London Child Guidance Clinic as a child psychiatrist
- 1937 – Qualified as an analyst, began supervision with Melanie Klein

- 1938 – Anna Freud, along with her father Sigmund Freud, moved to London to flee persecution
- 1940 – Became an Army psychiatrist, wrote paper "Forty Four Juvenile Thieves: Their Characters and Home-Life" (published in 1944)
- 1941–1944 – The Controversial Discussions took place
- 1944 – Elected Training Secretary of the British Psycho-Analytic Society (served for three years)
- 1946 – Appointed to direct the children's department at the Tavistock Clinic
- 1948 – Commissioned by Ronald Hargreaves, Chief of the Mental Health Section of the World Health Organization (WHO) to study the problems and needs of homeless children; Also hired James Robertson that year
- 1950 – Mary Ainsworth hired by John Bowlby
- 1951 – Wrote the WHO report, two years later published the report in paperback titled "Child Care and the Growth of Love"
- 1952 – Bowlby and Robertson presented the film *A Two-Year-Old Goes to Hospital* to the Royal Society of Medicine in London and to the British Psycho-Analytic Society
- 1953 – Learned of Lorenz and began the study of ethology
- 1954 – Ainsworth moved with her husband to Uganda and began the Ugandan Project
- 1956 – Ainsworth moved to Baltimore
- 1957 – Presented first ("The Nature of the Child's Tie to His Mother") of three papers on Attachment Theory to the British Psycho-Analytic Society
- 1958–1963 – Harlow conducted his monkey studies; Bowlby formally began formulating attachment theory
- 1963 – Ainsworth began the Baltimore Project from which she devised the Strange Situation
- 1964–1979 – Wrote trilogy Attachment (1969), Separation (1973), and Loss (1980)
- 1977 – Mary Main completed her doctorate from John Hopkins University, having studied with Mary Ainsworth, accepted a position at Berkeley and began the Berkeley Longitudinal Study
- 1978 – "Patterns of Attachment" by Ainsworth was published
- 1985 – Main, Kaplan, and Cassidy published the article "Security in Infancy, Childhood, and Adulthood: A Move to the Level of Representation"
- 1990 – Bowlby died.

Past circumstances affect present functioning and more specifically, maternal deprivation could possibly be linked to later disturbed behavior

The roots of Bowlby's interest lie in his own life story. His thinking was shaped by his own experiences as well as by his clinical work and the research he conducted. Born in 1907 to upper-middle class British parents, Edward John

Mostyn Bowlby was the fourth child of six. His was a typical upper middle-class upbringing where he saw his mother at appointed times and was raised primarily by nannies. He was not close to either parent, perceiving his mother as self-involved and distant and his father as rejecting. However, he was particularly attached to a nanny and was devastated when she left her position. At eight, Bowlby was sent to boarding school. Though Bowlby himself didn't acknowledge the impact, it seems likely that his relationship with his parents, the loss of his favorite nanny, and his separation from home at an early age all contributed to his quest to understand the attachment bond and the impact of maternal separation.

Following high school, Bowlby continued his academic journey, studying medicine at Trinity College in Cambridge. However, soon after he began, he took a break and volunteered at two progressive schools, Bedales Junior School and Priory Gate, a school for maladjusted children. It was during this time that the seeds of attachment theory germinated (Karen, 1994; Austrian & Mandelbaum, 2008). "And when I was there, I learned everything that I have known: it was the most valuable six months in my life, really" (Van Dijken, 1998, p. 40), he said of his experience at Priory Gate School. One boy in particular affected him. This boy was expelled from public school for repeated stealing and was friendless and emotionally isolated. As it turned out, his mother had abandoned him as a baby and he had not had a consistent home since. Those at this very progressive school understood that this boy and others like him were reacting to not having had the proper care by a mother figure in their early years. This notion, unusual for the time period, greatly influenced Bowlby's thinking. He came to understand that *past circumstances affect present functioning and more specifically, maternal deprivation could possibly be linked to later disturbed behavior.* His journey towards formulating attachment theory had begun.

Unresolved conflicts from a parent's own childhood can influence his or her interactions with progeny

Once Bowlby left Priory Gate School, he completed his medical degree, trained as a psychiatrist and became a psychoanalyst. From 1936 to 1940, he worked at the London Child Guidance Clinic at Canonbury. Here, he learned a great deal from his social work colleagues Molly Lowden and Nance Fairbairn, more than he would ever learn from his analytic colleagues he has said. Whereas most analysts at that time treated children alone, Lowden and Fairbairn focused on parents' issues as well as the presenting problem in the children. Bowlby recalled two cases that were particularly influential to his developing thinking. The first case involved a father who was very concerned about his son's masturbating and would punish him whenever he caught him touching himself by putting him under cold water. It turned out the father himself had issues with masturbating for most of his life. In the second case, a mother was extremely punitive to her three-year-old daughter because she was envious of a new sibling. The mother soon disclosed that she had always been jealous of her younger brother. Thus, Bowlby recognized that *unresolved conflicts from a parent's own childhood can influence his or her interactions with progeny* (Karen, 1994; Austrian & Mandelbaum, 2008).

Real-life experiences have a very important effect on development

In 1938, Bowlby was extremely honored when he was told he would be supervised by Melanie Klein, a prominent child psychoanalyst, as part of his psychoanalytic training. He very quickly realized he disagreed with her views completely. His first case was a young boy that was hyperactive. Bowlby noticed that the boy's mother, who waited for the boy in the waiting room, seemed extremely anxious. Klein forbade Bowlby to meet with the mother, believing that parents were insignificant to a child's treatment. Three months later, the boy's mother was taken to a mental hospital because she had a breakdown. Melanie Klein was exasperated by this, because now no one could bring the child to treatment. Klein held that the environment was of far less consequence than the inner life of the child. Bowlby has said "'and from that point onwards my mission in life was to demonstrate that *real-life experiences have a very important effect on development*'" (Karen, 1994, p. 46). This demonstrates another critical realization in Bowlby's thinking. He believed that contrary to what his colleagues of the era touted, environment affects development. Because of this, he ascribed to another ideal that Lowden and Fairbairn advocated for: that *families should be involved in the treatment process*, something that was not typically done at that time. One could say that Bowlby was one of the first to practice family therapy. Meanwhile, Bowlby's thinking was becoming more and more dissonant with psychoanalysts of the day.

Maternal loss or separation in early life has devastating consequences

Bowlby began to think about what exactly it is in the environment that affects development. Being a researcher at heart and frustrated by the lack of empirical testing on the part of the British analytic community, he initiated a research project at the Child Guidance Center. He observed young thieves at the center and continued to build upon what he had noticed at Priory Gate School, that something in these kids' backgrounds was contributing to their current behavior, "'an idea that was regarded as mad at the time'" (Karen, 1994, p. 50), he said. From 1936 to 1939, while at the London Child Guidance Clinic at Canonbury, he collected data on 44 juvenile thieves and 44 controls. What emerged from this study was remarkable. In 1944, he published his paper, the first psychoanalytic paper to include statistics. It was titled "Forty-Four Juvenile Thieves: Their Characters and Home-Life." In it, Bowlby reported that of the

44 thieves, 40% had suffered a prolonged separation from a maternal figure in early childhood. In the control group, only 5% had suffered such a loss (Bowlby, 1944). This supported his growing belief that *maternal loss or separation in early life has devastating consequences.*

Bowlby set to work to explore this idea more. Because separation and loss were measurable, he initiated two studies examining these constructs. One study involved children in sanatoriums for tuberculosis who had been separated from their parents for long periods of time. The other study was commissioned by The London Advisory Committee to examine whether or not children should be visited by their parents while in hospital. He hired James Robertson, a social worker, who began to systematically observe children's reactions to separation from parents. He noticed that typically children went through three stages of behavioral responses: protest, despair, and detachment. During the protest stage, children screamed, cried, or exhibited clinging with the threat of separation. The child is anxious and confused at this time, actively seeking the missing parent. During the next stage, despair, the child becomes disinterested in his surrounding environment and seems sad and apathetic. The child seems to be losing hope of a parent's return and seems to be in a state of mourning. During the final phase of detachment, the child actually seems to interact more. However, he becomes nonreactive to his parent upon return (Bowlby, 1969; Karen, 1994).

In 1952, Bowlby and Robertson paired up to make a seminal movie to address maternal separation, a movie that would have an enormous impact on hospital policies and the ideas of attachment theory. It was called *A Two-Year-Old Goes to Hospital*. The film follows a happy but unusually controlled two-year-old girl, Laura, during her nine-day hospital stay for routine hernia surgery. Though visiting typically occurred once a week, Robertson arranged for Laura's parents to visit her every other day. The film documents Laura as she struggles to maintain her composure during this time. She plaintively asks for her "mummy" several times and bursts into tears when she sees her parents on their first visit, begging to return home with them. She grows more and more withdrawn from her parents with each visit, but her quivering lip as she says goodbye reveals her true feelings. On her last day, she independently packs up all of her belongings and walks out of the hospital, declining to take her mother's hand (Robertson, 1953; Karen, 1994).

The film was first shown to a large audience of nurses and doctors and, to the surprise of Bowlby and Robertson, it was not well received. It was criticized for everything from saying that Laura was not distressed at all, to claiming it slandered the medical profession, to declaring that the subject of the film did not represent the general population. Some chastised the film makers for ignoring the fact that Laura was upset by her fantasies towards her pregnant mother and not by the actual separation (Karen, 1994; Van der Horst & Van der Veer, 2008). It would take years for hospitals to implement any changes. But the stage was being set and Bowlby had some more proof of the incredibly negative effects of maternal separation.

Mother's (or a primary caregiver's) love is critical for mental health

As the war ended, more and more children were displaced or homeless. Because of his 44 thieves paper and because he was now known to be interested in maternal deprivation, in 1950, Bowlby was commissioned by Ronald Hargreaves, the chief of the Mental Health Section of the World Health Organization (WHO) to write a report on the psychiatric aspects of the issue of homeless children. Bowlby traveled through Europe and to the United States. Here, he met others who were also noticing that the lack or loss of a mother had grave consequences (Austrian & Mandelbaum, 2008; Van der Horst & Van der Veer, 2008). At the end of his data gathering, he wrote the monograph *Maternal Care and Mental Health* (1951) which was published in the book version *Child Care and the Growth of Love* (Bowlby, 1953). This was to make him a household name. In this monograph, he coined the term "maternal deprivation" and wrote of the devastating consequences of socioemotional deprivation. Based on his prior work and a careful analysis of the available literature in the area, he made strong recommendations on how to avoid or at least mitigate the effects of such deprivation. He concluded with "*What is believed to be essential for mental health is that the infant and young child should experience a warm, intimate and continuous relationship with his mother (or permanent mother-substitute) in which both find satisfaction and enjoyment*" (Bowlby, 1951).

There is a built-in need to form an attachment bond with a specific individual and this bond ultimately promotes survival

At this point, Bowlby had his belief in the necessity of maternal care, but he had no theory to explain why a mother's love is so important to adequate development. There were four main prevailing theories explaining the nature of a child's tie to a caregiver. The first theory, termed Secondary Drive by Bowlby, was proposed by classical psychoanalysis and learning theory. According to this theory, a baby was purported to have two kinds of drives: primary and secondary. Food was thought to be primary and relationships, secondary (Bowlby, 1969; 1988). Also known as the "cupboard-love theory," this model hypothesized that a baby learns to love his mother because she fed him and satisfied his primary drives. Another theory argued that a child has a built-in tendency to orient towards a human breast and to suckle it. In doing so, the baby learns to attach to the breast and to the mother because she has a breast. Bowlby termed this theory Primary Object Sucking. A third theory, termed Primary Object Clinging, talked of an innate need to touch and cling to another human being, and a fourth theory, Primary Return-to-Womb Craving, supposed that babies hankered after returning to the womb and this desire drew them to their mothers (Bowlby, 1969; Karen, 1994). These hypotheses were all inadequate in Bowlby's view.

Bowlby was at a loss of how to explain why a child loves his mother until he happened upon ethology, or the study of animal behavior. The observational style of ethologists appealed to Bowlby, who was frustrated by the limited scope of study by psychoanalysts at the time who mainly delved into case studies. In the 1930s, Konrad Lorenz, considered the founder of modern ethology, pioneered studies of duckling and gosling behavior. He noted that there is a critical period during which animals instinctually form an attachment to an object following exposure to that object. Typically, the object is a parent. Thus, during a specific time period, attachment is directed to a particular, discriminated figure. Once this bond occurs, the specific object will be preferred to others. This process of learning is known as "imprinting" and is established irrespective of any food that is offered (Bowlby, 1969). This was a first strike against Secondary Drive theory.

The results of Harry Harlow's experiments helped consolidate Bowlby's thoughts. Harlow, another ethologist, observed eight infant macaque monkeys, separated from their mothers hours after birth and raised in a laboratory at the University of Wisconsin. His team constructed inanimate mother surrogates, half made of wood covered by cloth and half made of wire. For four infant monkeys, the wire surrogate offered a bottle and the cloth mother did not and for four other infants, the cloth surrogate lactated and the wire mother did not. After 165 days, both groups displayed a noticeable preference for the cloth surrogate, whether they were fed or weren't. This was more evidence that drive-reduction theory may not explain the development of attachment. Furthermore, when faced with fear-producing stimuli, infant monkeys actively sought out cloth mothers, not wire surrogates, in order to allay their fears, indicating that cloth mothers offered a sense of security to startled infants (Harlow & Zimmermann, 1959). Drawing on these observations, Bowlby concluded that the *attachment bond occurs irrespective of oral gratification. There is a built-in need to form an attachment bond with a specific individual and this bond ultimately promotes survival.*

Bowlby wrote about his growing conclusions concerning the nature of the tie between child and caregiver and in 1957, he presented the first of several papers to the British Psycho-Analytic Society titled "The nature of the child's tie to his mother" (Bowlby, 1958). He proposed that an attachment bond is formed with the repetition of genetically based behaviors that, with time, become directed towards a specific caregiver, typically the mother. These behaviors are initiated and terminated when interacting with the attachment figure and eventually form organized patterns. He purported that for human beings attachment behavior was as critical as sexual behavior, and served to ensure protection and survival (Ainsworth & Bowlby, 1991). Two further papers, "Separation anxiety" (1960a) and "Separation anxiety: A critical review of the literature" (1961a), followed, where Bowlby explicated his ideas of the manifestations of distress occurring with the separation from a maternal figure. There were two more papers still, "Grief and mourning in infancy and early childhood" (1960b) and "Processes of mourning" (1961b), detailing the grief and mourning that can ensue with separation and the defenses that arise from the anxiety of loss. Bowlby's ideas were so horribly received that he ultimately stopped attending any meetings to do with the British Psycho-Analytic Society. He was accused of being overly simplistic, of ignoring the internal world, of equating people with animals. With the break from the society, Bowlby spent from 1964 through 1979, writing his trilogy Attachment, Separation, and Loss. In these volumes, he expanded on the ideas he presented in his papers and penned what has come to be known as attachment theory.

Attachment theory

Attachment theory states that a child is predisposed to forming an attachment bond with a caregiver. Bowlby (1973) defined the bond as a relationship that provides a safe haven in times of distress and a "secure base" (Ainsworth, Blehar, Waters, & Wall, 1978) from which to explore the environment when feeling safe. Utilizing control theory and analytical biology to further his understanding, Bowlby proposed this bond to be regulated by adaptive, goal-directed behavioral systems (a term taken from ethology) that have proximity to a caregiver as well as maintaining that caregiver's responsiveness and availability as the expected outcome (Bowlby, 1969; 1973). The attachment bond, a subclass of affectional bonds, comes to have emotional importance for the individual such that closeness and security (labeled felt security by Sroufe & Waters, 1977) is sought and separation induces distress (Fonagy, 2001). The evolutionary function of the child's tie to a caregiver is to ensure survival (Bowlby, 1969).

Behavioral systems

The caregiver–child bond incorporates several classes of behavior, some of which belong to the child and some of which belong to the caregiver. For instance, a caregiver has retrieving behavior designed to maintain proximity to the infant, while the infant has an attachment system that serves to maintain closeness to a caregiver as well as an exploratory system that allows exploration, learning, and play in the surrounding environment. There is a fear system too, the activation of which disables the exploration system and enables the attachment system (Bowlby, 1969). These behavioral systems interact together to achieve a homeostatic balance, moderated by feedback from the involved systems and the surrounding environments. Though the bond evolves into a goal-corrected partnership, or an equal partnership where both parties work together, the bond is asymmetrical at first with the caregiver assuming most of the responsibility for providing security and safety. Thus, a frightened child will seek proximity to an attachment figure (attachment system) and temporarily curtail exploration until he or she feels secure once more. Activation of the attachment system usually instigates behaviors to try to either reestablish contact with the caregiver or to ensure the attachment figure's availability (Kobak, Cassidy, Lyons-Ruth, & Ziv, 2006). Once the child is reassured, the exploration system is stimulated. The systems operate like a seesaw. If a child perceives his caregiver to be available, his attachment system does not need to be galvanized and he is free to explore his environment. As Ainsworth wrote, the exploration system allows growth and learning to occur (Ainsworth et al., 1978). The initiation of the fear system instigates the attachment system's activation. A child seeks proximity to a caregiver. At first, Bowlby only wrote of maintaining physical proximity, but later he developed a cognitive aspect to the attachment system. He believed that a sense of security was not only based on physical closeness. It was based on a child's cognitive appraisal of whether or not his caregiver would be available in times of distress (Bowlby, 1973; Kobak, 1999).

Secure and insecure bonds

Bowlby asserted that though the behavioral systems are instinctual and normative, they are influenced by the surrounding environment, leading to individual differences in each attachment bond (Bowlby, 1969). While everyone forms an attachment bond, Bowlby described each bond as being either secure or insecure (Bowlby, 1973). A child who is securely attached feels sure that his caregiver is available if needed. If a child perceives his caregiver to be available, his attachment system does not need to be activated and he is free to explore his environment. A secure child does a dance, where he explores the environment and then every once in a while checks back in with his caregiver. A secure child can be alone in the presence of the caregiver. It is the insecure child who either hovers around his caregiver or pays no attention to the caregiver. He may develop certain strategies to attempt to engage her and if these strategies do not work, he may develop maladaptive coping strategies. He may become overwhelmed by his distress or he may attempt to shut it down. A secure child is free to explore the environment and to develop. He can practice and master emotional regulation and begin to feel competent, knowing that he has a secure base in the background. An insecurely attached child is uncertain that his caregiver will be available. He expends a great deal of energy trying to preserve his attachment relationship. This may negatively impact his growth trajectory.

The attachment bond is transactional, meaning it develops within the context of a relationship. Bowlby proposed this bond to be mediated by several different behaviors, termed attachment behaviors, including sucking, clinging, following, crying, and smiling, all of which help the infant maintain proximity to an attachment figure. They can be grouped into two classes: signaling behavior, designed to bring the caregiver to the child, and approach behavior, which brings the child to the caregiver. Approach behavior develops later than signaling behavior (Bowlby, 1969). As part of the transactional system, a caregiver needs to accurately interpret these behaviors in order to stay close to her child. A child behaves or communicates in a certain way and, hopefully, the caregiver understands the communication signal. When communication is understood, the child feels secure in the caregiver's availability. He comes to understand that when he communicates his attachment needs, his caregiver will do her best to protect him.

Sroufe and Waters (1977) hypothesized that the attachment behavioral systems are mediated by feeling. They proposed that the affective bond is a metaphor that suggests the positive feeling that occurs within the security and comfort of an attachment bond. Building on Bowlby's work, they suggest that attachment behaviors are organized in the most adaptive way possible to reach the set goal of "felt security" (Sroufe & Waters, 1977) to a caregiver. The expression of feelings is used to aid in meeting this goal. Thus, feelings and behaviors are selected on the basis of which will be most effective, given the present situation. For instance, with a physical threat, such as a snake, the fear system is activated. The child may signal fear and distress to his caregiver by crying or physically trying to establish proximity in order to communicate to a caregiver that he or she needs protection. Expression of anger is another way to let the caregiver know that she is needed. With these behaviors and expressions of emotion, an infant signals that something is wrong and that the caregiver needs to restore proximity. A responsive caregiver accurately interprets these signals and provides the security the child is asking for. If, however, these signals are misinterpreted or if the caregiver is unavailable, a child is left to negotiate the fear or anger he feels without help. He may feel despairing. For example, take a situation where a child angrily yells at his caregiver when she returns from a weekend away. Instead of understanding this as an attachment behavior, that the child is asking to reconnect, the caregiver takes it personally and rebuffs the child. This is exactly the opposite of what the child needed. His protest has not worked and he feels hopeless that his caregiver will protect him. He also feels rejected. He may cry with sadness and this crying is yet another attachment communication signal. It is another opportunity for the caregiver to reestablish proximity and provide protection. Should a caregiver routinely be unavailable, the child will come to understand that he cannot rely on his caregiver for security and protection. His expectations will adjust accordingly.

Internal working model

Bowlby talked of attachment being important across the life cycle, stating "[a]ll of us, from the cradle to the grave, are happiest when life is organized as a series of excursions, long or short, from the secure base provided by our attachment figures" (Bowlby, 1988, p. 62). Bowlby (1973) hypothesized that, across the lifespan, early attachment bonds are internalized and become encoded as "internal working models" (IWM), or mental representations of expectations in interactions in future relationships. With repeated interactions between a child and a primary caregiver, the child's understanding of his caregiver's availability turns into a general paradigm, or a way of understanding himself alone and himself in relation to others. The internal working model becomes a lens through which that child views all subsequent self–other relationships, thereby guiding future encounters. Attachment security and insecurity imply different representational systems. For instance, if a caregiver consistently responds to and understands a child's attachment signals, the child will feel secure in the availability of his caregiver and will develop a secure internal working model. Additionally, he will also come to understand that he is worthy of being cared for and that he is able to have his needs met. However, if a caregiver consistently misinterprets attachment signals or is not available or responsive when a child is distressed, the child will come to feel unsure of that caretaker's availability and may operate with an insecure internal working model. He will feel unloved by his caregivers and may think of himself as unloveable in general. Bowlby believed that these internal working models could potentially be revised should new and different experiences occur with enough frequency. On the whole, however, he viewed mental representations as resistant to change because they usually remain outside of consciousness and often cause individuals to act in self-confirming ways (Main, 1995). Indeed, research has confirmed that, barring trauma, there is substantial continuity of the various attachment organizations throughout the life span (Waters, Weinfield, & Hamilton, 2000; Main, Hesse, & Kaplan, 2005).

Summary

In the context of current increases in loneliness and social isolation, with their concomitant increased toll on mental and physical health, Bowlby's attachment theory is highly relevant. His theory, formulated on the basis of observation of children and infants separated from their primary caregivers, postulates that there is a universal need for an attachment bond. Furthermore, a secure attachment in a child forms if a caregiver is responsive and available to his needs. Likewise, an insecure attachment bond forms if a caregiver is rejecting or unavailable to the child when he is in distress. The various ways of interacting are internalized as internal working models and then generalized to other relationships across the life cycle. Thus, it seems that having that safe haven and secure base is critical to our well-being.

Note

1 Recognizing that caregivers and children can be any gender, for fluency purposes, female pronouns will be used for caregivers and male pronouns will be used for children.

Chapter 2

Mary Ainsworth

Secure base concept

The story of the origins of attachment theory would not be complete without the contributions of Mary Salter Ainsworth (1913–1999), known as the co-author of the theory. It was during Ainsworth's tenure as an undergraduate at the University of Toronto that she met William E. Blatz. She was so influenced by his theory of security that when it came time to work on her dissertation, she eagerly agreed to work with Blatz and focus on studying this theory in more depth (Ainsworth & Bowlby, 1991). According to this theory, infants and children with "secure dependence" on parents are brave enough to explore new situations and environments and build towards "independent security." In other words, children who are certain that their parents will be available, responsive, and protective should they need them, have more courage to take risks by going out to explore the world independently. However, not all reach "independent security," with some remaining "immaturely dependent" and others utilizing defenses to shield against feeling insecure (Bretherton, 2003). Ainsworth's research eventually led her to formulate the concept of a "secure base" in attachment theory (Ainsworth et al., 1978), the bond which provides the springboard for a child to explore the environment when feeling secure.

Maternal sensitivity

After marrying Leonard Ainsworth in 1950, Ainsworth moved with him to England so that he could enter PhD training at the University of London. Shortly thereafter, she was hired by John Bowlby to work as a developmental researcher at the Tavistock Clinic. This was the beginning of an extremely fruitful collaboration. After reading Bowlby's WHO report and also studying ethology, Ainsworth decided she would like to test his theory empirically and effectively spent the rest of her working life doing so. In 1954, Ainsworth moved to Uganda, where her husband began a research appointment. She began a pioneering naturalistic study, where, with little help, she collected data on 26 mothers and infants and observed and documented what attachment really is. She concluded that mothers who tended to be responsive and sensitive to their babies' signals had infants who cried less and seemed more securely attached by the end of their first year. She noted that security was not due to the amount of time spent with a child, but rather to the contingency of a mother's reactions to a child's signals (Ainsworth & Bowlby, 1991). It was Ainsworth who defined maternal sensitivity, stating that

> [t]he optimally sensitive mother is able to see things from her baby's point of view. She is alert to perceive her baby's signals, interprets them accurately, and responds appropriately and promptly, unless no response is what he seems to want, and when she does not she is tactful in acknowledging his communication. Furthermore she makes her responses temporally contingent upon the baby's signals.
>
> (Ainsworth et al., 1978, p. 142)

Attachment styles

In 1963, shortly after having moved to Baltimore, Ainsworth began the Baltimore Study. Here, she revolutionized the study of attachment theory when she devised the Strange Situation. In a laboratory setting, an infant's fear system and attachment system are intentionally activated when his or her parent leaves the room. They are further activated when a stranger enters the room and the infant's behavior is then observed when the parent returns. Ainsworth said

> I thought, Well let's work it all out: We'll have the mother and baby together in a strange environment with a lot of toys to invite exploration. Then we'll introduce a stranger when the mother's still there, and see how the baby responds. Then we'll have a separation situation where the mother leaves the baby with the stranger. How does the baby respond to the departure? And when the mother returns, how does the baby respond to the reunion? But since the stranger was in the room during the first departure, maybe we'd better have an episode in which the mother leaves the baby entirely alone. Then we could see whether the return of the stranger would lessen whatever distress has occurred. Finally, we'll have another reunion with the mother. We devised this think in half an hour.
>
> (Karen, 1994, p. 147)

Ainsworth observed 26 infant–caregiver pairs, watching their behavior at separation and at reunion with their caregiver. She aimed to ascertain how the infant had organized his attachment behaviors when the attachment system is activated and sought to identify individual differences in behavior patterns. From her observations, Ainsworth noted three general patterns of behavior exhibited by the infants. She called them groups A, B, and C. Some babies showed signs of missing the parent during separation and then actively greeting the parent when the parent returned. They were also able to return to play. Though the stranger could somewhat comfort them, it was not as adequate as the comfort they received from their primary caregiver. These were termed securely attached (B). Some were preoccupied with the parent throughout the situation, seeming maybe angry or passive, and then were unable to settle down when their parent returned. They were called ambivalent or resistant in their attachment (C). And some babies avoided or ignored the parent on reunion, showing little emotion when the parent returned. If picked up, they did not cling to the caregiver or protest being let go. For most, the presence of a stranger was not distressing and they focused mostly on the toys or the environment throughout the procedure. They were called avoidantly attached (A) (Ainsworth et al., 1978). In general, 55–60% of children in community samples are securely attached, 10–15% are ambivalent/resistant, and 20–25% have an avoidant pattern (Steele & Steele, 2008).

Ainsworth gathered more evidence for maternal sensitivity, documenting a connection between secure infants and mothers who had behaved most sensitively during the first three months of life. Mothers of avoidant infants had tended to be more rejecting and mothers of ambivalent infants had been inconsistent in their availability to their infants, sometimes being sensitive while at other times rejecting their progeny (Bretherton, 2003).

Secure, insecure/avoidant, and insecure/ambivalent attachment behavioral patterns can be seen as situation-specific strategies developed by the infant in order to maintain proximity to the caregiver. With variations in caregiving environments, infants and children must develop differing conditional strategies to adapt to their particular circumstances (Main, 1990). Thus, an infant must customize his behavior, feelings, memory, perception, cognition, and attention in order to assure himself the optimal chance of staying close to his caregiver. An infant who has a responsive caregiver will learn that the primary strategies he implements to achieve the goal of felt security will work. This increases his sense of efficacy and with repeated interactions, he learns he has the ability to tolerate negative emotion and situations. However, if an infant's primary strategy doesn't work and he is consistently met with an unresponsive and/or unavailable caregiver, he must learn other ways of staying close to his caregiver if he is to ensure survival (Cassidy, 1994). Attachment theorists call these other ways of maintaining the attachment bond secondary attachment strategies, where primary strategies must be overridden in order to attain the main goal of proximity to a caregiver. In other words, secondary conditional strategies involve actively changing or manipulating the instinctive behaviors of an attachment behavioral system. Both primary and secondary strategies are seen as adaptive initially in that they aid the individual in achieving the necessary goal of proximity to a caregiver (Main, 1990).

Theorists hypothesize that the strategies have two different configurations: deactivation and hyperactivation (Main, 1990; Shaver & Mikulincer, 2009). Deactivation involves the minimizing of attachment needs. Studies suggest that insecure/avoidant infants have been often rejected by caregivers, particularly when they needed help with distress (Ainsworth et al., 1978). With the ultimate goal of any attachment bond being proximity to an attachment figure, it is suggested that minimizing emotions and attachment needs may help as it ostensibly decreases the risk of being rejected. In other words, if an infant with a rejecting caregiver makes few demands on that caregiver, the caregiver is less likely to reject him (Cassidy, 1994). Caregivers who punish bids for closeness discourage infants from seeking them out. These infants attempt to suppress their attachment systems and develop a strategy Bowlby termed compulsive self-reliance (Bowlby, 1969/1982), or "flight" reactions according to the fight–flight distinction (Mikulincer & Shaver, 2007). Thus, the deactivation strategy may be adaptive in that particular caregiving arrangement, but may develop into maladaptive ways of interacting in general.

Insecure/ambivalent infants may heighten their emotional expression in an attempt to engage an inconsistently available caregiver. It is hypothesized that hyperactivating strategies serve to engage caregivers who are unpredictable and difficult to engage. According to the psychology of learning, if a behavior is unpredictably or only sometimes reinforced, the behavior may intensify. This increases the odds of receiving the reward as the child cannot predict when it will happen and has to keep up the behavior just in case (Daniel, 2015). Thus, by increasing their dependence needs on an attachment figure, these infants may have a better chance of engaging a caregiver when needed. These infants may exaggerate fearfulness or emotionality so that they can increase their odds of having a caregiver who may respond to their needs (Cassidy, 1994). In terms of fight or flight, hyperactivating strategies are "fight" reactions, or as Bowlby (1973) stated, "protest" responses to unmet attachment needs. He suggested this strategy could be adaptive with an inconsistently available caregiver, but maladaptive because it can interfere in interacting with others as well as with learning and exploring the environment. Additionally, the child is not calmed by the caregiver, like a secure child would be (Daniel, 2015).

We can now understand the Strange Situation classifications in terms of primary and secondary strategies. The B (secure) infants are seen as utilizing primary strategies, while the A (avoidantly attached) and C (ambivalently attached) infants inhibit ineffective primary strategies in order to implement secondary strategies. In effect, secure infants only need to access the attention of their caregivers, while insecure infants must negotiate the environmental stressors as well as adapting to their caregivers' needs (Main, 1990). Another way of understanding this dynamic is by examining the infant's flexibility or inflexibility of attention. Securely attached infants can flexibly vary their attention between attachment and exploratory behavior. In contrast, avoidant infants consistently shift attention *away* from parents and focus on exploration and the inanimate environment, such as on the toys in the room. Again, this may be an adaptive strategy to maintain proximity to rejecting caregivers. Insecure/ambivalent infants persistently turn their attention *toward* a caregiver as a strategy to engage an inconsistently available caregiver and have difficulty exploring the surrounding environment. By focusing attention on the caregiver, the infant or child is maximizing the chance that the caregiver will respond positively to attachment needs (Main & Hesse, 1990). In other words, for those who are insecurely attached, there is an imbalance between exploration and attachment behavior where shifting or restricting attention is used to maintain proximity. This leads to a certain inflexibility in focus, whereas secure infants are able to flexibly shift attention to maintain the attachment bond (Main, Hesse, & Kaplan, 2005).

The Strange Situation has come to be used widely as a tool for assessing the quality of infant–mother attachment as well as for measuring attachment styles. Because of the results from the Strange Situation, attachment behavior was now divided into three categories: secure, ambivalent/resistant, and avoidant. Later on, a former student of Ainsworth's, Mary Main, along with Eric Hesse and Judith Solomon, introduced a fourth classification, that of disorganized attachment (Main & Hesse, 1990; Main & Solomon, 1990). In several earlier studies, there were children who were difficult to classify with the A, B, C system because they had no observable organized, coherent strategy to negotiate separations or reunions. When researchers forced an assignment to the best fitting traditional classification, many unclassifiable infants were misidentified as "secure." Main and Solomon (1990) reviewed the data and concluded that infants who were termed unclassifiable exhibited conflicted patterns of behavior where there were sequential or simultaneous attempts to approach and to avoid attachment figures. These infants often froze, displayed odd behavior, or had undirected or asymmetrical movements. Main and Solomon chose the term "disorganized and/or disoriented" (D) to describe these unclassifiable infants. Main and Hesse (1990) hypothesized that D infants may experience their primary caregivers as frightening. When their attachment systems are activated, the usual strategy of seeking proximity to these caregivers fails. These infants therefore are placed in an irremediable bind where the "secure" base is also a source of threat. This leads to the observed disorganized behavior, termed "conflict behaviors" by ethologists, or behaviors that occur because of the concurrent instigation of opposing behavioral systems. The four classifications, A, B, C, and D, continue to be used in the study of attachment.

Empirical research

Though the Strange Situation was proving to be a reliable measure, there was still no way of knowing whether measured attachment security or insecurity meant anything other than simply a discrete behavior existing in the context of the caregiver–infant dyadic relationship. For the most part, with the exception of the Strange Situation research, Bowlby's theory still remained a thought exercise, with little empirical data to back his hypotheses. At the same time, in the 1960s and 1970s, while attachment theory was still emerging, developmental psychology faced many challenges. Opponents of attachment theory, such as Jerome Kagan (1984), purported that early experiences did not impact later functioning, stating that life was like a recorder constantly recording new happenings and overriding earlier experiences, with no stability or continuity through the life cycle. Others asserted that the constructs of personality and attachment were meaningless because an individual's behavior was inconsistent and changeable across contexts and time (Sroufe, 2016; Sroufe, Coffino, & Carlson, 2010). The scene was set for researchers like Alan Sroufe, Byron Egeland, Everett Waters, and Karin and Klaus Grossmann to *prove* what Bowlby proposed; that early experience matters and that the caregiver–child dyad is critical to adaptive, psychosocial functioning throughout the life cycle.

First in line to challenge the concept of a lack of continuity in attachment was Everett Waters, a graduate student of Mary Ainsworth's in the 1970s. Using the Strange Situation, he assessed 50 babies at 12 months old and then again at 18 months and found that remarkably, 48 out of 50 classifications remained constant over the six month period (Waters, 1978). Galvanized by these results, Alan Sroufe, a professor at the Institute of Child Development at the University of Minnesota, took the baton and ran with it, instigating the first longitudinal outcome study of attachment. Because of Waters' study, Sroufe had access to a group of toddlers with known attachment histories. He gathered a team and set up a study to investigate the competence of two year olds. Each subject had to figure out how to put two sticks together to make a single stick inside a tube, a task that invariably required assistance from an adult. The researchers were amazed by the results. In comparison to those who were insecurely attached, those who were securely attached managed their stress better, demonstrated more enthusiasm for the task, took instructions better, were more persistent, and were able to cooperate better with their caregivers. While securely attached children did demonstrate opposition when asked to clean up, when it came to performing the task, not only did they comply, but they were able to successfully engage the help of their caregivers to achieve success. Insecurely attached children, on the other hand, were noncompliant during the task as well as during cleanup (Matas, Arend, & Sroufe, 1978; Karen, 1994).

Up until this point, studies were conducted on middle-class subjects. In 1974, Byron Egeland, Sroufe's colleague at the University of Minnesota, initiated a study of high-risk, low-income expectant mothers. Soon, Sroufe and Egeland combined their efforts to form what became known as the Minnesota Study of Risk and Adaptation from Birth to Adulthood. The study followed 180 individuals in poverty from infancy to age 34, utilizing a broad and comprehensive range of measures examining many domains of development (Sroufe, Egeland, Carlson, & Collins, 2005a; Sroufe, Egeland, Carlson, & Collins, 2005b; Sroufe et al., 2010).

Does the Strange Situation measure more than random behavior? What does the measured behavior mean for later functioning?

From the beginning, results of the Minnesota Study were startling. Children in school with secure attachment histories had better self-esteem and possessed more ego resiliency. Socially, securely attached children, in comparison to insecurely attached children, were more able to initiate contact with other children, responded better when approached, displayed more empathy for those who were upset, and had more friends. Despite counter-predictions from behaviorists, it was the ambivalently attached children who demonstrated high levels of dependency, while the securely attached children were more independent. Furthermore, those with secure attachment histories were more able to play creatively and imaginatively. These children were less likely to bully or to be bullied, while ambivalently attached children tended to be victimized and avoidantly attached children were inclined to bully. Adolescents with secure attachment histories continued to display more adaptive relational skills (Karen, 1994). They were able to better negotiate the dynamics of mixed gender groups and in early adulthood, to experience more intimacy in romantic relationships. Furthermore, better school achievement was also related to attachment security. Indeed, based on attachment, researchers were able to predict by age three and a half who would later drop out of school. Lastly, signs of psychopathology were found to be related to the early infant–caregiver attachment patterns, where disorganized infants were more likely to display indications of psychopathology as adolescents and adults (Sroufe et al., 2010; Sroufe, 2016).

Thus, after 34 years, Sroufe and his colleagues (2005a) accumulated enough empirical evidence to assert that Bowlby's original supposition had merit and that "nothing is more important in the development of the child than the care received, including that in the early years" (p. 2). The early caregiver–infant relationship was now shown to directly affect differences in attachment quality and to impact many aspects of developmental functioning. What is more, assessments of the early attachment relationship were better than any measure of individual infant behavior at predicting later functioning in relationships as well as individually (Sroufe et al., 2005a; Sroufe, 2016). All of these results were irrespective of an infant's temperament. In fact, no studies have yet found a link between Ainsworth's Strange Situation's attachment patterns and temperament, further supporting the idea that the quality of attachment is related to the relational experience with a primary caregiver (Sroufe et al., 2010).

While Sroufe and his colleagues were studying a high-risk sample in the United States, the Grossmanns (Grossmann, Grossmann, & Kindler, 2005) teamed up to investigate a middle-class sample in Germany. They initiated two longitudinal studies in the mid-1970s: the Beilfeld Project and the Regensburg Project. Their results confirmed what Sroufe's group had found; that a child's attachment strategy significantly predicted young adult and partnership representation. At age 22, in comparison to those with insecure attachment histories, those with secure attachment histories were more able to ask for help, communicate emotions when distressed, regulate emotions when facing challenging social encounters, and to value relationships. Groh and colleagues (2014) recently conducted a meta-analytic review of the research on the emotional and social sequelae of early attachment security. Their results provided further evidence that there is a relationship between early attachment security and higher levels of social competence. These predictive effects endured from childhood into adolescence.

What is the role of the caregiver in the quality of attachment?

Study after study confirmed that mothers of securely attached children demonstrate a high degree of sensitivity over time. Indeed, mothers of secure toddlers in Matas, Arend, and Sroufe's (1978) study were supportive and helpful during a difficult task, while mothers of insecure toddlers were not as helpful and were either too intrusive, interfering when a child struggled, or were uninvolved, hanging back and offering little aid. In comparison to mothers of ambivalently attached children, mothers of those who were securely attached were more cooperative and sensitive when feeding, showing more awareness of their children's cries and pacing the process by accurately reading cues. They also demonstrated more physical affection. Meanwhile, mothers of avoidantly attached children displayed the least amount of insight and psychological awareness. They tended to be less effective when feeding their children and often seemed to avoid physical affection. Caregivers of ambivalently attached children had more trouble setting limits and boundaries and mothers of disorganized infants displayed insensitive and often-times intrusive caregiving. They also were more likely to mistreat their children (Sroufe et al., 2005a; Sroufe et al., 2005b).

The longitudinal study conducted by the Grossmanns analyzed mothers and fathers and their interactions with their children. The study emphasized that a secure attachment relationship not only provided a haven in times of distress, but also encouraged exploration when feeling safe. Thus, sensitivity was defined as not only providing support and appropriate scaffolding during difficult tasks, but also included the promotion of exploration and becoming competent in the environment. With this expanded definition, the researchers confirmed that maternal sensitivity and support during the early years predicted later security of attachment. With regards to fathers, the researchers chose to use the word "facilitation" instead of "sensitivity" because they noticed that while most fathers would not try to provide comfort themselves, they would respond to their children's distress by handing them off to their mothers. Results indicated that fathers' facilitation and support during childhood, especially when combined with maternal sensitivity, significantly predicted attachment classifications in early adulthood, meaning fathers were just as influential as mothers were in defining internal working models of attachment. This can be extrapolated to mean that all caregivers play a role in a child's later attachment representation (Grossmann et al., 2005).

Is there evidence of an "internal working model"? Along those lines, does attachment behavior remain constant throughout development?

Thirty-four years after the start of their longitudinal study, Sroufe and his colleagues (2005a) concluded "that change, as well as continuity, in individual development is coherent and lawful" (p. 2). Across development, attachment patterns were likely to remain stable, barring major occurrences or fluctuations. For instance, increases or decreases in perceived stress as well as changing levels of social support impacted attachment security across the life cycle (Sroufe, 2016). In their longitudinal study, Crowell and Waters (2005) found the same thing; there was a 72% correspondence between the four-way classifications of the Strange Situation and the Adult Attachment Interview results 20 years later. Change in attachment status was lawful in that it only occurred with significant challenges, such as a death or serious illness of a close family member.

How does early experience interact with later experience and affect development? How does attachment fit into the developmental process?

With regards to this question, Sroufe and his colleagues (2005a) concluded from their longitudinal study that not only are "individuals … always impacted by the entire history of cumulative experience, and even following periods of dramatic change, early experience is not erased," but "that ultimately, the individual person can only be understood within a model of continuing transactions between developing persons and the supports and challenges they are facing" (p. 2). Evidence supports that early experiences are never erased, as Kagan (1984) had suggested. As Bowlby (1973) had proposed, the development of attachment can be viewed with the lens of a pathway/process model, where early and later experiences interacted together to shape outcomes.

When interpreting the results of the Minnesota Longitudinal study, some caution is necessary. It is tempting to conclude that the attachment relationship predicts all aspects of psychosocial functioning. However, this is not the case. Attachment is a critical component in the dynamic development of a person's adaptive functioning, but it is not the only factor to affect development (Sroufe et al., 2010). For instance, while attachment was a predictor of who would drop out of school, parental support during the problem solving task at age three and a half was a far better predictor. Furthermore, though attachment history explained being able to form and keep reciprocal friendships, adding the quality of parental scaffolding into the mix explained "friendship competence" far better than attachment alone (Sroufe, 2016).

To reiterate, the definition of an attachment bond is a relationship that provides a safe haven in times of distress and a "secure base" (Ainsworth et al., 1978) from which to explore the environment when feeling safe (Bowlby, 1973). However, in addition to serving as a secure base, parents have many other purposes, such as providing a child with stimulation, guidance, limit-setting, and encouraging socialization. Though these abilities may relate to attachment security, they are not one and the same. Even when providing a secure base, a caregiver can be competent in some areas and not as competent in others. For instance, a mother may be sensitive to feeding cues, but be unable to discipline clearly. Too, a caregiver can be insensitive to a child when he is upset, but may be able to facilitate outside friendships for that child. In addition to parental influences on attachment, there are other factors that predict outcome. These include the external environment, neighborhoods, cohorts, schools, and income level, all of which are known to impact development (Sroufe, 2016).

Additionally, attachment experiences impact the interpretation of social interactions. The lens through which an individual looks at all relationships affects how he or she approaches specific relationships. It is a recursive experience, where expectations of availability or lack of availability can govern an individual's actions and thereby affect the elicited response. This can be seen in the caregiver–child relationship, where parental sensitivity reinforces a sense of security, which then leads to a child's responding well to a parent, which encourages the parent to continue to be sensitive (Thompson, 2016). In social situations, for example, an individual who expects to be rejected because of prior experience may retreat from the approach of someone who is trying to befriend him. That can cause the "befriender" to pull back too, and may then be perceived by the "befriendee" as a rejection. This interaction will reinforce that individual's expectations that he should withdraw in the future because he will be rejected. In other words, security of attachment may not only predict psychosocial outcomes, but may influence or moderate aspects of relationships that may impact outcomes (Thompson, 2016). Because there are multiple factors influencing an attachment relationship, the development of attachment is hardly linear. Overall, it can be viewed as a dynamic, transactional construct, one that influences and is influenced by early and later relationships, family experiences, and social factors (Sroufe et al., 2005b). According to this line of thinking, personality is not predetermined, but shaped by experience and interactions with the environment and according to attachment theory, it is the quality of the attachment relationship in particular that affects development.

Summary

Ainsworth's work was critical to the development of attachment theory. Her Strange Situation was monumental in that it provided a way to measure infant attachment and enabled researchers to contribute to the growing empirical body of knowledge in the field. Ainsworth's division of attachment into secure, ambivalent, and avoidant was even more monumental, as there was now a more in-depth framework to understand different attachment patterns. And her focus on the construct of maternal sensitivity has also served as a foundation for our understanding of a caregiver's role in the development of attachment security. The longitudinal studies that emerged because of the work of Bowlby and Ainsworth have allowed us to grasp what underlies optimal socio-emotional functioning.

Chapter 3

The Adult Attachment Interview

Up until this point, the focus of study had been on infant *behavior*. The next wave of research moved the study of attachment from behavioral observation to the *representational* world. The field of attachment was to change once more. In 1985, Mary Main, along with her colleagues (Main & Goldwyn, 1998), revolutionized the study of attachment when they devised a measure called the Adult Attachment Interview (AAI). The seminal paper "Security in infancy, childhood, and adult-hood: A move to the level of representation" (Main, Kaplan, & Cassidy, 1985) detailed the interview and moved the study of attachment from behavioral obser-vation to glimpses into the representational world. The interview had evolved somewhat by chance when a group of researchers, led by Mary Main, noticed a pattern between a mother's linguistic responses to an interview about attach-ment experiences and that mother's child's strange situation classification. It seemed that an individual's use of language around attachment-related material was somehow related to his way of organizing his attachment system. Until this time, research in the attachment field had focused almost exclusively on beha-viors. The AAI allowed investigators to gain insight into the underlying orga-nizational structures of the self, or what Bowlby had termed the internal working model (Bowlby, 1969/1982, 1973, 1980). Language became a window into an individual's representation of attachment.

Now known as one of the most influential thinkers in attachment theory, Main's path to studying attachment theory was somewhat circuitous. She began her career hoping to obtain a doctorate in linguistics, having a lifelong passion for language. After completing her bachelor's degree at St. John's College in Annapolis, she married one of her professors and therefore, ended up staying in the area. She applied to Johns Hopkins, hoping to study psycholinguistics with James Deese, a prominent linguist. Instead, Main was accepted by Mary Ains-worth to study infant–mother attachment. Main's husband convinced her that studying babies would further her understanding of language (Karen, 1994). This decision was to change the course of the study of adult attachment.

Main's ideas around attachment were influenced by a Robertson film she happened to see. In 1971, James Robertson filmed *Thomas: Ten Days in Foster Care* (Robertson & Robertson, 1971) where he documents two-year-old

Thomas's reactions during his ten day stay with the Robertsons while his mother was in hospital having her second child. When watching this movie, Main was particularly struck by Thomas's changing responses to a photograph of his mother. At first, he kissed the photograph and seemed happy to see the depiction of his mother. As time went on, however, he seemed increasingly agitated by the image and eventually completely avoided the photograph. Main concluded that because the actual photograph had remained the same, it must have been Thomas's perception or feelings about his mother or about himself in relation to her that had changed. Something internal seemed to have shifted (Karen, 1994).

Based on this observation, Main hypothesized that individual differences in behavior may be the result of differences in thinking, language, memory, and attention; factors that guide and influence resulting behavior. Thus, in the mid-1970s, when Main relocated to the University of California, Berkeley, she and another graduate student, Donna Weston, began a longitudinal study of middle-class families that ultimately focused on better understanding children's representational products, such as language and drawings of families, and responses to attachment representations. One hundred eighty-nine Bay Area middle-to upper-middle-class families were chosen from birth records and 84% of those participated in the study. During the first phase of what became known as the Berkeley Longitudinal Study, children at 12 or 18 months received a strange situation classification with both mother and father. Six years later, in 1982, Main and graduate students Nancy Kaplan, Carol George, and an assistant named Ruth Goldwyn assessed the same children for their under-lying attachment patterns. They examined the responses to the parents after an hour-long separation. Additionally, using an adapted version of the Separation Anxiety Test (SAT), Kaplan showed each child several drawings of children and parents separating and then a photograph of that child with his family when they had first arrived at the lab. The child was asked what the child in the picture might feel as well as what he may do and their responses were recorded. The SAT text was scored as secure if (1) the child expressed sadness, anger, or any other type of distress, and if (2) the child could suggest an adaptive solution. Main and Kaplan suggested that the way that these children spoke about the drawings and the photographs represented their internalized attachment experiences, particularly if they were able to show valuing of attachment and to autonomously construct a resolution to their distress (Karen, 1994; Main, Hesse, & Kaplan, 2005).

This line of thought indicated how Main had begun to think of individual differences in attachment. It was not a result of different behaviors, she hypothesized. In fact, she was becoming increasingly convinced that behaviors are actually manifestations of how attachment experiences have been internally structured and organized. Whereas Bowlby's conceptualization of internal working models centered on a structure that enabled the appraisal of accessibility and availability of attachment figures and influenced the individual's actions accordingly (Bowlby, 1969/1982, 1973), Main and colleagues (Main, Kaplan, & Cassidy, 1985) saw the construct as encompassing much more. They expanded the definition to include "a set of conscious and/or unconscious rules for the organization of information relevant to attachment and for obtaining or limiting access to that information, that is, to information regarding attachment-related experiences, feelings, and ideations" (p. 67). The development of the understanding of individual differences in attachment allowed Main and her colleagues to begin investigating attachment representations in older children and in adults. Now internal models could be seen as not only affecting behavior as part of a behavioral system, but also affecting memory, cognition, and attention in relation to attachment. Thus, the representational level of speech came to be seen as a reflection of underlying representational attachment organizations (Main, Kaplan, & Cassidy, 1985).

With this in mind, Main suggested that two of her graduate students, Carol George and Nancy Kaplan, conduct interviews with the parents of the six-year-olds, asking attachment-related questions in order to gather life histories. Initially, Main was struck by a particular interviewee's responses to the attachment-related questions, noticing a remarkable similarity between how the subject spoke related to her child's behavior (Hesse, 2016). Ruth Goldwyn and Main set to work analyzing these interviews. Amazingly, the researchers noticed a consistently strong connection between parents' responses to the interviews and their children's strange situation classification. In other words, how an individual spoke about attachment-related experiences was related to his child's attachment organization. Parents who answered in a coherent manner were more likely to have secure children whereas incoherence in parents was associated with insecurely attached children (Main, Kaplan, & Cassidy, 1985; Karen, 1994). Thus, Main returned to her first interest, the study of language, and the stage was set for the Adult Attachment Interview, a measure that continues to be one of the best ways of evaluating adult state of mind with respect to attachment.

The Adult Attachment Interview (AAI)

What is the AAI?

The AAI is a structured, 20-question, semi-clinical interview that focuses on an individual's early attachment-related experiences and the resulting perceived effects. The questions are given in a specific order, asking interviewees to describe their relationships with their parents, to speak to salient separations that may have occurred, to discuss any feelings of rejection they may have felt, as well as to address any experiences of loss, abuse, or trauma. Early in the interview, speakers are asked to produce five specific adjectives describing the relationship with each parent and then are asked for specific incidents or memories for each chosen adjective. They are asked how their parents reacted to them being upset, hurt, or ill. At the close of the interview, speakers are asked whether they have suffered any setbacks and how they feel these experiences have impacted their development. The interview takes one to one-and-a-half hours to administer and once finished, is transcribed verbatim, including any pauses, to be readied for coding. There is no mention, however, of bodily reactions or nonverbal occurrences, which is in keeping with Main's return to her linguistic roots (Main & Goldwyn, 1998; Hesse, 2016).

The following is an example of a shortened version of the AAI protocol. While it is not the actual AAI and should not be used as such, it gives an idea of how the interview flows.

Brief Precis of the Adult Attachment Interview (AAI) Protocol

1 To begin with, could you just help me to get a little bit oriented to your family – for example, who was in your immediate family, and where you lived?
2 Now I'd like you to try to describe your relationship with your parents as a young child, starting as far back as you can remember.
3 Now, I'd like you to choose five adjectives or words that reflect your relationship with your mother, starting as far back as you can remember in early childhood – as early as you can go, but say, age 5 to 12 is fine. I know this may take a bit of time, so go ahead and think for a minute …. Then I'll ask you why you chose them. I'll write each one down as you give them to me. (Repeat for father and/or any other adult involved in raising the speaker.)
4 To which parent did you feel closer, and why?
5 Could you describe your first separation from your parents?
6 How do you think your overall early experiences have affected your adult personality? Are there any aspects you consider a setback to your development?
7 Why do you think your parents behaved as they did during your childhood?
8 What is your relationship with your parents like for you currently?
(Adapted from Hesse, 2016, p. 554)

The goal of the interview is to ascertain the speaker's current state of mind with respect to attachment, or his strategy for organizing behavior, feelings, and thoughts around attachment-related material. This is done by examining the way language is used (Steele & Steele, 2008). George and colleagues (Hesse, 2016) have noted that the interview can be seen as "surprising the unconscious," where the interview actually creates a stressful situation that initiates the interviewee's attachment system. In doing so, the individual's underlying attachment organization, as represented by language, comes into play. Hesse (2016) has stated that the "central task the interview presents to participants is that of (1) producing and reflecting on memories related to attachment, while

simultaneously (2) maintaining coherent, collaborative discourse with the interviewer" (p. 556). In other words, speakers are asked to function at a cognitive level
by providing semantic, or evaluative, memories of attachment-related experiences
that must then match their episodic, or sensory, memories of the same events
(Main, Hesse, & Goldwyn, 2008; Steele & Steele, 2008). This is challenging for
most. Throughout the protocol, the speaker must provide succinct, consistent, and
clear evidence for what is said. Not only must the participant access stories to
support what he is saying, but he must integrate these stories into an overall
coherent presentation (Hesse, 2016).

Think back to the concept of attention shifting. Just as in the Strange
Situation where an infant must flexibly shift attention between the inanimate
environment and a caregiver who provides a safe haven, during the AAI, an
individual is required to fluidly alternate attention between attachment-related
memories and interacting with the interviewer in a coherent manner (Hesse,
1996). Inevitably, emotions are aroused by the content that is elicited. To
maintain a coherent discourse, the speaker must move attention away from
overwhelming emotion and talk with perspective about his experiences. He must
fluidly shift between presenting his story to a third party and then evaluating the
effects of these attachment-related experiences. Those who are unable to flexibly
and successfully shift attention tend to utilize one of two "maladaptive" strategies:
minimizing or dismissing difficulties by shifting attention away from past attachment experiences or maximizing or paying too much attention to attachment-
related troubles by focusing insistently on them (Hesse, 2016; Main, Hesse, &
Goldwyn, 2008; Steele & Steele, 2008).

Categories of the AAI

A classification and coding system was devised for the AAI based on patterns
of speech. At first, adult states of mind with respect to attachment were
divided into three: secure (F), dismissing (Ds), and preoccupied (E). The
secure category was identified by organized, singular strategies and coherent
discourse, whereas the two insecure categories (Ds and E) were identified by
coherent, but disorganized strategies of minimizing or maximizing attention
towards the attachment-related material. Later on, two more categories were
added: unresolved (U) and cannot classify (CC). These two categories
involved incoherent discourse. Whereas the unresolved category involved a
collapse of a coherent strategy only when speaking about loss or trauma, the
cannot classify category is assigned when there is no evidence of any particular
attentional strategy. When coding the AAI, speakers are assigned to specific
categories based on how they talk about their attachment-related experiences
(Hesse, 1996; Main & Goldwyn, 1998).

The AAI categories correspond to the classifications of the Strange Situation.
Those who fit into the F category have similar characteristics to infants designated as secure (B). Dismissing (Ds) adults match up with avoidant (A) infants

and preoccupied (E) adults match up with resistant or ambivalent (C) infants. Lastly, adults who are deemed unresolved with respect to attachment have similar characteristics to infants classified as disorganized/disoriented (D) (Hesse, 1999). The following section explains this further.

Secure (F)

Those who are secure in their state of mind with respect to attachment present plausible, cohesive, and coherent narratives when interviewed about their early childhoods. In fact, the most defining feature of an individual with a secure state of mind with respect to attachment is coherence of discourse, which turns out to be the strongest correlate with infant security. Such coherence implies the individual is working with a singular model of his attachment-related experiences (Main, 1991). Given that Main viewed the AAI as a conversation between speaker and interviewer, she hypothesized that a coherent interview would follow certain guidelines for conversation. For elaboration of these "rules," Main turned to the work of the linguistic philosopher Grice. Grice had developed four conversational maxims he deemed necessary for rational and cooperative conversation to occur between people: quality, quantity, relation, and manner. Utilizing these principles, Main suggested that interviews that adhere to these precepts be deemed secure. Following is an elaboration of what each maxim means.

Quality – refers to truthfulness of discourse; should be truthful and provide evidence for what is said
Quantity – refers to quantity of information imparted; should be succinct, yet complete
Relation – refers to relevance of subjects presented; should be perspicacious, presented in a way that is plainly understood
Manner – refers to speech being clear and orderly (Grice, 1989; Main, Hesse, & Kaplan, 2005)

For the most part, though there are other factors at play, a text that adheres to these overarching precepts is classified as secure while a text that violates them will most likely be classified as insecure with respect to attachment (Hesse, 2016).

EARNED OR EVOLVED SECURITY

There are five overall subcategories of the secure category: F1, F2, F3, F4, F5. Though speakers deemed secure maintain overall coherence in the interview, there is a spectrum of what secure states of mind may look like. There are speakers who tend to restrict their feelings while others tend to show mild preoccupation with attachment. Some speakers suffer loss (Main & Goldwyn, 1998) or come from traumatic backgrounds, but are still able to maintain coherent strategies when discussing these events. Some are solidly secure in their state of mind with respect to attachment, while others evidence resentment or anger, but are still involved with attachment relationships (Steele & Steele, 2008). In 1989, a new subcategory emerged, one that is of particular interest to clinicians; that of "earned security" or as Eric Hesse (2016) suggests "evolved security." Individuals who meet criteria for this category present a coherent narrative of their attachment-related history even though it is clear they have suffered with either difficult childhood relationships, experiences of great loss or separation, or abuse (Hesse, 2016; Main & Goldwyn, 1998).

AN INDIVIDUAL WITH A SECURE STATE OF MIND WITH RESPECT TO ATTACHMENT

Secure individuals tend to be objective in their discourse. They have autonomous thoughts, are balanced in their perception (i.e. they can see both positive and negative aspects of their upbringing), and they value attachment. A person who is free to explore and learn is also free to develop thoughts and ideas, free to understand his feelings, and free to incorporate the negative and positive. A securely attached individual has learned affect regulation, both because it has been modeled to him by his parent, but also because his parent has allowed him to express both "negative" and "positive" emotion and helped him to contain these feelings. He is more comfortable with all emotion and has been allowed to understand both negative and positive. A securely attached individual's attachment interview will be coherent. Coherence means consistent. It means adhering to Grice's maxims, where there is evidence for what is said, the information is relevant, and the manner of speech is easy to understand. Basically, it means the interview makes sense, the interviewee provides support for what he says, and is able to say it well. A securely attached individual will have a fresh interview. He will think on the spot, change answers, and come up with new ideas while he is being interviewed. One will get the sense that he knows who he is, that he is an autonomous person, that his ideas are his own, and that he is objective when telling his life story. He is not full of blame and can take credit or admit fault when talking. He can see the negative in his parents and he doesn't feel he will fall apart if he does this. He can be forgiving, even for terrible things. Valuing attachment is one of the most important facets of a securely attached individual. To sum up, security means the exploration system has been activated much of the time. The person has developed, has learned about the environment and about himself. He has been and is free to explore (Main & Goldwyn, 1998; Main, Hesse, & Goldwyn, 2008).

METACOGNITIVE MONITORING

Another sign of security is the idea of "metacognition," or "thinking about thinking in the moment." This process involves not only representing an experience, but having the ability to flexibly examine these representations

(Main, 1991). Main and her colleagues believe that active awareness of representational change underlies metacognitive monitoring (Gopnik & Astington, 1988). The following three subcategories demonstrate metacognitive monitoring: appearance–reality distinction, representational diversity, and representational change. The recognition of an appearance–reality distinction involves understanding that what one perceives may not in fact be the truth of the situation. For instance, a speaker states that though, as a child, she thought her mother was stupid, this may not have been the case. She now realizes that it may just have been that her mother was not educated. Representational diversity is the recognition that the same thing may be viewed differently by different people. An example of this would be a person acknowledging that he felt his father was strict, but that his sister didn't perceive him that way, and that perhaps his perception was clouded by his mother's opinion of his father. Recognition of representational change occurs when an individual acknowledges a change in beliefs about an object or an idea. For instance, what she thought was a normal childhood, she now realizes wasn't typical or "normal." Those individuals who possess the ability to utilize metacognition typically have a secure state of mind with respect to attachment, though one can be securely attached without being able to utilize metacognitive monitoring.

Peter Fonagy and his colleagues (Fonagy, Gergely, Jurist, & Target, 2002) extended the study of metacognition, focusing on the processes involved in developing coherent narratives. They write about "mentalizing" and "reflective functioning," and in so doing, have provided a platform for the clinical application of mentalization theory (Hill, 2015). Chapter 10 will elaborate on reflective functioning and mentalization theory.

Key identifiers of secure individuals:

Coherent
Objective
Forgiving
Autonomous
Balanced in perception – can see both negatives and positives in their caregivers
May exhibit metacognition
Value attachment

Dismissing (Ds)

A dismissing person has an organization of thought that is designed to keep attachment feelings deactivated. They tend to be cut off from feelings, to deny hurt and to idealize their parents. They normalize their experiences a lot and exhibit a lack of memory of childhood attachment events. They may devalue attachment relationships. They tend to violate Grice's maxim of quality and often of quantity too, where they are too succinct, providing little evidence for what is said. There are three subcategories of the dismissing category. Ds1 individuals have difficulty remembering details in relation their attachment experiences. Ds2 speakers tend to derogate and devalue attachment relationships and often claim overall personal strength, while Ds3 subjects are clearly restricted in their affect, even though they maintain a cognitively cohesive discourse (Main & Goldwyn, 1998; Main, Hesse, & Goldwyn, 2008; Steele & Steele, 2008).

AN INDIVIDUAL WITH A DISMISSING STATE OF MIND WITH RESPECT TO ATTACHMENT

A person who is classified as dismissing will speak differently from a secure individual. This is a person who has found emotion too painful. It assumes a parent who was rejecting and unavailable. The child presumably found this so upsetting that he developed a strategy to deal with his unmet needs. He decided to try not to feel. His interview will have very little feeling acknowledged. He will deny feeling hurt. He will idealize his parents because he couldn't afford not to do so growing up. He had to see them as perfect so that he could keep his disappointment at bay. He will have few memories, again because it is easier to have just blocked off his feelings and memories, rather than experiencing them. He will normalize his experience so that he doesn't feel bad about himself, meaning he wants to believe that everyone is like he is. He will emphasize his strength, again a coping mechanism to deal with feeling so powerless and unprotected. There is a sense that he does not have his own viewpoint. He has never challenged himself to do so because it would have meant feeling something. He will tell us what his parents told him. He did not have the freedom to explore his feelings while growing up and he seems unexplored emotionally. He did not develop good affect regulation. He cannot tolerate emotion. It is simply too much for him.

Incidentally, one should not think that dismissing individuals don't feel things as intensely. It is easy to assume this when a dismissing speaker makes claims to having had an idyllic childhood or minimizes the impact of upsetting events. However, Mary Dozier and Roger Kobak (1992) found that during the interview, dismissing participants showed a specific increase in electrodermal response which was interpreted as affective suppression coupled with high arousal. The interview challenges the typical deactivating strategy utilized by dismissing individuals by forcing them to focus on thoughts, memories, and feelings that they attempt to restrict, minimize, or avoid. This can be very anxiety-inducing. Thus, though dismissing speakers may attempt to "shut down" their emotions, Dozier and Kobak (1992) found evidence of larger rises in skin conductance in these individuals when they spoke of threatened separations or experienced rejections by caregivers. The same pattern occurred for questions of reflection about the influence of attachment relationships. In a later study, Roisman and colleagues (Roisman, Tsai, & Kuan-Hiong, 2004) confirmed these findings. Thus, it can be concluded that dismissing clients are often very aroused, even though they may not appear so.

Key identifiers of dismissing individuals:

Cut off from feeling
Denial of hurt
Idealize parents
Lack of autonomy in thought-endorse parent's point of view
Normalize experiences
Lack of memory

Preoccupied (E)

A preoccupied person is designated by "E" which stands for enmeshed. They appear to be flooded with emotion and preoccupied with the past and attachment figures, so much so that they are unable to fully process their feelings with objectivity. There are three different subcategories of preoccupation: passive (E1), angry (E2), and fearful (E3) (Steele & Steele, 2008). Passive individuals are vague in their discourse. Though they may adhere to Grice's maxim of quality in that they acknowledge childhood difficulties, they often violate Grice's maxim of quantity (speaking too long), relevance (vacillate between topics), and manner (often have vague, nonsense-like speech). Thus, they may speak like a child, use nonsense words, and/or wander from topic to topic. Angry speakers exhibit current, unanalyzed anger towards a caregiver, using entangled speech, run-on sentences, and/or extensive wordy discussion of the offending caregiver with an underlying intent to enlist the support of the interviewer. Those who are fearful in their state of mind with respect to attachment have intruding frightened images and discourse, but still maintain a coherent story (Main & Goldwyn, 1998; Main, Hesse, & Goldwyn, 2008; Steele & Steele, 2008; Hesse, 2016).

AN INDIVIDUAL WITH A PREOCCUPIED STATE OF MIND WITH RESPECT TO ATTACHMENT

A person who is classified as preoccupied is overwhelmed by emotion. His affect overwhelms any structure or organization he may have and feelings, memories, and cognitions relevant to attachment are under-regulated. Most likely, he had an intrusive caregiver or one who was overprotective and, furthermore, there was probably some role reversal present. There were few boundaries in attachment relationships and he has never had the space to gain understanding with regard to what he thinks or feels. He is unobjective, seems stuck in his emotion and often, seems stuck in his past. He'll give you one point of view in one breath and then in the very next breath tell you something completely different. When talking, he'll lapse into memories as if they were in the present. He may forget he is talking to you and address someone else in that moment. He may exhibit a great deal of anger in the present that concerns a past happening. He may use pseudo psychological terms, but one gets the sense that he doesn't really know what he is saying and he is grasping at words in an attempt to organize himself. A preoccupied individual talks a lot in vague terms. He is tangential. He may express many different viewpoints, directly contra- dicting himself and may seem unable to have any objectivity. Oftentimes, inter- viewers feel a pull from the speaker to "side" with him in his view of his attachment figures. He talks and talks and one often cannot follow what he is saying. He has a vague, inchoate sense of identity. He does not know who he is. Growing up, he probably had to focus on a confusing caregiver. He could not explore his environment or himself. He is not autonomous.

> **Key identifiers of preoccupied individuals:**
>
> Diffusion of identity
> Tangential
> Oscillate
> Speech is vague, using many meaningless expressions
> Seem stuck in the past

Unresolved (U)

There is a strong relationship between the unresolved/disorganized category and the infant D classification. As in the case of disorganized infants, this category is only assigned in conjunction with another category. For instance, someone can be unresolved in their state of mind with respect to attachment, but can also be deemed secure. An individual is assessed as unresolved if when speaking about a death, a trauma, witnessing a trauma, or abuse that occurred more than two years before, there are linguistic signs of mental disorganization or disorientation. Ratings are given on a scale of 1 through 9, with 9 being the most extreme of reactions (Main, Hesse, & Kaplan, 2005; Main & Goldwyn, 1998).

UNRESOLVED WITH RESPECT TO EXPERIENCE OF LOSS

As previously noted, according to Bowlby (1969/1982), loss of an attachment figure can be devastating and can possibly cause a disorganized or disoriented response. Bowlby (1980) understood adult bereavement to be motivated by the same mechanisms that guide children to seek proximity to an attachment figure within the context of the attachment behavioral system. The protest and searching behavior exhibited by adults who have suffered a loss are seen as reactions to the unavailability of an attachment figure. Up until the AAI was devised, atypical mourning was divided into one of two groupings: "chronic mourning" where grief does not lessen with time and the individual is unable to re-engage with daily life, or "failed mourning" evidenced by minimizing or complete avoidance of the loss (Kosminsky & Jordan, 2016). Main and her colleagues noticed that linguistically, those who were unresolved with regards to loss had signs of mental disorientation and disorganization. In particular, during the discussions about loss, these individuals had indications of (1) lapses in metacognitive monitoring of reasoning, (2) lapses in metacognitive monitoring of discourse, or (3) they report excessively disoriented or disorganized behavioral responses to a death or trauma and there is no suggestion of later successful integration of mourning. Such lapses came to be seen as the tell-tale signs of an unresolved state of mind because they were interpreted as indications of interference in being able to integrate the losses or trauma into a working model. These interruptions or state of mind shifts seem indicative of changes in the speaker's overall organizational strategy. Whereas the overall discourse of the subject may be coherent, when addressing loss or trauma, there are signs of lack of coherence.

Lapses of metacognitive reasoning processes can be evidenced by a seeming suspension of plausibility, such as believing the dead person is alive. Another example occurs with signs of magical thinking, such as feeling responsible for a death because the individual was angry and wished for the person to die. A third example of lapses in metacognitive reasoning processes can be seen when the speaker demonstrates efforts to influence the mind to attempt to "erase" the facts. For instance, an individual states "I moved away from the city I grew up in so that a lot of the time I can imagine she is still there if I needed her." Confusing the dead person with the self is yet another way a speaker shows signs of lapses in the monitoring of reasoning. An example of this would be if the individual mixes up who he is talking about, such as saying "I died when I was 13." Disorientation with regard to time and to space may occur, where subjects appear muddled as to when things happened or where they were when events occurred. They may place themselves at scenes when they weren't there or they may mention conflicting dates at different points in the interview for the same death. General confusion with regards to the loss is also an indication of unresolved loss (Main & Hesse, 1990; Main & Goldwyn, 1998; Hesse, 2016).

Lapses in the metacognitive monitoring of discourse processes can be seen in a variety of ways. There may be unusual attention to detail specifically when telling the interviewer about the circumstances of the death, such as listing the date, time, and year of the death, together with other facts that don't add any meaning. There can be poetic phrasing and one may get the sense one is hearing a prepared eulogy and not an individual's genuine thoughts and feelings about the death. Lastly, signs of behavioral disorganization, such as suicide attempts or redirected grief toward a pet for example in the absence of a reaction to the loss of the attachment figure, are signs of being unresolved with respect to loss (Main & Hesse, 1990; Main & Goldwyn, 1998; Hesse, 2016).

UNRESOLVED WITH RESPECT TO TRAUMA OR ABUSE

Speakers are analyzed for this state only when they are talking directly about having or witnessing a frightening or abusive experience that involves a caregiver. A mentally disorganized response is evidenced in much the same way as for experiences of loss. There will be lapses in the monitoring of reason, or behavior. The subject may feel he caused the abuse or he may exhibit unsuccessful attempts to deny the occurrence of any trauma. He may appear confused when discussing the events. In this way, a speaker's usual adaptive strategies fail and his discourse becomes disorganized, only when speaking about the traumatic experience (Main & Goldwyn, 1998; Hesse, 2016).

> **Key identifiers of unresolved state of mind:**
>
> Lapses in monitoring of discourse
> Lapses in monitoring of reason
> Extreme behavioral reactions

Cannot classify (CC)

Like the unresolved classification, cannot classify interviews are related to the disorganized category in the Strange Situation. These are speakers that don't meet criteria for any other category of the AAI. There may be signs of idealization, indicating a dismissing state of mind, but then also indications of being highly angrily preoccupied. Likely, these are individuals who have experienced so much chaos in early life that it was not possible to develop a coherent attachment strategy. Thus, in 1992, Main and Hesse added the category of CC, deeming certain transcripts unclassifiable or "cannot classify" (Hesse, 1996; Hesse, 2016).

Qualities of the AAI

In the initial Berkeley Longitudinal Study, 48% of parents were classified as secure, 39% as dismissing, and 13% as preoccupied (Hesse, 2016). Van IJzendoorn and Bakermans-Kranenburg (2008), in their meta-analysis conducted across a combined sample of 1,012 nonclinical mothers, similarly found that in their studied population, 56.3% were secure, 25.4% dismissing, and 18.3% preoccupied. When examining the distribution while including the unresolved category, of the 889 nonclinical mothers, 55.2% were secure, 19.6% dismissing, 10.4% preoccupied, and 14.9% unresolved.

The distribution among nonclinical fathers was analogous to the distribution among nonclinical mothers and these proportions held fairly constant among adolescent samples. However, once samples were combined with those from lower socioeconomic backgrounds, it was found that dismissing and unresolved categories were overrepresented while the secure-autonomous category was underrepresented. In clinical populations (sample of 685), only 27% of the sample were deemed secure, 35% were found to be dismissing, and 38% were preoccupied. With the addition of the unresolved category, 41% were coded as unresolved.

The link between a parent's AAI state of mind with respect to attachment and that parent's child's classification has been confirmed many times over. In fact, in a meta-analysis across 18 samples, van IJzendoorn (1995) documented a 75% concordance rate between classifications of parents and their children. A later meta-analysis (Verhage et al., 2016) confirmed this exceedingly high correlation between AAI status of parents and their children's Strange Situation classification. Even when the interview was conducted with pregnant mothers before the birth of their child and compared to that parent's child's attachment classification at 12 months old, this strong relationship held true (Steele, Steele, & Fonagy, 1996). Investigators have explored why this is the case. Why is there such a strong association between a caregiver's attachment classification and that caregiver's child's attachment pattern? How is an attachment classification transmitted through the generations? Maternal sensitivity has been proposed as one of the factors explaining the "transmission gap" (van IJzendoorn, 1995). Recently (Verhage et al., 2016), the intergenerational transmission of attachment was reviewed with a meta-analysis. The analyses confirmed the transmission of attachment and found caregiver sensitivity to partially, but not fully, explain this transmission. This suggests that multiple mechanisms explain how parental attachment representations influence children's attachment patterns and is an area for further study. Later on, in Chapters 9 and 10, we will examine the role of affect regulation as one possible mechanism involved in understanding the passing on of attachment patterns.

The coherence of the AAI has been found to be unrelated to intelligence, general memory abilities, and verbal fluency. Additionally, the coded state of mind is not associated with qualities of the interviewer (Main, Hesse, & Kaplan, 2005). Social desirability does not affect AAI classification while social adjustment is only modestly associated with it. Not surprisingly, those in clinical populations are more likely to be classified as insecure as compared to those in nonclinical populations. As opposed to the Strange Situation where attachment patterns with mothers were unrelated to those with fathers, states of mind with respect to mothers have been found to be significantly related to states of mind with respect to fathers (Hesse, 2016).

Research has documented that AAI classifications, barring intervening trauma or major life events, tend to remain stable over the years (Crowell, Treboux, & Waters, 2002; Crowell & Hauser, 2008). There have been four U.S. studies exploring individual differences in attachment and in all four of these studies, individuals' AAI classifications have consistently been related to earlier Strange Situation statuses with their mothers (Main, Hesse, & Kaplan, 2005).

Scale estimating experiences with parents

When coding the AAI, a researcher infers to the best of his ability the subject's actual experiences with each parent. On a scale of 1 through 9, with 9 being the highest score possible, each parent is rated on the degree of "loving" behavior, whether or not he or she was rejecting, role-inverting, neglecting, or pressurizing in terms of achievement. For instance, did a parent interact with their child? Did a parent comfort the subject when he or she was upset? Is there evidence that a parent took care of the speaker when he or she was sick? Or are there signs that the parent actively rejected the speaker? Was there little affection growing up? Did the parent expect to be taken care of by the subject? Or did the speaker feel an inordinate pressure to achieve in order to be loved? For the purposes of coding the AAI, a researcher examines the evidence presented by the speaker against her best estimation of the actual circumstances, coding for overall coherence.

Clinical uses for the AAI

To become a certified coder of the AAI, one must go through an intensive training period that takes up to two years to be proficient. Trained coders take between four to six hours to code each transcript. However, a clinician has much to learn from this instrument. The following are case examples of the differing states of mind with respect to attachment. Though Chapters 11 and 12 will delve much further into doing therapy using an attachment framework, these examples are provided to give an idea of how to begin viewing clients from an attachment perspective.

Case examples[1]

Kathy

Kathy entered the room laughing nervously. She was long and thin, dressed stylishly, but in an unassuming way. She was unsure how to begin, but stated that there were two pressing issues she needed to address. Firstly, two people that were close to her had died within the past year and secondly, she and her husband had not had sex in two years. She insisted her husband was the love of her life, that she would not want to consider whether the relationship was working for her because it most certainly was. It was just this one problem which was becoming more of an issue because she was deciding whether or not to have children. As she talked about her husband, she stated that she was sure other people had this issue, that it wasn't such an issue really, and that she was strong and able to manage her feelings with regards to this relationship. Because she was so defended against exploring issues in her romantic relationship, we decided to focus on her mourning her two losses. The next few sessions went really well as Kathy delved into her unexplored feelings about her grandmother's death and her friend's passing away. She had admittedly thought she was fine, had not talked about her feelings with anyone, and had tried to continue on with her life as usual. As we spoke, we began to touch upon her family history. Initially, when I asked her about her mother, she told me that her sister had been scarred by how her mother had acted, but that she herself was unscathed. She talked calmly about how, when she was 18, her mother had been upset with her for making some popcorn at an inopportune moment and had chased her down a street with a gun, telling her to never return. Kathy had been homeless for six months, until she had begged her parents to return. Again, she said though, that she really was fine, that she had gotten over any of the possible negative effects, that she was a coper. In the scheme of things, her life had not been that bad. She had pursued a college degree, had been the first in her family, a working class family, to graduate from college and that again, she was fine. I attempted more delving into her past and met with a brick wall. She had few memories to substantiate her claim to normalcy and often fobbed me off, saying "I don't know" to my many inquiries. At first, when I asked what she felt about talking about her past, she replied that it was no problem. As therapy progressed however, she reported feeling numb. She told me that she had realized that either she felt nothing or that her emotions were so extreme, she felt embarrassed to own them. When I asked for examples of extreme emotion, she told me how she had been upset by the recent Kavanaugh hearing and the fact that Kavanaugh was eventually sworn in as a Supreme Court judge. She stated this in one sentence and her description of her upset feelings were far from extreme, but any feeling seemed to overwhelm her.

Discussion

Kathy had a dismissing state of mind. She had protected herself from a rejecting mother and an inept, quiet father, by telling herself that everything was fine. She had told me that this was her defense. She would pretend she was normal and would tell herself this over and over again until she felt that the problem went away. She also lacked memories of her childhood and blocked attachment feelings by trying not to feel. As she stated, she felt numb most of the time. After realizing that her attachment style was dismissing, the process of therapy became clear. It involved enabling her to find a safe haven in which to explore her true feelings, something she had never been able to do because she focused her energy on trying to preserve herself. It would have to be really slow because letting her feelings through would have meant acknowledging a marriage that wasn't working and also admitting to a painful past. She also would have needed to open up more in therapy, something else that was difficult for her to do. She was scared to feel close to anyone, scared to feel safe.

Andy

Andy walked into his first session with an air of arrogance. He was there to fix his marriage, he stated. He hid things from his wife and she wanted him to be able to communicate better. He also had been having difficulty performing when they were having sex. He felt bad about this because it was making his wife feel unattractive. He explained though that they simply had different sex drives where she wanted sex much more than he did. At the end of the first session, I realized I knew his wife's perspective on things, but almost nothing about how he felt. In subsequent sessions we talked about sex but never got very far. He had described sex as "scary" and constantly felt pressure, he admitted, to protect his wife, though from what he was not sure. This pressure was incapacitating. His level of metacognitive monitoring regarding sexuality was quite low, and he could not articulate anything other than his view that sex was "scary." I decided to delve into his family of origin, hoping I would be able to access more of his true self. He spoke clearly and descriptively. When asked to give five adjectives to describe his relationship with his mother, he was cooperative and interested in the process. He gave both positive and negative adjectives, adjusting what he was saying as he talked. He had fresh thinking and was coherent in his speech. He had had an admittedly tough childhood, where both his parents had been alcoholics. They had divorced when he was 12 and a nasty custody battle had ensued, one that lasted until he left for college. He was glad to go to college on the west coast. Andy talked about things he had never talked about before. He seemed interested and engaged in the therapy process. I was still having trouble formulating a hypothesis as to why he was unable to perform sexually, until one session, where things suddenly became clear. Andy usually entered the therapy room and sat casually on the couch across from me, at times draping his legs across the couch and at other times moving around to demonstrate a point. This session, he sat huddled in the corner of the couch, his air of arrogance gone. He was tearful as he spoke of a memory he had of a fight between his parents. When he was two, he had witnessed a scary alter-cation. He had hidden in the coat closet and no one had known he was there. His father had come home drunk as usual and for no apparent reason, he had started physically attacking his mother. As Andy talked, he became more and more tense. He was talking about who was home when he made a startling statement. He told me that his mother was two years younger than he is, so his mother was not born yet. I knew he meant his sister wasn't born yet, but he did not catch himself. He was so caught up in what he was saying, he had not noticed this.

Discussion

When scoring an AAI, this would rate high as a lapse in monitoring of discourse. I had the key to why he was having trouble with his wife. He was unresolved regarding this traumatic event that he had witnessed. His previous descriptions of sex as "scary" and his reports of constantly feeling pressure to protect his wife from an unidentified threat began to make sense. This pressure to protect his wife was incapacitating because it stemmed from his unresolved exposure to trauma. Through therapy, he was able to see that it was his mother he had felt unable to protect and that he was projecting this onto his wife. He felt enormous relief in this realization.

Tania

When Tania attended her first session, she spoke solidly for an hour. At the end of the hour, I struggled to piece together why she had come to therapy. She said she was there to address her issues and what not. She was unable to specify what her issues were; rather, she seemed content to rephrase herself saying that she needed to deal with her family of origin. I got the feeling that she expected me to understand what she meant even when she seemed to lack clarity herself. The second concern she raised was a lack of direction she felt in her life. She had just graduated from college and was not sure how to proceed in life. She felt she had no place in society. She was 33 years old and had an 18-year-old son, yet she could not speak openly about her experiences as a young mother and seemed to lack any identity as a parent. She said she felt grown up and then she felt insecure. She talked in vague generalities and used many psychological terms which in the end left me even more confused about what was bothering her. For example, she talked about her issues with other people not respecting her boundaries, and in the same breath described how her boyfriend had broken up with her because she was too clingy. During her discussion of the break-up I tried to formulate a hypothesis about her behavior in intimate relationships. I struggled to track her and became frustrated when she ended up describing her boyfriend's sister-in-law's new dog, a topic Tania had somehow stumbled upon as she wandered away from the topic of intimate relationships. Tania had many odd manners of speech, phrases such as "that kind of thing" popped up in odd places. She would also refer to her mother as "mama" at times. I asked a few sparse questions and was regaled with verbose answers that again meant nothing. The next session, I attempted to ground Tania by asking closed-ended questions and reminding her what she was talking about when she wandered off. Even with this, Tania was difficult to follow. Her parents had separated before she was born and she had been raised by her mother, living in poverty and existing on welfare. Her father had remarried and had acquired a new family, almost replacing Tania and her siblings. She had little interaction with her father. Tania reported that becoming pregnant at 15 was no big deal. There were several girls who were pregnant at the same time and she felt very supported in having a child. Tania was vague when talking about her mother. I suspected a lot of role reversal and that her mother did not function well after her father left, but again, Tania talked about her mother in a vague, hallowed light. Reading between the lines, her mother sounded incapacitatingly depressed. At one point she said that her mother was very angry at her father and she did not want to be like this, but then in the next sentence told me that her mother handled the separation from her father like a lady, showing no bitterness. She talked as if she had questioned her past, but it was clear she had not delved deeply. When asked her feelings on her father's absence and apparent rejection, she said it wasn't bad, that it was the norm for her neighborhood, and gave a 20-minute long description of the other children in her neighborhood, again obfuscating the issues at hand. When talking about her past, she used the word "we" a lot, referring to her brother and herself.

Discussion

Tania had never individuated and was very much stuck in her past relationships with her father, mother, and brother. She was not her own person. Tania was clearly preoccupied with her past relationships. She had never had a secure base from which to develop herself and her development had been even further impeded by the birth of her son at such a young age. There was a vague sense of her identity. Her feelings were so present in the room that they clouded her ability to think about her past. Therapy involved enabling Tania to become more objective by structuring the sessions more, questioning her part in things, and highlighting and allowing her feelings about the loss of her father, her anger at her mother, and her difficulties with having been a teenaged mother. She presents a much more coherent story these days and has talked of how much she values our relationship. She has a secure base.

Summary

In the 1980s, the assessment of attachment was extended to adults through the work of Main and her colleagues and their development of the Adult Attachment Interview (AAI). With this, the study of attachment moved from behavioral observation to gaining insight into adults' internal representations of attachment. Main and her colleagues described states of mind with respect to attachment, dividing up the various states into secure, dismissing, preoccupied, and unresolved states of mind. A fifth classification, cannot classify, designated transcripts that didn't fit into any other category. Each state of mind can be viewed as the result of a strategy developed to cope with the availability of attachment figures. Secure individuals will most likely develop adaptive coping strategies. However, in response to unavailable caregivers, preoccupied individuals tend to utilize hyperactivating strategies, where they magnify their attachment needs, and dismissing individuals tend to use deactivating strategies, where they shut down their attachment needs. Those with unresolved states of mind have no coherent coping strategy for negotiating a trauma or loss. The AAI provides clinicians with a good assessment tool, or a window into underlying attachment representations and the strategies that result.

Note

1   All case examples in this book are either completely fictional or mostly fictionalized and are very loosely based on actual cases.

Chapter 4

Self-report measures

History of self-report measures

While Ainsworth, Main, Sroufe and other developmental psychologists furthered their understanding of the attachment bond and its correlates, social and personality psychologists took another direction. They turned their attention to romantic love. Based on a hunch that romantic love could be seen as an attachment process, Phillip Shaver, a social psychologist at the University of Denver, and Cindy Hazan, a doctoral student, devised a "love quiz" to test out their theory (Hazan & Shaver, 1987; Mikulincer & Shaver, 2007). In July of 1985, the *Rocky Mountain News*, a local newspaper in Denver, Colorado, published their "love quiz," with three statements that Hazan and Shaver hypothesized would correspond to the secure, avoidant, or ambivalent attachment styles of infancy. The statements were as follows:

> – I find it relatively easy to get close to others and am comfortable depending on them and having them depend on me. I don't worry about being abandoned or about someone getting too close to me. [Secure]
> – I am somewhat uncomfortable being close to others; I find it difficult to trust them completely, difficult to allow myself to depend on them. I am nervous when anyone gets too close, and often, love partners want me to be more intimate than I feel comfortable being. [Avoidant]
> – I find that others are reluctant to get as close as I would like. I often worry that my partner doesn't really love me or won't want to stay with me. I want to merge completely with another person, and this desire sometimes scares people away. [Ambivalent].
>
> (Hazan & Shaver, 1987, p. 515)

Readers were asked to endorse the statement with which they most identified. There were also questions about childhood relationships, their parents, and important romantic relationships. Upon analyzing the responses, Hazan and Shaver noticed a connection between those who felt secure with others and the increased satisfaction they felt with their partners. The respondents who identified most with the first description reported longer lasting relationships, less divorce, more trust and happiness, and more acceptance of flaws in their significant others. Those who felt more akin to the second description, suggesting avoidant attachment, expressed skepticism about the existence of romantic love, had jealousy, and were fearful of intimacy. Lastly, those who seemed ambivalently attached became involved in intense relationships with highs and lows, and often became obsessed with their partner. Not only was there this connection, but roughly 56% of respondents rated themselves as secure, 25% as avoidant, and 19% as ambivalent, almost exactly mirroring the proportions of infant–mother attachment in American studies. And there was an obvious parallel between a respondent's endorsed attachment style and descriptions of childhood rapports with parents. Taken together, the results of the "love quiz" suggested what Hazan and Shaver had proposed; that adult romantic love may indeed be an attachment process akin to infant–caregiver attachment processes (Hazan & Shaver, 1987; Karen, 1994). This study was to catapult research about romantic love into the attachment arena, providing evidence for Ainsworth's (Ainsworth et al., 1978) infant attachment classifications serving as possible determinants of adult romantic attachment styles. In essence, Hazan and Shaver had succeeded in outlining both a normative model of romantic love as well as a way to conceptualize individual differences in adult attachment relationships (Feeney, 2016).

Since the publication of the "love quiz," numerous self-report measures have been developed in an effort to measure adult romantic love. Quickly realizing the limitations of the original forced-choice, three category measure, researchers, including Hazan and Shaver themselves, explored other possibilities. Continuous rating scales such as the Adult Attachment Questionnaire (AAQ) and the Adult Attachment Scale (AAS) were developed. The Attachment Style Questionnaire (ASQ) was yet another self-report measure that emerged on the scene (Mikulincer & Shaver, 2007). The AAQ, AAS, and ASQ were all based on a three-category model of attachment. In reviewing these self-report measures, it became clear that there were two core dimensions of insecurity that were fundamental to romantic attachment: avoidance and anxiety. Attachment-related avoidance speaks to those who are uncomfortable with intimacy and utilize distancing and self-reliance as defensive strategies to deal with distress while attachment-related anxiety speaks to those who have an intense wish for closeness and proximity, worry about separation or abandonment, and experience self-doubt (Mikulincer & Shaver, 2007). Based on this understanding, Kim Bartholomew (Bartholomew & Horowitz, 1991) developed the Relationships Questionnaire (RQ), based on a four-category model of attachment. She reevaluated Bowlby's (1973) original definition of the internal working model and noted that he delineates two important factors:

(a) whether or not the attachment figure is judged to be the sort of person who in general responds to calls for support and protection; [and] (b) whether or not the self is judged to be the sort of person towards whom anyone, and the attachment figure in particular, is likely to respond in a helpful way.

(p. 204)

A child internalizes whether another person will be responsive to him and also whether he is worthy of getting a response. Bartholomew hypothesized that both the model of the self and the model of others are important features of an adult's attachment style and they generated a scale that measures people along dimensions for security with positive models of the self and of others (low anxiety and low avoidance); preoccupied with positive models of others and negative models of the self (high anxiety and low avoidance); dismissing with negative models of others and positive models of the self (low anxiety and high avoidance); and fearful with both the self and of others (high anxiety and high avoidance) (Gentzler & Kerns, 2004; Mikulincer & Shaver, 2007).

In the late 1990s, Brennan, Clark, and Shaver (1998) conducted a factor analysis, a statistical procedure used to ascertain underlying "factors" or dimensions, on all the non-repetitive items of the self-report attachment measures that had been devised up until that point. As had been suspected, they found two orthogonal, higher-order factors: *attachment-related avoidance* and *attachment-related anxiety*. Based on this, Brennan and his colleagues constructed the Experiences in Close Relationship scale (ECR) which, together with the revised version, the ECR-S (Wei, Russell, Mallinckrodt, & Vogel, 2007), is currently the most widely used self-report measure of adult attachment and has generated much empirical research. The scale has two sets of questions; one that assesses attachment-related anxiety and the other that measures attachment-related avoidance. The attachment-related anxiety dimension evaluates an individual's tendency to hyperactivate the attachment system, while the attachment-related avoidance dimension assesses an individual's tendency to deactivate the attachment system. Fraley and Shaver (2000) believe that these two dimensions can be conceptualized as involving the two components of each attachment behavioral system: the monitoring and appraisal of a caregiver's availability and the operating and regulating of attachment-related behavior once a threat is detected. Increased attachment-related anxiety with lower thresholds of monitoring for rejection and increased attachment-related avoidance encourages the use of withdrawing as a way to regulate the attachment behavioral system. Thus, those who score high on attachment-related anxiety are prone to heightening their vulnerabilities and emotions in an attempt to solicit attention. In contrast, individuals who score high on attachment-related avoidance downplay their vulnerabilities and try to suppress their emotions in order to be more self-sufficient. Those who measure high on both dimensions seem to alternate between the two tactics and ultimately may seem to lack any coherent strategy, while those who score low on both dimensions can be deemed securely attached, with the capacity to maintain close, supportive relationships (Mikulincer & Shaver, 2007; Wei, Russell, Mallinckrodt, & Zakalik, 2004).

Narrative vs. self-report measures

Because of the different tacks taken in understanding adult attachment, the different terminology used throughout the attachment literature can be confusing.

Authors refer to dismissing attachment and avoidant attachment as one and the same, as they do for preoccupied and anxious attachment. One could wonder what the difference between disorganized, unresolved loss, and fearful attachment may be. To address this, it is useful to explore the differences between self-report measures (i.e., ECR) and narrative measures (i.e., AAI). To reiterate, the developmental psychologists, such as Ainsworth, Waters, Main, and Cassidy, used observational methods and then interviews to study attachment. Social psychologists, such as Hazan and Shaver, utilized Bowlby's and Ainsworth's theories to study romantic attachments and developed self-report measures based on these theories. Though both schools of thought are based on similar conceptualizations of secure and insecure attachment strategies, only modest correlations exist between the different measures developed from these two lines of thought. Furthermore, the measures appear to be related with somewhat discrete characteristics of adult relationships. In other words, they may be measuring different constructs (Shaver & Mikulincer, 2002; Roisman et al., 2007).

The measures developed from these two lines of research diverge from one another in several ways. Firstly, attachment can be measured in categories or along a continuum. Narrative measures such as the AAI tend to be coded categorically. Though Main described attachment strategies as dimensions, for simplicity's sake, she chose to use categories for the AAI measure (Brennan, Clark, & Shaver, 1998). There are some who argue that categorical approaches to attachment do not capture the natural structure of attachment representations and that the adult experience of attachment is more varied (Fraley & Waller, 1998). As already suggested, there are those who believe that adult attachment can be described along the two dimensions of attachment-related anxiety and attachment-related avoidance (Wei et al., 2004). Self-report measures, such as the ECR, are based on continuous scales resulting in these two attachment dimensions. Though self-report measures can yield discrete attachment categories such as secure, avoidant, or anxious, most researchers who use these measures ascribe to a dimensional approach and understand adult attachment patterns as occurring along continuums (Daniel, 2015).

Another difference is suggested by the notion that the AAI is supposed to tap into unconscious processes, whereas self-report measures reflect conscious appraisals of relationships. The AAI, and other measures like it, evaluate defenses associated with an adult's current state of mind regarding childhood relationships with parents, while self-report inventories assess an individual's feelings and behaviors in the context of a romantic partnership or other close relationships. Roger Kobak suggests that self-report inventories seem to pull for feelings in current relationships, which can change depending on the attachment style of a partner. Thus, a clingy partner can elicit avoidant behavior, whereas a distant partner can engender clinginess. Therefore, he feels, the results of self-report measures may more accurately represent current relationships rather than childhood attachment experiences (Karen, 1994). Along similar lines, Shaver and his colleagues (Shaver, Belsky, & Brennan, 2000) concluded that the two measures were more related than others had supposed, but conjectured that the AAI may be more a measure of caregiving than attachment style. However, this interpretation is subject to disagreement (Roisman et al., 2007).

In the end, it is not clear that either method truly captures these representations (Steele et al., 2014). One thing with which most concur is that both lines of research attempt to assess individual differences in adults' representations of attachment relationships and it may be that each measure captures different aspects of internal working models of attachment (Dykas, Woodhouse, Cassidy, & Waters, 2006). Again, there are two critical constructs that are central to Bowlby's attachment theory: the secure base idea and internal working models. Though the precursors to secure base behavior are well understood, the nature of and mechanisms underlying internal working models are less clear (Waters & Waters, 2006). Recently, there has been a move towards more accurately assessing the underlying architecture of attachment representations. This has led researchers to investigate individual differences in secure base script knowledge.

The secure base script assessment is a measure of attachment based on a third research tradition. This measure, which is correlated with the AAI coherence score as well as to the ECR (Dykas et al., 2006), is based on the theory of secure base scripts. Again, according to Bowlby, an attachment relationship provides a secure base from which to explore the environment and a safe haven to return to in times of distress. A caregiver is either available or unavailable to a child. Based on a caregiver's responsiveness, the child develops paradigms, or cognitive representations, of the self in relationships and these representations guide future interactions. Lately, researchers have hypothesized that an individual's heuristic that is developed within the attachment bond is organized or represented as a secure base script. This theory is based on Bretherton's work suggesting that experiences are encoded as cognitive structures, or summaries of commonalities in events that occur in particular situations. These summaries result in a script, or a map that guides expectations and behavior in the future (Waters & Waters, 2006). For instance, going to a restaurant can evolve into a "restaurant script," where an individual understands that examining a menu, placing a food order, paying, and then leaving are part of this script that guides expectations and interactions in restaurants in general (Steele et al., 2014). With respect to attachment, these secure base scripts are thought to be the cognitive building blocks of attachment representations (Coppola, Vaughn, Cassibba, & Constantini, 2006). The scripts are assumed to be organized around the following three central affect-regulating strategies: the recognition and manifestation of distress, engaging and resolution-seeking, and soliciting support (Shaver & Mikulincer, 2002). Thus, when a stressor is encountered, presumably the secure base script is activated and the individual will expect script-consistent behavior in close relationships. Also, the individual will use the script to organize his or her reactions to the stressor (Waters & Waters, 2006). Hence, secure individuals feel confident that either they can rely on attachment figures for support or that they can solve their own distress. Insecurely attached individuals will be uncertain of the attachment figure's availability and will doubt his or her ability to resolve the issue at hand. Research supports the fact that early caregiving experiences manifest in individual differences in secure base script knowledge and that the script assessment can measure this abstraction (Steele et al., 2014). Secure base scripts are linked with attachment in adolescents and adults (Waters & Rodrigues-Doolabh, 2001; Dykas et al., 2006).

These different ways of measuring attachment reflect the various ways in which adult attachment is understood. Researchers tend to choose a path of understanding based on which subfield of psychology to which they ascribe (Mikulincer & Shaver, 2007). Central to these differing traditions though is the notion that romantic love can be seen as an attachment process. According to attachment theorists, there are three key features of an attachment bond that distinguish it from other types of relationships. Firstly, in an attachment bond, an individual seeks proximity to an attachment figure in times of distress. Secondly, an attachment figure serves as a safe haven when under threat. Thirdly, an attachment figure provides a secure base from which to springboard into exploring the environment. According to the theory of attachment across the life cycle, these functions are transferred from a caregiver to a peer and finally to a romantic partner (Fraley & Shaver, 2000). However, though seeming variants of a single process, it is important to note that attachment in a romantic relationship differs from the attachment between an infant and a caregiver in important ways. Of primary significance, romantic love is usually between two equal partners, whereas there is a clear hierarchy between a caregiver and a child, with the onus on the caregiver to ensure security and safety in the attachment bond. In other words, there should be a give and take between adults in a relationship, where partners take turns between giving and receiving comfort and security. And, sexual attraction is almost always a part of a romantic partnership. In fact, Bowlby (1979) and Ainsworth et al. (1978) hypothesized there to be a distinct sexual behavioral system that together with the attachment system and the caregiving system, interact to create the biological process of romantic love with the goal of ultimately ensuring reliable care for progeny (Hazan & Shaver, 1987; Mikulincer & Shaver, 2007).

Attachment patterns in the self-report tradition

In comparison to attachment in children, which is considered to be relationship-specific, the adult attachment patterns described by social and personality researchers can be seen as more trait-like based on the internalization of attachment-related experiences thus far (Daniel, 2015). As opposed to the AAI which assesses states of mind with regards to attachment, the self-report tradition generally measures individual dispositions that result from varying attachment histories. According to Mikulincer and Shaver (2007), attachment styles are:

patterns of expectations, needs, emotions, and social behavior that result from a particular history of attachment experiences, usually beginning in relationships with parents. A person's attachment style reflects his or her most chronically accessible working models and the typical functioning of his or her attachment system in a specific relationship (relationship-specific attachment style) or across relationships (global or general attachment style). As such, each attachment style is closely tied to working models and reflects the underlying, organizing action of a particular attachment strategy (primary or secondary, hyperactivating or deactivating.

(p. 25)

The following section explores the body of research resulting from the social and personality psychology researchers surrounding secure, avoidant, and anxious attachment styles. In each section, the goals, behaviors, cognitions, and relational aspects will be explored. The same fictional example will be given, viewed from all different variations in attachment. It is helpful to use the same case example and analyze it from different perspectives to enable the reader to fully grasp the differences between each attachment pattern.

Secure attachment

Goals

A secure individual seeks a partner who will serve as a secure base in times of distress and a safe haven from which to explore the environment. The person who serves as a safe haven encourages and supports this exploration.

Behaviors

Secure individuals tend to have close, intimate connections with others. Most likely, they are able to comfortably express feelings of vulnerability and fear, have open communication, and make self-disclosures. These individuals tend to give clear messages and have better strategies for negotiating interpersonal conflict. Forgiveness comes easily and they are more likely to accept their partners' flaws. They are more likely to ask for help and find supportive interactions more beneficial when trying to cope with stress. A secure mindset is associated with better performance on general tasks and academically in school settings. Additionally, they are involved in more altruistic activities and demonstrate a greater eagerness to help others (Mikulincer & Shaver, 2007; Levine & Heller, 2011; Daniel, 2015). In terms of sexual behavior, secure individuals are less likely to participate in one-night stands or extra-marital relations and they're more likely to take pleasure in their sex life with their partner (Feeney, 2016).

Cognitions

Secure individuals have more positive views of themselves and an increased sense of self-efficacy. They are more likely to assume the best of others' intentions, are more trusting of others, and have a positive memory bias when thinking of interpersonal interactions. In terms of conflict, they tend to attribute hurtful actions as a one-time offense or as situation-specific, such as "He was upset by his boss, so he overreacted to me." They view others with more compassion and empathy. Additionally, secure individuals have a more positive attitude towards their studies (Daniel, 2015; Mikulincer & Shaver, 2007).

Relational aspects

Secure individuals tend to be more satisfied in their relationships, are more committed, and experience interdependence. Additionally, they are more likely to be supportive when resolving problems and less likely to evidence signs of rejection (Feeney, 2016).

Example of a first session

Ruth stepped into my office and asked where she should sit. I told her she could choose a seat that felt most comfortable to her. She sank into her chair and started talking softly. She had been feeling overwhelmed since going back to work three months after the birth of her first child, Annie. She felt resentful towards her husband, as he left her to do the majority of the housework. In exploring her childhood, she reported that her mother and father had few confrontations. In general, she remembered that though her mother and father worked full-time, her mother bore the brunt of childcare and housework and didn't complain. She had a lot of good friends, but happened to be the first of her friends to have a baby, so she felt she couldn't discuss her issues with her friends. It became clear that Ruth and her husband had a solid, loving relationship where she felt her needs were met. However, once Annie arrived, Ruth felt abandoned by him. He slept through the night, while she bottle-fed Annie. He didn't do much housework and Ruth was unclear as to how much she was entitled to ask for. She loved him and believed he wanted what was best for her but couldn't understand why he wasn't helping more. When I asked her if she had talked to him about her feelings, she replied she had not. I asked what it would be like to discuss her concerns with her husband. All of a sudden, she realized that it was valid to ask for more and that unlike what her mother had done, she could maybe ask her husband to participate more in house chores and in parenting. She sat up and said she felt empowered. She looked at her watch, thanked me for my time, and scheduled her next session.

Attachment-related avoidance

Goals

Those with attachment-related avoidance have two main goals in relationships. Firstly, they seek out "felt security" by avoiding distress, trying to meet their needs on their own without the help of a secure base, and by maintaining distance and control. Even when their attachment system is preconsciously activated, they inhibit any behavioral expressions of need for another. Secondly, they try to ignore their needs and avoid any feeling that may activate their attachment-system. They are usually focused on exploring the environment and distancing themselves from their secure base in order to prevent the anticipated rejection (Hazan & Shaver, 1994; Mikulincer & Shaver, 2007).

Behaviors

Individuals with attachment-related avoidance tend to utilize deactivating strategies. They distance themselves from others, avoid any sign of dependency or intimacy, and practice little self-disclosure, tending to be secretive. In fact, they may feel uncomfortable with others self-disclosing to them (Hazan & Shaver, 1994; Mikulincer & Shaver, 2007). They tend not to ask for help and are less likely to volunteer help. Avoidantly attached individuals are less likely to commit, more likely to terminate relationships, and find it easy to suppress feelings in order to move into their next relationship. They are less cooperative, show deficits in conflict management, and are less likely to forgive, instead often seeking vengeance. In fact, conflict causes so much anxiety that a study found that avoidant individuals had increased ambulatory diastolic blood pressure when experiencing interpersonal discord. Even with no conflict, those with attachment-related avoidance tend to feel uninvolved during day-to-day interactions, often feeling either anxious or bored by them. In terms of sex, avoidantly attached individuals report more one-night stands, view sexual encounters as unimportant, engage in more casual sex, and have more sex outside of committed relationships. In general, avoidant individuals have been found to have less frequent sex, to focus on their own enjoyment during sex, and to masturbate more often, a solitary activity (Gentzler & Kerns, 2004; Mikulincer & Shaver, 2007; Feeney, 2016).

Cognitions

Those with attachment-related avoidance direct attention away from attachment-related signals. Because of this, they may not accurately process or integrate incoming information. These individuals may have inflated self-esteem as a protection against feeling any negative feelings, including vulnerability. However, in social situations, they see themselves as less confident, feel less connected, and more unemotional (Klohnen & Bera, 1998). They are more likely to denigrate others in order to make themselves feel better. They tend to see others through a negative lens, with less empathy, and often attribute malintent or excessive dependence to partners' actions (Mikulincer & Shaver, 2007). According to a diary study (Pietromonaco & Barrett, 1997), avoidantly attached individuals view most daily interactions negatively, even those that are objectively positive. Though they are likely to suppress any thoughts related to rejection or separation, they continue to view others as rejecting and because of this, may interpret kindness and supportiveness from others negatively. Avoidant individuals tend to be distrusting of people in general (Mikulincer & Shaver, 2007; Mikulincer, Shaver, Bar-On, & Ein-Dor, 2010).

Relational aspects

Individuals with attachment-related avoidance have lower levels of relationship satisfaction (Li & Chan, 2012). Interestingly, avoidant individuals seem to gravitate to those who are anxiously attached. Presumably the styles reaffirm their negative beliefs, where those with attachment-related avoidance feel stronger and more independent, viewing their partners as overly needy, and those with attachment-related anxiety repeat the cycle of feeling rejected (Levine & Heller, 2011).

Example of a first session

Ruth came into my office hesitantly. She sat down and pushed her chair a little bit away from me, picking up a pillow on the couch and placing it on her stomach as if to shield herself from me. When I asked what had brought her to therapy, she replied that she wanted to feel better. I asked what she meant by that and she answered that she had not been feeling herself since the birth of her daughter three months ago. After many more questions from me, I eventually pieced together that she seemed angry at her husband for his lack of support. I asked her directly if she felt that he was not supporting her enough and she replied that he was supportive, but just not enough. They had a good relationship, she said, one where they never fought. She wanted to keep it that way. I asked questions about her childhood and she was able to tell me that her parents both worked and that she often was home alone. In fact, she took care of most of the household chores from the age of 12 onward. It wasn't terrible, she said. However, she felt tired now. And again, not herself. She had few friends, saying that she was used to being on her own and so it hadn't been a problem for her. Though sometimes she felt lonely, but she quickly said, she was fine with taking care of herself. Something about the birth of her daughter and going back to work though had made it more difficult to do things on her own. Her husband was a busy man and she was reluctant to ask him to do more. But managing the house and a baby on her own was tiring for her.

There was a lot of silence in the room while I tried to probe more. The session ended slightly early with Ruth saying she had to rush back to work. As she was leaving, she asked if she could meet every other week because she wasn't sure she would be able to make it to a weekly appointment.

Attachment-related anxiety

Goals

Those with attachment-related anxiety seek a feeling of "felt security" with a secure base. They require excessive attention and care, almost wishing to merge with another. They frequently are not looking to explore the environment (Hazan & Shaver, 1994).

Behaviors

Individuals with attachment-related anxiety exhibit hyperactivating behavior. They are often clingy and controlling, trying their best to get their partner's attention. They may exaggerate their vulnerabilities, overly self-disclose, and declare an inability to cope by themselves. These individuals may seem childish and excessively needy, tending to inhibit support-seeking behaviors in favor of appearing helpless. They manifest intrusive behavior that can be perceived as aggressive at times. Ironically, this behavior can elicit rejection, the very thing they are trying to avert. These individuals may express inappropriate amounts of anger in conflict, are often hypersensitive to disapproval, and may take blame for negative interactions even when they aren't at fault, hoping to maintain contact with their partner. Though they may notice others in distress and report more distress themselves because of this, they are less likely to help others. Attachment anxiety is related to more self-centered reasons for volunteering, as opposed to altruistic intent. In terms of sex, anxiously attached women tend to be more promiscuous, are a younger age when they begin having sex, have more sexual partners, and have an increased likelihood of having extradyadic sex. Both men and women with attachment-related anxiety often engage in sex just to please a partner and tend to view it as a way to increase intimacy (Hazan & Shaver, 1994; Mikulincer & Shaver, 2007; Feeney, 2016).

Cognitions

Those with attachment-related anxiety tend to have low self-esteem and to view themselves as less competent than others. They tend to have a negative lens and to interpret many interactions as signs of rejection, even if this is not the case. Additionally, they may misinterpret positive actions from others, distortedly seeing them as negative, and may have trouble inhibiting thoughts of rejection (Mikulincer & Shaver, 2007; Mikulincer et al., 2010). For instance, a diary study (Pietromonaco & Barrett, 1997), where subjects logged their reactions to daily interactions, found that anxiously attached students had increased negative self-views after most social encounters, even those that weren't confrontational. In general, these individuals often are self-focused and have a pessimistic view of their partner's intentions, dependability, and trustworthiness. They can also be obsessively preoccupied with their romantic partner's reactions to them, feel overwhelming jealousy, and also increased loneliness. This can interfere with relationship satisfaction (Hazan & Shaver, 1994; Mikulincer & Shaver, 2007). Interestingly though, unlike avoidantly attached individuals, those with attachment-related anxiety can also value relationships and feel happiness when they are absolutely secure in the availability of their partner (Li & Chan, 2012).

Relational aspects

In general, anxiously attached people experience decreased satisfaction in their relationships (Feeney, 2016). The same has been found true for men's and women's same-sex relationships (Mohr, Selterman, & Fassinger, 2013). Attachment-related anxiety is correlated with increased conflict (Feeney, 2016). Interestingly, Pietromonaco and Barrett (1997) found that those with attachment-related anxiety actually reported feeling more satisfied with the relationship following conflictual behavior with their partner. In fact, they reported that as the level of discord increased, so did their positive feelings about their interactions. This can possibly be explained by the notion that anxiously attached individuals interpret conflict as increased involvement and attention from their partner.

Example of a first session

Ruth arrived at her first session in tears. She sat down and then scooched her chair closer to me. When I asked what brought her to therapy, she began sobbing. Her daughter Annie was born three months ago, she said, spitting out the words. Her husband did nothing to help around the house. She told him again and again that he wasn't pulling his weight, but it just seemed to make him withdraw more. She was the first of her friends to have a baby, she reported. But come to think of it, she had never really been able to depend on her friends anyway. She had thought she could count on her husband, but, and here she broke down again, he was proving to be just like her father. Uninvolved and uncaring. When I did a relationship history with her husband, she confessed that she hadn't known him all that well. Theirs had been a love story, she said with a smile. She had seen him from across campus and had fallen instantly in love with him. She had found out his name. A friend happened to know him and after just a little research, she had managed to meet him in person. He was everything she had imagined and within just four months, they were planning their wedding.

Just her luck though, she fell pregnant on her honeymoon. And now, here she was, with a baby and a husband who was unsupportive. She repeated that she had tried many times to tell him that she wasn't coping, that the baby was too much for her to manage. He just seemed cold and distant in response to her pleas for help. They fought constantly now, she told me sadly. And the strange thing was, she sometimes was only able to feel cared for when they were in the middle of screaming at each other. At least, he was taking notice of her, she said. I had to tell Ruth that our time was up multiple times before she got up to leave.

Fearful attachment

Goals

Typically, those with fearful attachment have had frightening caretakers serving as secure bases. They have opposing goals, alternating between attachment-related anxiety and attachment-related avoidance, trying to feel safe while at the same time trying to maintain distance and never feeling safe (Daniel, 2015).

Behaviors

Those who are fearfully attached use both hyperactivating and deactivating strategies. Either both or neither strategy is employed, which results in random, contradictory, and arbitrary reactions when the attachment-system is activated. This leads to generally poor coping mechanisms as well as problem-solving abilities. More than others, fearfully attached individuals have a tendency to dissociate, or to disconnect or detach from what is happening in the moment. It can seem as if the individual is entering a trance. This is both protective and scary to the individual. They feel safer because they have retreated, but frightened because they feel out of control. They exhibit low amounts of empathy for others and are more likely to have severe personality disorders as well as to suffer from poor mental health (Mikulincer & Shaver, 2007; Daniel, 2015). They tend to suffer more than others and long for connection, but feel anxious about this need and are fearful of any impending rejection from those with whom they connect. They are likely to have only a few close relationships that are usually dysfunctional. They are often-times controlling and critical when interacting with others (Daniel, 2015).

Cognitions

Individuals with fearful attachment tend to be rigid and closed in their thinking (Mikulincer & Shaver, 2007). They tend to view themselves as helpless and inadequate (Daniel, 2015). They overestimate the risks of getting involved with others and tend to exaggerate negative traits and attribute negative intentions to others (Mikulincer et al., 2010).

Relational aspects

Fearfully attached individuals tend to be involved in violent or highly conflictual relationships (Mikulincer & Shaver, 2007). They tend to feel unconnected to their partner (Daniel, 2015).

Example of a first session

Ruth walked into my office and asked if she could switch some chairs around. She explained that her back was hurting and she needed to be a certain distance from my chair. I obliged. She sat down and began talking. She and her husband had been fighting constantly since the birth of their first child. Well, she acknowledged, they'd always fought, but this was somehow different. She felt overwhelmed by going back to work and resentful of her husband for making her do so. He worked as well, but she had been under the impression that he would allow her to be home with their daughter. Should have known, she muttered. Story of her life. No one lives up to their word. In the middle of talking of her childhood, telling me that her father had been strict, her eyes glazed over and she momentarily stopped talking. She blinked and then asked where she was. I reminded her that she was talking about her father and she said no, she was talking about her husband. She continued to complain that he was not meeting her needs, but then said she was fully self-sufficient, always had been. So she would just continue to do her own thing. She had few friends, saying they were never able to live up to her standards. But this did leave her feeling lonely. She wanted to do things differently to how her parents had done things and she was afraid she wouldn't be able to do so. When I reminded her of the fee at the end of the session, she got an edge in her voice, saying she didn't know there was a copay. She got up to leave and said she would call to schedule another appointment.

Summary

While developmental psychologists were studying states of mind with respect to attachment and the resulting attachment strategies, social and personality psychologists were studying attachment patterns. Hazan and Shaver's focus on romantic love sparked the beginnings of self-report measures in the attachment world. According to these researchers, attachment patterns can be viewed along a continuum of two underlying dimensions: attachment-related anxiety and attachment-related avoidance. The attachment-related anxiety dimension evaluates an individual's tendency to hyperactivate the attachment system, while the attachment-related avoidance dimension assesses an individual's tendency to deactivate the attachment system. Increased attachment-related anxiety with lower thresholds of monitoring for rejection and increased attachment-related avoidance encourages the use of withdrawing as a way to regulate the attachment behavioral system. Thus, those who score high on attachment-related anxiety are prone to heightening their vulnerabilities and emotions in an attempt to solicit attention. In contrast, individuals who score high on attachment-related avoidance downplay their vulnerabilities and try to suppress their emotions in order to be more self-sufficient. Those who measure high on both dimensions seem to alternate between the two tactics and ultimately may seem to lack any coherent strategy, while those who score low on both dimensions can be deemed securely attached, with the capacity to maintain close, supportive relationships. Still other measures resulted from this new line of inquiry, including the secure base assessment, which measures an individual's heuristic that is developed within the attachment bond and is organized or represented as a secure base script. These measures can also be used in therapy to better understand our clients.

Chapter 5

The developmental pathway of attachment

As one can gather, a great deal of attachment research has focused on classifying or categorizing children and adults as secure, insecure, or disorganized with respect to attachment. Overall, this has been incredibly beneficial to the field, allowing empirical research to flourish, validating more concepts and aspects of social science than had ever been validated before. However, the emphasis on classification has often allowed researchers to overlook the process of how an attachment bond forms, develops, and functions dynamically (Slade, 2004). As Fonagy (2001) notes, while many of Bowlby's cohorts' theories led to new schools of psychoanalytic therapy, Bowlby's ideas did not. His focus on empirical investigation created increased distance between him and the psychoanalysts of the day, setting a trend that continued until fairly recently.

It was developmental researchers who began to further their thinking and to attempt to better understand the *process* of attachment formation. Did the attachment bond develop in a linear manner and become fixated at certain points, as Freud had posited? Was the caregiver completely in charge of the attachment bond's development while the baby remained a passive participant, or did the baby have the ability to have a say in the matter? Do babies and caregivers communicate? If so, how do they do this without words? *How* does a secure or insecure baby become a secure or insecure adult, as empirical research seems to indicate? And, what role did social relationships, and in particular the caregiver–child dyad, play in the emergence of the self?

These were some of the fundamental questions developmental theorists began to tackle. They turned to the work of Louis Wilson Sander (1918–2012), a child psychiatrist, who studied personality development, and whose research provided evidence to attachment theorists that the self is a social creation, emerging from within the caregiving relationship system (Sroufe, 1989). When Sander completed his training in child psychiatry at the Judge Baker Guidance Center, a Harvard Medical School affiliate, he joined a research team studying the early mother–child relationship. Launched in 1954, this was a naturalistic, longitudinal study in much the same vein as was Ainsworth's naturalistic, observational study. From this study, Sander (1962; 1975) was able to chart a basic course of development for babies from age zero to 36 months. He emphasized that though there is a general path for development (see below), each infant develops in a unique way in order to adapt to its unique dyadic caregiving system and external surroundings. The caregiver needs to adapt to and accommodate the changing needs of the child across development (Sander, 2000; Sroufe, 2000). In the end, much like Bowlby had concluded, Sander determined that the quality of the infant–caregiver relationship is essential to an individual's developmental trajectory (Sroufe, 2000).

Systemic thinking

Like Bowlby, Sander very much believed that development occurred within a relational context. His was a systems model. According to systems thinking, an individual's inner experiences are organized by dynamic transactions. The individual continually grows and adapts to his context, which in the case of the attachment bond is the dyadic relationship. Sander turned to cybernetic theory to frame his thinking, seeing the caregiver–infant dyad as a coordinated system that adapts to change, where each member of the system modifies and is modified by the other's needs and behavior (Sander, 1975; 2000). It is through this interactive regulation within the dyadic relationship that the infant learns to self-organize and ultimately becomes integrated (Beebe & Lachmann, 2002). As Sroufe (2005) later wrote, development can best be viewed from an organizational perspective, where behavior is organized and then reorganized when the system is perturbed, achieving new equilibriums. All in all, the self, or an inner organization, emerges as a consequence of the dynamic, dyadic configuration of which it was a part (Sroufe, 1989; 2000). We are not separate entities living in vacuums. We influence and are influenced by each other.

Take a football team as an example. Why do they need to train together as a team? Quarterbacks throw to receivers and receivers adjust their playing to be able to catch the throws. Basic skills are learned within this interaction that are practiced again and again. Plays are organized and strategies adapted. The team players function within a system that works in a coordinated manner only after practicing together. If a specific quarterback is traded to another team, the system is disrupted. With the addition of a new quarterback, a new equilibrium must be reached.

Layered model of development

Another idea that was new at the time Sander came on the scene was that of the layered model of development. At the time, in the 1950s and 1960s, Freud's theory of stage development predominated. This view purported that an individual progressed through the following series of fixed psychosexual stages in a linear manner: oral, anal, phallic, latency, and genital. Each stage was associated with a specific conflict requiring resolution in order to progress to the next stage. However, not all are able to proceed from one stage to the next. Some are frustrated by unmet needs and are therefore unable to resolve the particular conflict and some experience being overly indulged, and because of this, are hesitant to move on. Both situations can result in what psychoanalysts have termed "fixation," or being stuck in a specific stage until the conflict is resolved. Sander's perspective on psychosocial development differed in that he, in line with Bowlby's thinking, suggested a layered, or hierarchical model of development. Here, development is viewed as a cumulative process where each successive layer builds on the other, with many layers remaining active across the life cycle. In other words, stages don't get "passed." They just become part of the individual's journey to self-cohesion. Not surprisingly, as an individual ages, the tasks he must accomplish become more complicated (Stern, 2000; Sroufe, 2005; 2016). As Bowlby (1973) stated, the developmental pathway "turns at each and every stage of the journey on an interaction between the organism as it has developed up to that moment and the environment in which it then finds itself" (Bowlby, 1973, p. 412). Phases of development are viewed in terms of *adaptive* tasks that are negotiated by the infant where the ability to negotiate each stage is determined by the infant's physical and emotional developmental capacities and successful negotiation of one stage allows for the resolution of previous stages (Sroufe, 2016). Thus, the approach is normative with the increment of adaptive behaviors, and not pathomorphic, relying on conflict resolution or overcoming disturbances to progress forward (Stern, 2000).

Adaptive issues across development as attachment bonds form

Sander's research on the development of regulatory abilities fits well with Bowlby's theory of attachment. In fact, attachment theory has been described as a theory of regulation (Kobak & Sceery, 1988), with the caregiver–infant interaction being viewed as critical to the development of affect regulation and to ultimate self-organization and integration (Kopp, 1982; Sroufe, 2000). Of course, the interactions are asymmetric at first, with the caregiver assuming more of the role of regulating the dyad than the infant can. However, responsive caregiver-orchestrated regulation paves the way for the infant to develop self-regulatory abilities (Sroufe, 2000). Infants co-regulate with their caregivers. Preschoolers become increasingly self-reliant, but with a great deal of support and scaffolding from a caregiver. Middle childhood can be said to be a time of personal effectance and increasing peer competence. Children at this age begin to develop friendships outside of the attachment relationship, but are still reliant on their attachment figures. They are capable, though, of having deep and loyal friendships. Adolescence is a time of transition. It is a time of balancing autonomy with connectedness. According to attachment theory, a normative task of adolescence is to strike a new balance between the exploratory system and the attachment system, with increasing autonomy from a caregiver and decreasing overt attachment needs. While developing autonomy, adolescents strive to maintain a secure relationship with a caregiver. Therefore, a caregiver, or a "secure base," is required to provide developmentally appropriate scaffolding to an adolescent as he or she negotiates the quest for autonomy. Whereas a caregiver is seen as providing "caregiver-guided-self-regulation" during the toddler and school-aged years, the "goal corrected partnership" becomes more of a mutually negotiated effort between parent and adolescent. Open communication is one way in which such negotiation takes place (Allen, 2008). Adulthood is a time for emancipation and for functioning individually (Sroufe et al., 2005a). A securely attached adult has a coherent and cohesive sense of self with a capacity to relate to others and maintain intimate connections. Security implies having the ability to internally experience, regulate, and integrate a wide range of emotions and to cope with the stressors of adulthood. How does one get there? What follows are Sander's observations of the course of development in the beginning, over the first three years of life.

Physiological development (0–3 months). During the first three months of life, the primary focus of caretakers is the physiological regulation of their infants' basic functions such as eating, sleeping, and eliminating, as well as day–night organization. In order to do so, the caregiver must learn to interpret the infant's cues. If the caregiver is reasonably accurate in this interpretation and is fairly consistent in meeting the infant's needs, the baby begins to show a preference for that particular caregiver and the infant state and caregiver's ministering become coordinated.

Regulation of reciprocal exchange (3–6 months). This stage has been termed "attachment-in-the-making" phase (Mikulincer & Shaver, 2007). The infant becomes a more active participant in routine tasks, such as getting dressed, diapering, and spoon feeding and thus, there is more of a reciprocal coordination between caregiver and infant. Furthermore, these interchanges between caregiver and infant, together with the baby's emerging ability to smile, often elicit joy and delight.

Initiative (6–9 months). Termed the "clear-cut attachment phase" (Mikulincer & Shaver, 2007), a baby is able to physically reach out and can initiate social interaction with the caregiver. The smiling response is at its zenith and interchanges are joyful. The caregiver–infant dyad can be seen as more like a relationship and not just interactions and the baby is more particular to his caregiver, experiencing increased negative responses to strangers. Also, the child is often more physically mobile and able to better explore the world. He has increased independence. A caregiver witnesses a child's developing initiative, where he moves toward her as well as away from her of his own accord. The caregiver must negotiate any feelings that may arise with the baby's activity, such as possible feelings of rejection as the baby moves away or feeling overwhelmed by the baby's needs when the baby moves toward the caregiver.

Focalization (10–13 months). The baby's ability to move is more developed than before and furthermore, he is able to be more goal-directed in his behavior. Bowlby (1973) posited the beginnings of the development of internal working models during this phase. The child exercises even more discrimination of his caregiver from other adults and begins to evaluate whether or not she is responsive to his bids for her availability. Predictable availability engenders more delight in interchanges with the caregiver as well as with the world at large. The caregiver assumes the role of a "secure base" (Ainsworth, 1973) where if the caregiver is perceived to be definitely available, the child increases exploratory activity. Should the baby encounter a threat, he will return to the caregiver for comfort. So, for example, if a secure baby is crawling away from his mother, but then is terrified by the sound of loud thunder in the distance, that baby will orchestrate his return to his mother in order to feel safe again. By the end of the first year, the baby is still only capable of "co-regulation" (Fogel, 1993), and not self-regulation. In other words, the baby needs his caregiver to help maintain his inner organization. The term "focalization" is used to convey the notion that the caregiver becomes the focal point, at the center of a growing world.

Self-assertion (14–20 months). The toddler experiences increased goal-directed behavior and assertiveness. He will often modify his behavior until he achieves his desired result. Clashing of wills often occurs during this phase. Whereas before, the child may have avoided disagreement with or separation from a caregiver, he may now actively initiate it. At the same time, the caregiver is required to curtail the toddler's behavior, imposing various rules and constraints of socialization. An example of this is toilet training, which can become a battle ground, or simply when a caregiver says "no" to a child begging for a piece of candy. In fact, it has been documented that between 13 and 17 months of age, a caregiver inhibits her child's behavior every nine minutes (Schore, 2003). As a result of this kind of limit-setting, negative emotion, such as shame, may enter the interchanges between caregiver and child. During this period of development, the child is constantly trying to balance his need for increased independence and autonomy with his need for attachment. A sensitive caregiver must allow for exploration all the while providing a secure base. She must provide what Sroufe (1996) called "guided self-regulation," or appropriate scaffolding to support the child in adaptive development.

Recognition (18–36 months). The ability to verbally communicate rapidly develops during this stage. The child gains increased awareness of his inner self organization and can now better express his feelings and thoughts. The increase facilitates the infant's move to what Sander termed "self-constancy" and also allows the child to understand the caregiver's state of mind as separate from his. The child can now move toward what Bowlby called the "goal-corrected partnership," where caregiver and child become equal participants in the coordination of the dyadic relationship (Sander, 1962; 1975; Sroufe, 1989).

Daniel Stern (1934–2012)

The infant is an active participant

Sander set the stage for other developmental attachment researchers to follow. In particular, infant researchers now had a platform to build upon. They had a general growth trajectory, but still needed more understanding of the *process* of development. In the early 1970s, Daniel Stern, a psychoanalyst and infant researcher, introduced into research the microanalysis of film and videos of caregiver–infant face-to-face interactions. Here, mothers and babies are seated face-to-face with one another. There are two cameras, one on each dyadic member's face, and there is a split screen to view both faces. The new technique allowed researchers to focus on the *process* of communication, as separate from *content*, though both could be explored. This way of researching was different to the focus of other researchers on behavior or on language. It was a move that would revolutionize the way we think of infants and of regulation in general (Beebe & Steele, 2013; Karen, 1994).

Stern's seminal book *The Interpersonal World of the Infant*, originally published in 1985, was named the book of the decade because of its incredible impact on psychoanalytic theory. Up until then, it was presumed that infants were passive during interactions with caregivers. However, with the ability to closely observe caregiver–infant relationships, Stern concluded that a sense of self is present from the start of life. Even before the development of language and self-awareness, the infant possesses some sense of self which is evidenced in the nonverbal interchanges within the caregiver–infant dyad. And not only that, the infant is able to communicate with the outside world, using vocalizations, silences, eye contact, and gestures to do so (Carr & Nachman, 2017; Stern, 2000). He can avert his gaze or smile or coo to engage another. In other words, the infant is an active, complex, and social being whose interactions with his caregiver are bi-directional from the start.

Intersubjectivity and nonverbal communication

Stern's upbringing explains his interest in early life as well as in nonverbal communication. Stern's father passed away while he was still a baby and in the year that followed, his mother remained mute. Though he was born in Manhattan, his first language was Czech because of his Czech nanny. Thus, when he was hospitalized at age two for a few months, he was unable to understand the English spoken to him by the hospital workers. He was forced to rely on reading nonverbal cues and behaviors (Carr & Nachman, 2017). Thus, years later, when examining caregiver–infant dyadic interaction, Stern was drawn to the nonverbal, implicit communication he witnessed.

Stern was the first to write of "intersubjectivity," or the active pursuit of the sharing of experiences. He grouped intersubjectivity into three forms: joint attention, shared intentions, and affect attunement. An example of joint attention is when a caregiver points somewhere and the baby looks at where the mother is pointing as opposed to simply looking at her finger. The baby then looks back at the caregiver's face to confirm that he is looking in the correct direction and in order to validate that they have a joint focus of attention. Sharing intentions usually involves some form of language and the most common example of this is making a request. For instance, an infant indicates that he wants the cookie his mother is holding by reaching out a hand to his mother and saying "Eh!" The infant is assuming that his mother understands his intention to eat the cookie. This becomes interintentionality, or joint intention. The third form of intersubjectivity is of the most interest to clinicians. Affect attunement is similar to the concept of empathic responsiveness, almost like "getting inside" other people's experiences. It is more than mere imitation. It is conveying that a feeling is communicated and shared. As Stern (2000) writes, "[a]ffect attunement … is the performance of behaviors that express the quality of feeling of a shared affect state without imi-tating the exact behavioral expression of the inner state" (p. 3). A nine-month-old boy sees a toy train and becomes excited. He pulls it towards him, smiles, and exclaims "Tatata!" His mother widens her eyes, smiles, and breathes in deeply for the exact length of time her son says "Tatata!" conveying excitement and joy. This is an example of affect attunement. The focus of the attunement is not on the behavior alone, but on the feeling behind the behavior (Stern, 2000).

Beatrice Beebe

Just how much the infant engaged with his caregiver was a matter for further inves-tigation and Beatrice Beebe was poised to do just that. Her career trajectory began in the early 1970s, when, as a graduate student, she had the good fortune to join Daniel Stern as he filmed mothers and infant twins in their homes. On one of those days, Beebe was particularly overwhelmed with emotion as a baby tracked her face and then responded to her joy in kind. She decided at that point to do her dissertation with Stern, and would ultimately use microanalysis of film to explore the process of positive facial affect. While Beebe conducted research with Stern, she continued her clinical training. Both her research and her clinical training led her to a deeper understanding of self- and interactive regulation (Beebe & Lachmann, 2002).

Exactly what is self-regulation? Beebe and Lachmann (2002) state that

> [f]rom birth onward, self-regulation refers to the management of arousal, the maintenance of alertness, the ability to dampen arousal in the face of over-stimulation, and the capacity to inhibit behavioral expression. It includes var-iations in the readiness to respond and in the clarity of cues, such as how clearly a baby conveys hunger, sleepiness, or approach-avoidance. Self-touching, looking away, and restricting the range of facial expressiveness are examples of self-regulation strategies that dampen arousal.
>
> (p. 28)

Self-regulation incorporates the management of both negative *and* positive affect. The ability to adaptively self-regulate is crucial to an individual's engagement with others and with the world at large and it is critical throughout the life cycle.

However, one needs more than just the ability to regulate the self. One needs to be able to regulate while engaging with others. In fact, attachment theory proposes that it is through interactive regulation that self-regulation develops. This implies that it is not only about being able to self-regulate while communing with others, but it may be that it is the communing with others, and in particular, caregivers, that enable self-regulatory abilities to function and grow. After years of study, Beebe and Lachmann (2002) became certain that dyadic interaction plays a large role in the organization of early experiences. Furthermore, not only did infants seem capable of regulating themselves, but they also seemed able to adjust their interactions to adapt to the dyadic system.

In an effort to find empirical validation, Beebe began tracking vocal rhythms. It was something that was measurable. Actual data could be collected to answer questions such as "how tightly do infants and caregivers match vocal rhythms with one another?" Eighty-eight infants and their mothers were studied, comparing the vocal coordination during face-to-face interactions when the infants were four months old and those infant's Strange Situation classifications at 12 months of age. The team of researchers were not surprised to find that at four months old, mother–infant pairs and stranger–infant pairs co-regulated with one another. What was surprising were the attachment classification results. In ascribing to Stern's concept of affect attunement, it may have made sense that the mother–infant pairs who better matched each other's vocal rhythms would be more securely attached later on. However, this was not the case. It turned out that the pairs with a midrange score of bidirectional mother–infant vocal coordination at four months predicted more secure attachment at 12 months. In fact, a high degree of coordination within the dyad was a risk factor for developing disorganized attachment and low degree of coordination predicted attachment insecurity. Midrange coordination was optimal (Jaffe et al., 2001).

Midrange model of coordination

These results point to the notion that interactions between caregiver and infant are "co-constructed," where infants regulate themselves as well as interactively regulate with caregivers. Thus, caregivers and infants "contingently" follow each other, each individual adapting his or her behavior to the other's prior behavior (Beebe & Steele, 2013). Based on the findings of vocal coordination study, Beebe and Lachmann (2002) posited a midrange model with three interacting units: the caregiver, self-regulating part; the infant, self-regulating part; and the caregiver–infant dyad as a system on its own. Midrange coordination of interactive regulation predicts secure attachment, and midrange self-regulation is seen as optimal. This implies that in the midrange, there is a balance of interactive coordination and self-regulation where neither is excessive. There is flexibility to navigate between self- and interactive regulation, allowing the infant to balance his attention, affect, and levels of arousal without becoming overwhelmed. Infants signal their needs to a caregiver in various ways. For instance, it has been found that infants turn away from their caregivers' gaze in order to reregulate themselves. There is a dynamic interplay between caregiver and infant to keep the infant's arousal within tolerable ranges. Consequently, caregivers and infants gaze at each other, but not constantly. An infant's heart rate has been shown to decelerate with gaze aversion, presumably to recover from the heart rate acceleration that occurs just before the infant looks away. Thus, gaze aversion is a form of self-regulation. Again, optimal infant–caregiver coordination is midrange, with caregivers and infants doing a dance, where they gaze at each other for a period of time which is stimulating to the infant, either positively or negatively. The infant then averts his gaze and only returns his gaze to his caregiver when he is ready to engage once more (Field, 1981).

A baby who cannot rely on a caregiver to appropriately respond to his cues may adapt accordingly. Take for instance a caregiver who is intrusive or overbearing and cannot allow her baby a chance to recover from the stimulation of attunement. This baby is unable to adaptively focus on self-regulation and may have to focus exclusively on the caregiver's movements in order to protect himself. This can lead to "interactive vigilance" which occurs with babies with ambivalent attachment, where a mother may only sometimes be available for the baby. Worse, a caregiver may personalize a baby's gaze aversion, feel rejected, and intrude upon the baby's space in an attempt to reconnect too soon, thereby overstimulating the baby. On the other hand, a baby who is only focused on self-regulation may become withdrawn or inhibited. This may happen for a baby who is avoidantly attached, where a mother is oftentimes rejecting and unavailable. The baby is forced to rely on himself when in distress and may learn to withdraw in order to cope with any affect that may overwhelm his system. Supporting this, Beebe and colleagues found that avoidantly attached infants used self-touch to self-regulate in order to stay visually engaged with their caregivers (Beebe & Lachmann, 2002). Thus, with insecure attachments, the infant experiences maladaptive levels of attention, affect, and arousal.

Chase-and-dodge

Beebe had a particular interest in what happens to a baby when he is overstimulated. How does this affect his ability to modulate or regulate himself? In a study designed to investigate this question, mothers were told to play with their four month olds as they would have at home. The following pattern of interaction of intrusive mothering was noted: a mother "looms" into the infant's face and the infant reacts by moving his head away from the mother. This instigates the mother's "chasing" by moving her body and head toward the infant. The baby continues to move further away, as the mother continues to "chase." At the end of this split-second sequence of behaviors, the mother usually picks the infant up. While she is doing so, the infant centers his head without looking at his mother and then as she places him in her lap, the infant moves his head away again. The infant keeps "escaping" from the mother. These movements are predictable, with the mother's behavior affecting the infant's behavior and vice versa. Beebe termed this interaction "chase-and-dodge" and it is an example of misattunement, where the mother is not regulating the infant's level of arousal and in fact, may be overstimulating the infant (Beebe & Lachmann, 2002).

Edward Tronick

The more these researchers micro-analyzed caregiver–infant dyadic interactions, the more questions were answered, but also the more questions were generated. For instance, exactly how does the integration of self-regulation processes and interactive regulation occur? In other words, *how* does an infant balance the regulation of his own state with the influencing of and being influenced by another's state? Does it all occur at the same time? And how is this related to the attachment bond's development? Edward Tronick, a developmental psychologist and infant researcher, committed himself to answering these questions. Beginning his studies in the 1970s, at the same time as Beebe and Stern, he developed the still-face paradigm (explained below), an experiment that would transform our understanding of infant coping as well as the effects of maternal anxiety and depression on infant social and emotional development. Currently, Tronick is a professor of psychology at the University of Massachusetts Boston, a lecturer at Harvard Medical School, and the director of the Child Development Unit.

Self- and interactive regulation (mutual regulation model)

According to Gianino and Tronick (1988), self-regulation and interactive regulation happen at once. They believe that the infant uses the same abilities to engage a caregiver as he uses to regulate himself. Gianino (Tronick, 2007) documented six different coping mechanisms an infant uses to re-engage with a caregiver following a disruption.

1   Signal – The infant signals his caregiver with emotional shows that are either positive (i.e., coos), negative (i.e., fussing), or neutral (i.e., gesturing to be picked up).
2   Alternate focus – The infant shifts attentional focus away from the caregiver, either examining an object (i.e., the seat he sits in) or the self (i.e., his hand).
3   Self-comfort – The infant turns to his body to self-soothe. This can be an oral behavior (i.e., sucking a finger), a self-clasp (i.e., holding own hands), or rocking (i.e., swaying from side to side).

4   Withdrawal – The infant disengages from the caregiver, either motorically (i.e., slouching) or perceptually (i.e., looking "dull").
5   Escape – The infant physically distances himself from his caregiver by turning away.
6   Avert/scan – The infant shifts his gaze elsewhere, away from his caregiver.

When signaling, the infant is still trying to interact with the caregiver. All signaling behaviors were termed "other-directed regulatory behaviors" by Gianino and Tronick (1988). The rest of the coping strategies occur when the infant gives up on his goal of maintaining engagement with his caregiver. These have been labeled "self-directed regulatory behaviors" (Gianino & Tronick, 1988). Overall, these coping strategies point to the fact that the infant is not completely dependent on the caregiver to manage his levels of arousal.

The still-face experiment

Tronick set to work to better understand when an infant disengages from interactive regulation. Thus, while Beebe focused on intrusive caregiving, in 1975, Tronick began examining the opposite. He wondered what would happen to a baby if a caregiver was unresponsive to his cues to engage. Tronick developed the 'still-face' experiment. Here, after interacting naturally with her infant, a mother is instructed to suddenly become stone-faced. The results were striking. The mother remains unresponsive while the infant desperately tries to reengage her. After failing at re-engaging the mother, the infant averted his gaze, withdrew, and became sad and angry (Tronick, 2007). The infants who had experienced more "interactive repairs" (Gianino & Tronick, 1988) in the past were better able to cope with the lack of a responsive caregiver in the still-face paradigm. Those who were used to unrepaired mismatches gave up trying to repair the mismatch more quickly and resorted to focusing on self-regulation. This often occurs with infants whose mothers are depressed.

Interactive error and interactive repair

The results of the 'still-face' paradigm confirmed for Tronick (2007) that, first and foremost, an infant's optimal developmental outcome is dependent on the effective functioning of the dyadic affective communication system. He highlighted that in all dyadic pairs, both those who function adaptively and those who function maladaptively, regulatory interaction is not totally in sync. It, in fact, consists of the caregiver–infant pair cycling between coordinated states, which only occurs between 30% and 50% of the time (Ammaniti, 2018), and miscoordinated states. The cycle from coordinated to miscoordinated and back to coordinated states happens every three to five seconds or so. In a study designed to examine how much coordination occurs between the infant and his caregiver, Tronick and Cohn (1989) found that once the pair enter a mismatched state, 70% of these states are repaired within two seconds. Rather than defining normal interaction as synchronous and coherent, it is more apt to define it as cycling between coordination and miscoordination.

What is more, they found that both the caregiver *and* the infant coordinated the repair, meaning it is an interactive process. It is important to note, however, that at first, the caregiver bares much more of the responsibility for ensuring that repair occurs. How the caregiver manages the transition between the states of miscoordination and coordination is critical (Tronick & Cohn, 1989). Tronick purports that if this transition is continually managed well, infants feel more of a sense of self-efficacy in meeting their goals and are able to develop better coping mechanisms when interacting with others. Supporting this, he found that babies who are able to cope better during the still-face scenario and who, in general, experience more repairs following mismatched situations, are more securely attached to their caregivers at age one year of age (Tronick, 1989). On the other hand, if disrupted coordination is not often repaired, infants may feel a lack of self-efficacy as well as despair. This occurs for those who are insecurely attached.

When repair doesn't happen as it should, an "interactive error" (Tronick, 1989) occurs. Imagine, for example, a mother initiating peek-a-boo with her baby. In the middle of the most exciting part of the game, the baby suddenly turns away from his mother and expressionlessly gazes into the distance. The mother leans back in her seat and waits patiently for the baby to give her a signal of what he wants to do. The baby returns to the game quite quickly and the mother leans in, restarting the game with a smile. The baby repeats his turning away at some point and the mother waits again for her baby to reinitiate play. Both have big smiles on their face. Now picture a situation where the baby turns away from the mother and the mother looms in. The baby moves further away and the mother continues to put her face in front of her baby's face. The baby exhibits negative affect. This is an example of an interactive error. In each example, differing emotions are elicited. In the first, the baby experiences joy, while in the second example, the baby experiences negative emotion.

What happens to a baby who repeatedly experiences the adaptive repair of interactive errors? A baby is motivated to feel positive emotions and therefore, will seek out interactive repair. As caregiver–infant dyads move from disruption to repair, they experience their negative emotions changing to positive ones. A sequence begins as positive with attunement, turns negative with interactive error, and transforms to positive once again upon repair. Over time, the ability to turn mismatches into matches builds coping strategies and a sense of efficacy. The positive sequences also develop representations of others as reliable and available should they need support. However, if an infant does not experience the repair of mismatches often enough, there can be several harmful consequences. Firstly, these infants begin to self-regulate, managing overwhelming levels of arousal without help. Because they may come to focus almost exclusively on self-regulation, their ability to achieve their goals may become compromised. They become used to experiencing long periods of negative affect and aren't given the experience of converting negative to positive affect. Secondly, they begin to feel unable to rely on their caregiver in general. Thus, they don't gain experience in managing stress and, as the failure to experience repair accumulates, they develop a representation of the self as ineffective and a representation of others as unreliable (Tronick, 1989; 2007). These representations become part of the internal working model and in this way, influence the trajectory of attachment styles across the life cycle.

Caregiving system

Before we continue, it is important to examine the role of the caregiver in the interactive process. Thus far, this chapter has focused on the infant's ability to self- and interactively regulate. When the infant is interactively regulating with the caregiver, what is required of the caregiver to ensure the proper development of their child? Bowlby (1969; 1982) proposed the existence of a caregiving system that interacts with the attachment system, but up until recently, most attachment researchers have focused on the attachment system and in particular the infant or child's behavior within this system. Few have examined Bowlby's notion of the caregiving system, a system that is closely linked to the other behavioral attachment systems. Bowlby believed a caregiving system evolved in tandem with the attachment system, whose function is to ensure protection of the young. Just as affect regulation is involved in the child's attachment systems, so too is emotion a part of the caregiving system. Presumably a mother experiences intense feelings of satisfaction and pleasure when she is able to provide security and support to her children and sadness or despair when separated from or when unable to provide necessary comfort to her young. Conversely, in a well-functioning system, she herself experiences distress when unable to provide protection (George & Solomon, 2008). In an effort to address this gap, George and Solomon (2008) have suggested that whereas children are motivated to maintain their protection, caregivers are motivated to provide protection to their young in order to ensure the survival of our species. Because of the transactional nature of the attachment dyad, a caregiver's emotions will influence and be influenced by the child. Co-regulation occurs with the interlocking of the caregiving system and the attachment systems and through this, a child's emotions will be regulated. A mother's sensitivity to her child's cues is seen as necessary in enabling a healthy co-regulation to occur.

Recall the concept of maternal sensitivity, or being able to contingently respond to a child's signals (Ainsworth & Bowlby, 1991). Maternal sensitivity includes "awareness of infant signals, accurate interpretation, appropriate response, and prompt response" (Beebe & Steele, 2013, p. 584). The sensitive caregiver picks up on the infant's signals, such as crying or reaching to be picked up. She intervenes appropriately and in a timely manner, neither overstimulating nor under-stimulating her child. It should not be surprising that maternal sensitivity is highly correlated with attachment security. During interactive errors and repairs, a caregiver must sensitively keep an infant's level of arousal from becoming overwhelming. This means the caregiver must facilitate the repair of interactive errors before the infant experiences prolonged distress. Additionally, the caregiver must settle the infant during recovery (Sroufe et al., 2005a). It turns out that a great deal of self-regulation is required from the caregiver if she is to provide sensitive and optimal care to an infant. As Slade (2002) proposes, in order to co-regulate, a caregiver should be able to understand and regulate her own emotion as well as have the capacity to understand her child's emotions. How well she is able to provide interactive regulation depends on her being able to maintain perspective on her own projections and experience empathy for her child (Sander, 1962).

Example

A case vignette may illustrate how coordination and miscoordination may occur with an adult woman and her mother. The vignette focuses on an adult to adult interaction as the same dynamic that occurs between infants and their caregivers traverses the life cycle. Thus, understanding infant–caregiver dyadic interactions can aid clinicians when working with adults. The following dyadic transaction illustrates the dance of attunement as it has developed from infancy. Keira, a 39-year-old single woman, was sitting across from her mother in a restaurant. Her mother was taking her out for lunch to celebrate a promotion she had just gotten at work. They had both talked about going to the Italian Eatery, a new restaurant that had opened up and had received rave reviews. Both Keira and her mother enjoyed Italian food, while Keira's father didn't like it. It was something special that Keira and her mother had shared together since Keira was a little girl. Keira felt very connected to her mother at that moment and decided to disclose a secret she had held on to for almost a year. She suddenly blurted out to her mother that though it wasn't noticeable now, her hair was falling out in small chunks. She had gone to the doctor, who had diagnosed her with alopecia areatta and told her that there was nothing that she could do about this autoimmune condition. It was just going to keep happening. As she spoke, Keira became more and more upset. Her voice began to shake and tears started spilling over, streaming down her face. She looked down in shame and confessed that this felt like the end of the world to her. She was single, and trying to date. Her mother seemed shocked. She took a deep breath of air, as if she couldn't get enough of it. She lightly patted her own hair as if to feel its presence and she then told her daughter that it wasn't the end of the world. After a brief pause, she continued in a stilted voice, saying that it would be alright, that she was sure there was another solution, and that Keira should seek another medical opinion. She just wanted Keira to be happy and she really couldn't see a reason why this would be a problem. She leaned over and put her hands through Keira's hair. "See, you can't feel it." By the end of her mother's rebuttal, Keira felt hopeless. Her situation felt worse than it had before. She quietly dried her eyes and tried to quash any feelings she had about the matter. After what seemed an interminable silence, Keira told her mother she was right, it wasn't that bad, and she was sure she would cheer up. She noticed this seemed to make her mother visibly relax her shoulders.

Keira and her mother had shared a coordinated, interactive regulatory experience before Keira's disclosure about her hair. They both enjoyed Italian food. Keira felt happy because her mother was celebrating her and her mother felt happy because she was doing something nice for Keira. The miscoordination occurred when Keira confided in her mother. Because her mother couldn't regulate herself, she was unable to tolerate Keira's pain and was quick to try to get Keira to feel better. Keira sensed that her pain overwhelmed her mother and that, therefore, her mother wasn't going to be able to soothe her. She felt more helpless and hopeless. She had needed an empathic, attuned response, but had received a miscoordinated one instead. Had Keira's mother distanced herself from the negative affect by "handing it over" to Keira, she would have aggravated the situation as well. As an example, had she said, "That is really awful. I'm so glad that I didn't have to experience that", Keira would have continued to feel unfelt. Furthermore, there would be no room to explore her own feelings as Keira would be saddled with negotiating her mother's response, which could be interpreted as rejection. A repair may have looked like the following scenario: Once her mother had recovered from her initial shock, she said "I'm sorry that I responded that way. It caught me off guard and also, to be honest, I'm never good in these kinds of situations. But this must be really hard for you and I want you to know I am here to listen to you for as long as you may need me to do so."

Summary

Attachment theory is inherently a developmental, systemic theory. Infant researchers elaborated on the process of dyadic development, documenting an infant's growth through a dance with a caregiver. The dance includes moments of attunement as well as moments of misattunement. In fact, it is necessary to have breaks in attunement to enable the baby to recover from the stimulation of being in sync. What is also essential, however, is the interactive repair that must occur following moments of misattunement. When there is a trend of adequate repair, a baby feels safe and secure. However, when there is a pattern of inadequate repair, a baby often develops an insecure attachment strategy to compensate for the overwhelming emotions he is left to negotiate on his own. Clinicians should be aware of this pattern of attunement, misattunement, and interactive repair. They should be able to join with their clients, allow for breaks in attunement with their clients, and also focus on the repair process. So much of the work happens in that repair process.

Chapter 6

The brain

The last three decades have ushered in new waves of attachment research beginning with linking neuroscience and psychology into a field that has come to be called interpersonal neurobiology (Siegel, 1999). The brain has come to be seen as increasingly plastic and as being affected by our experiences. We are not fixed upon birth. We change and continue to change until well into adulthood. There is now more evidence that our brains grow and develop with time and there is a developmental trajectory that is universal to all of us. However, we also interact with the environment in different ways which means we all have unique growth paths. With this understanding has come the idea that our connections with others, in particular our attachment figures, play a critical role in changing our brain over time. Just how our brain changes seems to be very much related to our relationships with others, and in particular with our attachment figures. Our attachment internal working models can be understood as the brain's consolidation of experience, as schemas created based on representations of our memories and our attachment-related experiences that are encoded by our brains. Not only do we seem wired to connect, but from an evolutionary perspective, it can be presumed that we are motivated to do so to ensure our survival. This need for connection ultimately drives how we grow and change. Thus, though much of the research connecting neuroscience and clinical applications is speculative and largely theoretical in nature, as clinicians, it behooves us to better understand just how change in the brain occurs.

The shift in thinking began when President George H. W. Bush proclaimed the 1990s to be the "Decade of the Brain." Because of this, the United States Library of Congress and the National Institute of Mental Health announced the beginnings of a large research initiative to increase awareness of and to encourage dialogue about cutting-edge brain research (www.loc.gov/loc/brain/). Together with the aid of new imaging technologies and an improved ability to measure brain functioning, this tremendous research thrust has greatly advanced our understanding of the human brain's inner workings and in particular, has transformed our thinking about the capacity for the brain to change, or neuroplasticity (Siegel, 2010b; Volkow, 2010). Brain size, neuron size, dendritic architecture, and gray matter density and volume all were observed to change with stimulation and external input (Jensen & Nutt, 2015). In fact, in a defining moment in 1997, Peter

Eriksson, a Swedish neuroscientist, discovered evidence that the adult human brain can actually generate new neurons, a process known as neurogenesis (Banks & Hirschman, 2015). Up until then, the brain was seen as fairly fixed from birth on with little to no changes occurring during development. However, with this evidence and other research to support these findings, neuroscientists now view the brain as highly malleable, constantly interacting with and responding to internal and external stimuli (Volkow, 2010). It seems that the brain can change and does so well through adulthood.

Over the years, evidence has continued to support the notion that experience influences and is in fact, necessary for proper brain development. Once neural plasticity could be assumed, the pressing question changed from "*Does* the brain change?" to "*How* does the brain change?" Scientists have proposed that there are two different processes that affect neural plasticity: those that are experience-expectant and those that are experience-dependent. Experience-expectant processes occur during major growth periods and are based on normative experiences to which everyone is exposed. These include visual stimulation, body movement, and sound. The brain "expects" these stimulating experiences to occur and utilizes them to grow and adapt. If all goes well, for example with visual input, an individual will develop normally. However, if something goes wrong, and for instance vision is obstructed during a critical period of development, the brain may not be able to form the necessary synapses to ensure adequate functioning. Thus, a baby may begin life with the potential to see, but because of a lack of appropriate stimulation, ultimately may not be able to see. Experience-dependent processing occurs throughout our life and impacts how experiences are stored. It can be seen as a refining process, where each individual encounters different experiences and stores this information in their own way (Greenough, Black, & Wallace, 1987). For instance, studies have shown that professional musicians have increased grey matter density in motor, auditory, and visual-spatial brain regions in comparison to amateur and non-musicians (Jancke, 2009). Experience has been shown not only to affect brain structure, but even to impact the expression of genes, something known as epigenetics (Siegel, 2010b; Sroufe, Coffino, & Carlson, 2010). Thus, we are all wired differently because experience shapes us in different ways.

According to advances made during the "decade of the brain," some experiences are more influential than others in shaping the brain. It seems the human brain is particularly sensitive to social and relational input (Volkow, 2010). In fact, Allan Schore, a preeminent neuropsychologist and attachment theorist, proposed that it is the primary caregiver who provides the necessary environmental input for the experience-dependent development of a child's socioemotional functioning (Schore, 1994). Furthermore, he suggested, this attachment-related input is crucial to the brain's development and in particular, to its evolution in managing emotional regulation, attunement, and stress. Scientists have confirmed this connection (Weaver et al., 2004; Cozolino, 2014) and with this, the field of interpersonal neurobiology, a merging of the fields of neurobiology and attachment, came into being (Siegel, 1999). We now understand that the mind is shaped by relational experiences, by attunement, and by attachment. Regulating our emotions and negotiating our dysregulation are part of how our brains grow, how we organize ourselves, and how we become who we are (Siegel, 2003; Cozolino, 2014).

This area of research revolutionized the attachment world, advancing our thinking from a behavioral and cognitive bent to an integrated mind–body approach. Whereas Bowlby and Ainsworth had originally focused on examining behaviors and cognitive internalizations and Main and her colleagues had explored attachment's intersection with the linguistic world, the focus of attachment theory shifted to focus on the connection between the mind, body, and the brain. Schore states that this is in line with Bowlby's original aim of combining the psychological and biological spheres and he argues that because of this expansion in understanding, attachment theory can now be termed "modern attachment theory," or a regulation theory (Schore & Schore, 2008).

Mirror neurons

A momentous discovery occurred in the early 1990s that suggests that we are indeed wired to connect with one another. Beginning in the 1980s, Giacomo Rizzolatti and a team of scientists at the University of Parma in Italy had been mapping out the F5 premotor cortex area in macaque monkeys' brains. They implanted electrodes in single brain cells and watched to see if the cells lit up in response to various movements. They were testing exactly which neurons fired when a monkey performed a specific task, such as reaching for or eating a peanut. From their observations, they came to understand that the F5 neurons fired only when a monkey had an interaction between an object and a biological effector, such as a hand or mouth. One day, quite by accident, one of the researchers noticed something else occurring. When the *researcher* reached for an object, the electrodes in the *monkey*'s F5 area lit up. The monkey's arm was by his side, not moving, but a neuron in his brain was activated. This made no sense to the group of scientists, who believed that motor neurons and sensory neurons were responsible for two entirely different tasks with the sensory neurons reading information from the external environment and the motor neurons acting on these stimuli. A motor neuron responding to sensory input did not fit in with this understanding. Somehow, the monkey's brain was "reading" the researcher's actions as if they were his own (Rizzolatti & Craighero, 2004; Goleman, 2006; Banks & Hirschman, 2015). These neurons that responded while witnessing another perform an action were named "mirror neurons."

There is evidence of mirroring in the brains of humans too, located in the frontal and parietal lobes. In one study (Hutchison, Davis, Lozano, Tasker, & Dostrovsky, 1999) a specialized cortical neuron responded not only when that individual was pinpricked, but also when that person watched the *examiner*'s fingers being pricked. And when a pinprick was then administered to the patient, the neuron began firing *before* contact with skin had even occurred, suggesting the brain reacts in anticipation of a stimulus and not only with the actual stimulus. This indicates that there is a version of mirror neurons in humans. However, given that the human brain is larger and more complex than a monkey's brain (and it is not possible to record from living human brains over long periods of time), it has proven difficult to isolate the firing patterns of particular living neurons and thus, to date, no singular mirror-neurons have been found in humans. It seems more accurate to describe a mirror-neuron system, and one that is more advanced than what we see in monkey brains in two ways. Firstly, non-goal directed movement seems to activate the mirror-neuron system in humans, whereas mirror neurons are only activated by goal-directed behavior in monkeys. Secondly, there is evidence to suggest that the human mirror-neuron system codes for the movements that make up an action, whereas for monkeys, it is only the action itself that is encoded. The human brain has many different mirroring systems, designed to mimic, to imitate, and to potentially understand and empathize with others. These attributes of various brain circuits are automatic and not under our voluntary control. But the existence of these circuits allows us to conclude that perhaps we aren't only built to imitate others' actions, but to actually resonate with what they are feeling (Rizzolatti & Craighero, 2004).

Our brain is designed to make sure we survive. Because we are communal mammals, we require social interdependence to thrive, meaning we survive best when connecting and collaborating with others (Van der Kolk, 2014). And it seems that mirror neuron systems may be at the root of our ability to experience and to act together. Emotions such as pain and grief become shared. As Rizzolatti (Rizzolatti & Sinigaglia, 2006) writes, mirror neurons demonstrate just how much we are interconnected with one another and "how bizarre it would be to conceive of an I without an us" (p. xiii). Therefore, from an evolutionary perspective, we are wired to connect. According to attachment theory, it is the caregiver–child relationship in particular that is critical in fostering and growing these connections. Louis Cozolino (2014), a leading psychologist in the field of interpersonal neurobiology, states "[w]e can now add a corollary to Darwin's survival of the fittest: Those who are nurtured best survive best" (p. 7). It is not only that we survive because of connection, but that we survive better because of our attachments.

The way a brain functions

Neurons

The question becomes not only how the brain changes, but how do attachment relationships facilitate changes in the human brain? In order to understand this, it is helpful to examine how the brain works in general. The human brain is made up of multiple types of cells, primarily including neurons (which are nerve cells), and glial cells (which are cells that help organize, build, and maintain neural systems). There are close to 100 billion neurons in the average brain that are constantly transmitting both chemical and electrical signals throughout the brain and the nervous system. In general, neurons are composed of three parts: dendrites, cell bodies, and axons. The dendrites are the input section and receive electro-chemical signals from other neurons. These signals travel through the cell bodies to the axons (the output sections), and in so doing, transform the cell bodies' biochemistry (the micro-machinery of the cell). When the signals reach the axon, this triggers the release of chemical neurotransmitters that are transmitted across synapses, or the gaps between cells that are at the most two-millionths of an inch wide. A layering of lipids and protein called myelin insulates axons thereby increasing the speed of transmission, often as much as a hundredfold. Multiple signals can be rapidly triggered and thus, the process continues (Cozolino, 2014; Jensen & Nutt, 2015).

How learning occurs

Neurons that fire together, wire together

Neuronal connections are continually forming and being eliminated as we develop through the life cycle. We all begin with our own, unique genetic code contained in our DNA that lays the initial groundwork for growth, what can be called our "nature." From there, cells and synapses are impacted by the environment in several ways, which can be seen as "nurture." New neurons are continually forming throughout the human lifespan, although at a much slower rate following birth. Upon receiving stimuli from either outside or inside the brain, synapses grow in a process called synaptogenesis, and cells become chemically connected together. It should be noted that most synapses in the cortex, the area responsible for higher cognitive functioning, are not fully formed at birth (Jensen & Nutt, 2015). They continue to form throughout the life cycle. When neurons in close proximity are repeatedly stimulated at the same time, they tend to link together through synapses to form a neural network. Donald Hebb, a Canadian psychologist, stated in 1949 that the more neurons fire together, the more they become linked together. Carla Shatz paraphrased this, creating the pithy

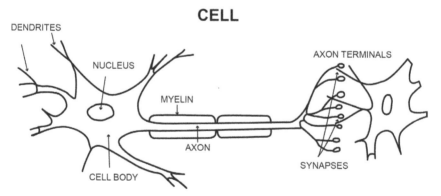

Figure 6.1 Cell, drawn by Toni Mandelbaum (2020), digitized by Chloe Amen © Toni Mandelbaum

saying "neurons that fire together, wire together," an aphorism that became known as Hebb's Law. With increasing stimulation of a neural pathway comes increasing strength. Myelin increases and axons and dendrites develop additional branches. The neural circuit becomes more efficient at transmitting signals (Siegel, 1999; Siegel, 2012; Banks & Hirschman, 2015). Thus, novel information excites the same pathway again and again until the connections solidify. This is how the brain changes and how we learn.

Use it or lose it

We start out life with an abundance of axons and dendrites, and our synapses (connections between neurons) proliferate continually throughout the first two years of life. Indeed, before birth, we have denser brains than at any other stage of life. This profusion of neurons is necessary to help an infant negotiate the onslaught of stimuli that occurs after birth. There are new sights, sounds, aromas, and experiences to adapt to and with each encounter, the neuronal connections in a baby's brain form. In fact, we grow around two million synapses every second soon after birth and the number of synapses we have in childhood is the most we will ever have in our lifetime. Many of the neurons in a baby's brain are not fully connected to one another because most synapses have not yet formed. Over time, synapses that aren't used or remain unconnected are pruned, meaning that weak connections are discarded. Likewise, neurons that aren't signaling to other neurons disappear through a process of cell suicide called apoptosis. Neurons that aren't stimulated strongly enough or for a long enough period of time may wither away (Cozolino, 2014; Jensen & Nutt, 2015; Coan, 2016). This is called the "use it or lose it" rule. This too is part of learning and growing. Neural networks become streamlined as unused neurons die off. Thus, with Hebb's Law and the "use it or lose it" principle, the brain grows via the interaction of genes and the environment. It seems both nature and nurture are heavily involved in brain development.

How this relates to attachment

Attachment theory proposes that the caregiver–child dyad provides the most critical influence on a child's brain growth. We may be born with certain innate tendencies, such as our temperament, but we interact with the environment, and most especially our caregiver, in a way that shapes our neural networks. Receiving care and support from a consistently available caregiver engenders the strengthening of the specific neuronal networks related to feeling supported. Synapses are generated and networks honed, so that the brain learns to respond appropriately and restore equilibrium after distress. Likewise, those who receive inconsistent care and support and have unavailable caregivers, may create different associations and cellular responses as a result of these experiences. Furthermore, in each case, the neurons that are not used go through apoptosis, while the unused synapses are pruned. One can understand how difficult it may be to change, given that these ways of interpreting and responding to our environments become hardwired into our brains.

Memory

As mentioned before, Bowlby proposed that the dynamic interplay between caregiver and child becomes internalized and schematically represented by something called an "internal working model." This paradigm, or model, guides expectations in future transactions through childhood and into adulthood. How do we understand the process by which a model becomes internalized? Memory plays a big part in the encoding of these representational schemas. Broadly defined as "the way past events affect future function" (Siegel, 1999, p. 19), memory by definition is affected and shaped by experience. When a neuron fires following an experience, an electro-chemical transmission is induced. This occurs with short-term memories. However, the electro-chemical transmission itself does not cause permanent change, meaning no structural brain alteration occurs. Only with continued repetition and practice, where neurons fire together and wire together, do structural changes ensue and memories become stored and encoded. These structural changes are how long-term memories are formed and, in terms of attachment, long-term memory is part of how our attachment representations become internalized working models (Siegel, 1999).

There are two main categories of long-term memory: *explicit* and *implicit* memory. *Explicit* memory requires focused attention to be encoded. There is a sense of "remembering" something. It includes narrative, semantic, sensory, episodic, and autobiographical memories. The ability to organize our stories through time is part of explicit memory, as is autobiographical memory, which include episodic, semantic, and emotional memories. It should be noted that those who experience lack of recall may have had high levels of anxiety or dissociative tendencies as a child which prevented the encoding of long-term memories. Often called late memory, explicit memory is organized as the brain matures by a region called the medial temporal lobe, which includes the hippocampus. It seems to be mediated by several regions in the brain, including the orbitofrontal cortex.

Implicit memory, often called early memory, is mediated by circuits not involving the hippocampus and can occur when the brain is still in its infancy. It includes automatic, emotional, procedural, and sensory memories. Skills such as riding a bike or even walking involve procedural memory. Involuntary emotional reactions, such as startling when you see someone you fear, can be seen as habitual emotional memories. With implicit memory, one doesn't "remember" how to, for instance, ride a bike. It does not require focal attention and though often it is conscious, there is no sense of actively recalling something. Attachment schemas are systems of social, implicit memories. Our internalized working models can become activated automatically and out of our conscious awareness, when our implicit memories are triggered. Thus, it seems that implicit memories shape our emotional and relational experiences (Siegel, 2003; Cozolino, 2014).

The structures of the brain

The triune brain

To better grasp the brain's structure as well as how the brain develops, it is helpful to explore the theory of its evolution. Neuroscientist Paul MacLean's concept of the triune brain, or the "three brains in one" (1985, p. 406), provides just this: a concise way of understanding how the brain's structure can be seen as a hierarchical progression of development. In this model, each layer is seen as managing increasingly involved functions and capacities. He proposes that the brain has three parts to it, each believed to have developed phylogenetically at different times during evolution. All parts of the brain are intricately connected and function with and in relation to each other and ultimately, we cannot understand any part of the brain as separate entities. We must understand the brain as a sum of the whole, which means that MacLean's model may be overly simplistic. However, it is a useful metaphor that can guide our thinking (Cozolino, 2014).

THE TRIUNE BRAIN

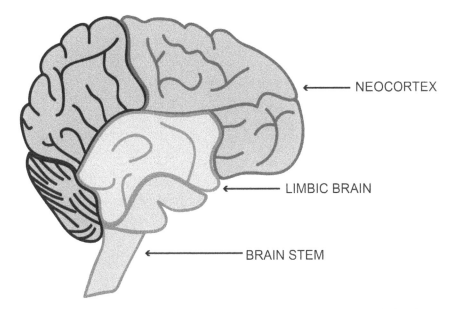

Figure 6.2 Triune brain, drawn by Toni Mandelbaum (2020), digitized by Chloe Amen
© Toni Mandelbaum

The brain stem. The brain stem, oftentimes referred to as the "reptilian brain," is thought to have developed first. Located just above the area where the spinal cord enters the skull, it includes the medulla, pons, mesencephalon, the globus pallidus, and the olfactory bulbs. The reptilian brain modulates arousal, reproductive drives, and the vital functions of the human body, such as body temperature, heart rate, balance, hunger, and sexual desire. Basic emotions seem to be generated in the reptilian brain. Overall, the brain stem is involved in our 'motivational systems' that organize us to satiate basic needs (Siegel, 2010b; Lanius, Paulsen, & Corrigan, 2014).

The limbic brain. The second structure of the brain is called the "paleo-mammalian" brain and is seen to have developed after the brain stem comes into being. Known as the limbic brain, it mediates emotion, self-regulation, memory, learning, and social functions. The limbic brain together with the reptilian brain can be called the "emotional brain" (Van der Kolk, 2014).

> *Thalamus.* The thalamus receives sensory and motor signals from the outside world via our eyes, noses, mouths, ears, or skin. It then sends the signals along, either directly to the amygdala (see below) or first to the frontal lobes to process and then to the amygdala. LeDoux, an emotions researcher, termed the fast path that goes directly to the amygdala the "low road" and the slower path that goes from the thalamus to the neocortex and then to the amygdala, the "high road" (Benson, 2002). These two paths may result in differing interpretations. For instance, the "low road"

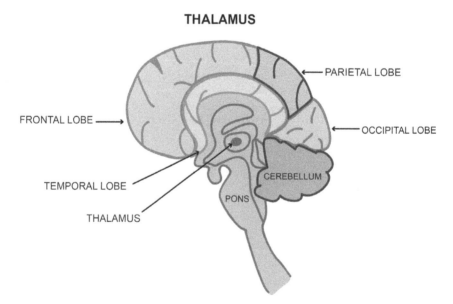

Figure 6.3 Thalamus, drawn by Toni Mandelbaum (2020), digitized by Chloe Amen © Toni Mandelbaum

path may cause an immediate fear response upon seeing an object that resembles a snake, whereas the "high road" path may allow the individual to ascertain that the object is in fact a piece of yarn that is lying on the floor and therefore, no fear response occurs.

Amygdala. The amygdala, the almond-shaped cluster of neurons located in the temporal lobe, is involved with attention, physiological arousal, and the processing of many emotions, such as fear, anger, and sadness. The amygdala is critical in helping an individual evaluate the meaning of incoming positive and negative emotional stimuli. Because of a bias toward appraising negative stimuli, the amygdala is particularly able to appraise danger and aid in negotiating fight or flight responses. This evaluation occurs outside of our conscious awareness. In this way, the amygdala enables us to protect ourselves by rapidly assessing what is dangerous and what signals are unremarkable, triggering our stress response (see Chapter 7) and enabling us to act swiftly. Because of its ability to appraise

AMYGDALA

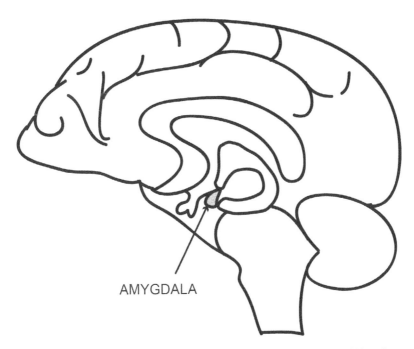

AMYGDALA

Figure 6.4 Amygdala, drawn by Toni Mandelbaum (2020), digitized by Chloe Amen © Toni Mandelbaum

threat, the amygdala is intimately involved in social connection, helping to sort out who is safe versus who is not. The amygdala "reads" nonverbal facial cues, tone of voice or prosody, and body language communications, constantly assessing for safety. Additionally, the amygdala is involved in consolidating long-term memories, by marking which memories are important and releasing certain neurochemicals which aid in memories' storage. In terms of its development, by the eighth month in utero, the amygdala is already quite mature (Cozolino, 2014; Baylin & Hughes, 2016; Coan, 2016). It continues to develop rapidly post-birth and, in girls in particular, it reaches maturity by age four (Tottenham, 2012).

Hippocampus. The hippocampus, a cluster of neurons shaped like a sea horse, links various areas of the brain together, and in so doing, relates new stimuli to previous experiences. It is critical to memory and conscious learning and is the area of the brain where explicit memory is processed. It is here that moments

HIPPOCAMPUS

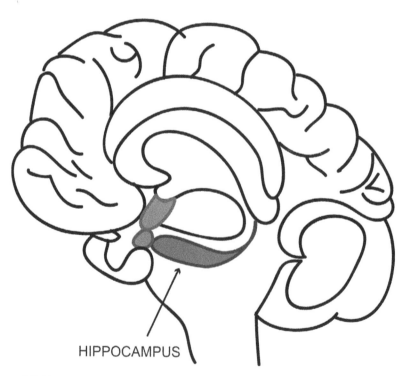

HIPPOCAMPUS

Figure 6.5 Hippocampus, drawn by Toni Mandelbaum (2020), digitized by Chloe Amen © Toni Mandelbaum

of experience are converted to memories and from here, as well as from the cortex, that these memories are retrieved. It is likely that both the amygdala and the hippocampus are involved in the encoding of internal working models, the consolidation of relationships with attachment figures, and the processing of emotionally significant events (Coan, 2016; Siegel, 2010b).

Hypothalamus. Some include the hypothalamus as part of the limbic system. Located at the center of the brain, it can be seen as a control center for the endocrine system, affecting the thyroid, adrenal glands, and the sexual organs. The hypothalamus is a regulator of functions such as body temperature, hunger, aggression, and sexual behavior and it is essential to the body's stress response, coordinating this response by secreting hormones (see Chapter 7). Additionally, it is critically involved in facilitating social soothing in the down-regulation of stress, and in particular coordinating interactions with attachment figures (Ogden, Minton, & Pain, 2006; Gunnar & Quevedo, 2007; Siegel, 2010b; Cozolino, 2014; Coan, 2016).

HYPOTHALAMUS

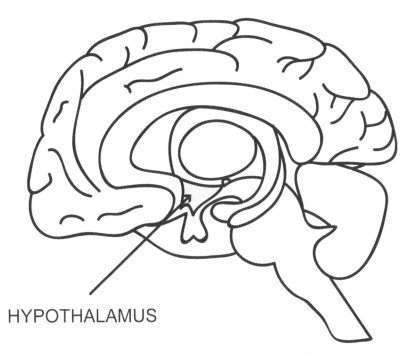

HYPOTHALAMUS

Figure 6.6 Hypothalamus, drawn by Toni Mandelbaum (2020), digitized by Chloe Amen © Toni Mandelbaum

Insula (or insular) cortex. Known as the limbic integration cortex (Cozolino, 2014, p. 47), it connects to limbic structures as well as to the frontal, parietal, and temporal lobes. The insula, together with the cingulate cortex, is involved with our negative emotions such as disgust, envy, hate, and jealousy, as well as our positive emotions such as love and empathy. It plays a crucial role in our ability to attune emotionally as well as being able to differentiate our selves from others. The insula enables us to pinpoint important stimuli, to activate our autonomic systems, and to initiate motor and behavioral responses. The insula starts out on the surface of the brain but once the frontal and temporal lobes expand, it becomes covered by them (Cozolino, 2014; Baylin & Hughes, 2016).

Cingulate cortex. This region helps integrate cognition and emotions and also is involved with activating and modulating motor activity. It comes into play around the second month of life (Cozolino, 2014).

Anterior cingulate. The frontal part of the cingulate cortex, the anterior cingulate, also part of the limbic area, connects the limbic region to the prefrontal cortex. It has a role in integrating and coordinating affect

INSULA

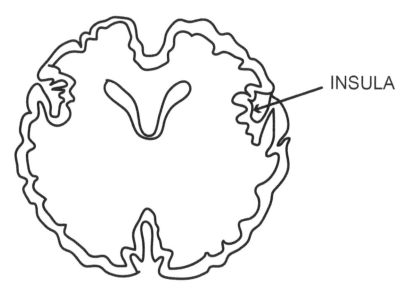

INSULA

Figure 6.7 Insula cortex, drawn by Toni Mandelbaum (2020), digitized by Chloe Amen
© Toni Mandelbaum

CINGULATE CORTEX

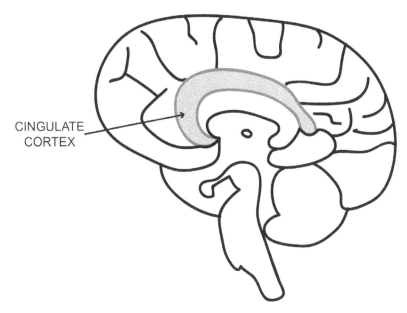

CINGULATE
CORTEX

Figure 6.8 Cingulate cortex, drawn by Toni Mandelbaum (2020), digitized by Chloe
Amen © Toni Mandelbaum

ANTERIOR CINGULATE CORTEX

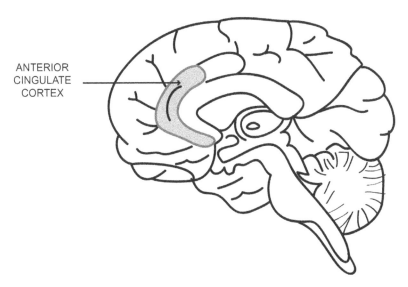

ANTERIOR
CINGULATE
CORTEX

Figure 6.9 Anterior cingulate, drawn by Toni Mandelbaum (2020), digitized by Chloe
Amen © Toni Mandelbaum

regulation. It becomes activated when we feel emotions such as compassion and empathy. Interestingly, not only does it respond to physical pain, but it also responds to social pain, such as the pain of social exclusion. Our brains register social rejection in much the same way as they register the pain of a physical injury (Way, Taylor, & Eisenberger, 2009).

The neocortex. From a phylogenetic perspective, the last part of the brain to develop is the "neomammalian brain," or the cerebral cortex or the neocortex. Known as the "rational brain" (Van der Kolk, 2014), the cortex is the outermost layer of the brain and is also the most developed part of the brain. It is concerned with a great deal of cognitive processes, including executive functioning, impulse control, judgment, planning, and insight (Jensen & Nutt, 2015). Basically, it is here that rational and abstract thought are believed to occur. The cortex is composed of gray matter, or the cell bodies of neurons, at the surface and white matter, or the myelinated axons, that is just beneath the gray matter. Gray matter is comprised of neurons involved in processing information as well as in thinking, perceiving, movement, and basic body functions. Neurons communicate to other neurons, both in the brain and in the rest of the body, through what is known as white matter. White matter actually looks lightly colored because it is largely made up of myelin, the fatty insulator that surrounds the long neuronal processes called axons (Jensen & Nutt, 2015). The cortex is generally functionally divided into four broad areas: the occipital, the parietal, temporal, and frontal cortices.

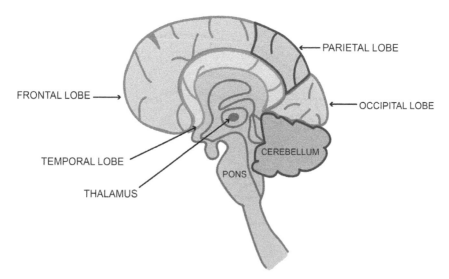

Figure 6.10 Occipital, parietal, temporal, and frontal lobe, drawn by Toni Mandelbaum (2020), digitized by Chloe Amen © Toni Mandelbaum

Occipital lobe (back). Visual processing occurs in the occipital lobe.

Parietal lobe (top back). The parietal lobe helps forge the experience of our sense of body in the environment.

Temporal lobe (sides). The temporal lobe is responsible for auditory processing, memory functions, and aspects of language. It also includes areas that regulate sexuality and emotions.

Frontal lobe (top front). The frontal lobe, part of the neocortex, together with the parietal lobes, helps regulate language, executive functioning, reasoning, judgment, insight, and planning. It facilitates associational processes and reasoning (Cozolino, 2014; Jensen & Nutt, 2015).

Prefrontal cortex. The front of the frontal lobe is called the prefrontal cortex and can be partitioned in a few ways. The dorsolateral or lateral prefrontal cortex is involved with working memory. The ventromedial prefrontal cortex, also known as the orbital medial prefrontal cortex, is essential in neural integration: it joins the neocortex, the limbic system, and the brain stem. It can be viewed as an extension of the limbic system even though it belongs fully to the cerebral cortex. It allows for the integration of external and internal inputs of emotion and motivation, and is connected with networks involved in learning, emotion, and memory. Growing evidence suggests it functions in conjunction with the amygdala and has the ability to consciously inhibit amygdala activation (Tottenham, 2012). This helps us to make sense of what we are experiencing and to inhibit what otherwise may feel like automatic responses, such as losing our temper every time our partner is late without waiting for an explanation. In this way, the prefrontal cortex aids in the regulation of the autonomic nervous system, modulating such physical mechanisms as breathing, digestion, and heart rate.

PREFRONTAL CORTEX

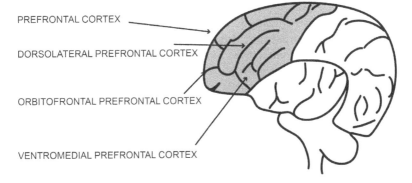

Figure 6.11 Prefrontal cortex, drawn by Toni Mandelbaum (2020), digitized by Chloe Amen © Toni Mandelbaum

The autonomic nervous system itself is divided into two components: the sympathetic nervous system and the parasympathetic nervous system (see Chapter 7). Generally, the sympathetic branch instigates activity and the parasympathetic branch quells activity. Both are regulated by the orbitofrontal region, which means this region is critical to enabling affect regulation. It should be noted that the connection between the amygdala and the orbital medial prefrontal cortex is shaped by experience and this experience includes our attachment interactions. Overall, the prefrontal cortex, together with the parietal lobe, is hypothesized to be involved in emotional regulation and social processing. (Siegel, 2003; Cozolino, 2014).

The brain's course of development

For the first few years of being, an infant relies on subcortical (brain stem and limbic system) regions for regulation. An infant's cortex has little myelin, while its brain stem is almost fully myelinated. At first, a baby is able to regulate basic functions such as its heartbeat, breathing, and eating. Because of the relatively undeveloped regulation circuitry, an infant requires external aid to effectively regulate less basic functions. This role is usually filled by a caregiver. In fact, having access to a caregiver at this young age can be critical in enabling the regulation of, for example, heightened amygdala activity (Gee et al., 2014). By two years of age, a lot of the "primitive" brain has been insulated, but myelination continues to occur in brain regions involved in higher order functions such as language and fine motor skills well into young adulthood (Jensen & Nutt, 2015).

Teenage brains, between 12 and 18 years of age, tend to evidence a loss of volume in the number of neurons, or gray matter, but an increase in its density. Furthermore, at first, teen brains tend to have an undersupply of the amount of myelinated connecting neural networks, or white matter, meaning adolescents are primed, but don't have adequate networks to manage their abundant density of neurons. As we continue to develop, with rapid pruning, increased synaptogenesis, and an increase in our white matter, our neural networks become speedier and more efficient at processing and regulating incoming stimuli. The connectivity moves from the back of the brain towards the front. So for instance, it has been shown that while babies need caregivers to help with heightened amygdala reactivity, adolescents do not seem to require the presence of a caregiver to reduce amygdala reactivity. They have begun to be able to self-regulate (Gee et al., 2014). In normal development, the amygdala, the hippocampus, and the prefrontal cortex all become better connected by the time a child reaches adolescence, with connectivity to the frontal lobe only fully developing later on. In fact, structurally, though a teenage brain is more developed than that of a child's brain, it can still only be viewed as having reached an 80% level of maturity, both in the development of the amygdala, which is fairly overactive, and the frontal lobe. It can take up to two and a half to three decades for the frontal lobe to fully develop (Barkley, 2012; Cozolino, 2014; Jensen & Nutt, 2015). Ultimately, cortical structures oversee subcortical structures. They become the "management" system for the process of regulation and in dysregulating situations, an individual who has developed adequately, can self-modulate reactivity quickly and take appropriate action.

As mentioned earlier, the right hemisphere develops fairly rapidly during a baby's first two to three years after birth. Attachment theorists suggest that the initial burst of growth in the right hemisphere is shaped by attachment relationships and therefore, shapes our early social and emotional growth. The repetition of the attachment dyadic interaction fosters the development of our abilities to regulate our affect and contributes to our attachment schemas. There is a tremendous amount of growth in the left hemisphere beginning in the second year of life, tying in with our increasing language abilities and our growing abilities to physically maneuver ourselves (Cozolino, 2014).

The brain's integration and attachment theory

The brain functions well when its neural networks are integrated. Information can flow between the top and bottom, meaning from the neocortex to subcortical regions and then back again. This is known as vertical integration. It also flows between the left and right hemispheres, which is known as horizontal integration. Vertical processes include the ability to inhibit, organize, and regulate emotions being passed along through the brain stem and the limbic system. The linkage between the left and right hemispheres enables individuals to name feelings, to become consciously aware of affect, and to maintain a balanced, holistic view of incoming stimuli. Should our neural networks be effectively integrated, we feel safe and secure. We feel confident in our ability to negotiate our inner world as well as the external environment. Even when feeling powerful emotional reactions of fear, anger, or sadness, states of being that typically increase the activation in subcortical brain areas and decrease the ability to engage the frontal lobe, those with more integrated brains are usually able to reengage the frontal cortex. However, should our neural networks be unintegrated, we may either favor bottom–up approaches or top–down approaches, which affects our abilities to effectively deal with inner or outer stimuli. When this occurs, we aren't able to develop a coherent approach to living in the world at large (Siegel, 2010b; Cozolino, 2014; Van der Kolk, 2014).

This is where attachment enters the picture. It is hypothesized that good care allows brains to develop the flexibility to shift between bottom–up and top–down approaches. Poor care discourages effective brain development, where a less integrated state of being favors bottom–up approaches that are more reactive and based on fear. For instance, a child who cannot rely on a caregiver for protection must protect himself. He can never be sure when to let down his guard and may remain constantly vigilant with his body ready to react to danger at any moment. This means his brain stem and limbic system are overactive and his prefrontal cortex is underactive (Baylin & Hughes, 2016). Research supports just this. In terms of neural activity, insecure attachment has been related to increased activation of the prefrontal cortex, which suggests that those with insecure attachments either have to work harder to regulate themselves or feel more of a burden when receiving stimuli such as stress. In another study, individuals with attachment anxiety had greater reactivity in the amygdala and parahippocampal areas and less activity in the orbitofrontal region when examining negative relationship situations. This seems to indicate that those with attachment anxiety may have difficulty regulating themselves when experiencing relationship turmoil (Coan, 2016). In terms of gray matter volume, it was found that those with anxious attachments had increased gray matter in their left orbitomedial prefrontal cortex and decreased gray matter in their anterior temporal area. Those with anxious attachments show more activity in their anterior cingulate and insula regions, and seem to be more activated by thoughts of loss in comparison to those with avoidant attachments (Cozolino, 2014).

In addition to affecting the brain's functioning, there is some evidence to suggest that attachment patterns may impact a brain's structures. This is another way that neural integration can be impacted. For instance, insecurely attached 18-month-olds predicted greater amygdala volumes in adulthood, in comparison to those who were securely attached as babies (Moutsiana et al., 2015). Furthermore, studies have shown that those with attachment avoidance have less cell density in their hippocampi (Quirin, Gillath, Pruessner, & Eggert, 2010). Thus, attachment schemas can be seen as a representation of our histories and stories that have shaped our experience-dependent brains, connecting the neocortex with the amygdala and the insula and cingulate cortices. Available caregiving helps to mold the brain in ways that encourage the ability to effectively self and co-regulate and to have optimal growth and development. Conversely, inconsistent and unavailable caregiving shape the brain differently, in ways that often are not optimal for development (Cozolino, 2014).

Summary

The "Decade of the Brain" once again revolutionized attachment theory. With growing evidence that the environment does indeed affect our growth trajectory, attachment bonds were suddenly at the forefront of explaining how our brains can change. The notion that neurons that fire together, wire together came about and thus, the repetition of our dyadic dynamic within our attachment relationships were now understood to be encoded in our brains. In this way, relational transactions shape the brain over time. As the brain does not fully form until well into our twenties, there is tremendous room for adaptation and therapy can actually help to create these changes.

Chapter 7

Psychophysiology

There was yet another trend in research that was to affect the development of attachment theory and that was a renewed interest in the biological implications of the attachment bond. Suddenly, the field of psychophysiology, the study of the relationship between physiological and psychological processes and behavior, became a major thrust for many researchers. With the advancement of technology and the improvement of measures, the past two or three decades have seen an enormous rise in this study. The reactions of the autonomic nervous system can be examined; levels of cortisol, a stress hormone, can be measured; and electrodermal (skin) responses and heart rate variability can be read more accurately. In essence, this line of research links neuroscience with the science of our bodies' reactions and behaviors (Hane & Fox, 2016). Attachment researchers have seized on this area of study, utilizing it to explore the intersection of attachment patterns with psychophysiological responses. Bodily reactions are seen as influencing and reinforcing the overall attachment system. Recall that according to attachment theory, there are several behavioral systems that interact together to achieve a homeostatic balance. The caregiver–child dyad forms an attachment system which interacts with a fear system as well as an exploration system. In times of distress, the fear system and the attachment system activate, while the exploration system deactivates. A securely attached individual will seek proximity to a caregiver to relieve the distress. The field of psychophysiology allows us to understand what is happening on a physiological level when the systems interact with one another. We now know that maintaining proximity to an attachment figure is rewarded physically. It feels good to be close to our loved ones. Fear serves a purpose too. It initiates a bodily wide response that propels us to seek safety so that we can down-regulate and achieve homeostasis once more. Thus, on a physiological level, the attachment relationship helps to regulate our sense of security, facilitates our coping with stressors, and enhances our motivation to maintain closeness to caregivers, all to ensure our optimal survival.

Physiology and neurobiology of social bonding

Our bodies are "wired to connect." We are rewarded when we seek proximity to a safe caregiver whereby we have physiological reactions that make us feel good. Our genetic predispositions together with our attachment-related experiences work together to create these psychophysiological responses. Neurotransmitters are released which reinforce our proximity-seeking behavior. In times of distress, our bodies react, disrupting our homeostasis. We do what we can to re-establish that homeostasis and these efforts are supported by our bodies. If our heart rates rise, we seek to decelerate our heart beats. If our stress levels rise, we do our best to quell our fears. It has been shown that social bonding helps decrease stress. Therefore, our bodies support our seeking social bonding, physically rewarding this adaptive behavior. The following section details some of the ways in which our bodies reinforce the attachment bond.

Heart rate

In their study, Spangler and Grossmann (1993) examined the relationship between infants' heart rates and their attachment styles as classified by the Strange Situation. All infants, no matter their classification, had heart rate increases when separated from their caregivers, with disorganized infants showing the most marked increase. This finding is notable as it suggests that secure infants may be just as distressed during separation as are avoidant and anxious infants, but they are able to better manage the distress they feel. Our body reacts to separation and propels us to seek proximity in times of distress.

Monoamines

Monoamines are types of neurotransmitters, or chemical substances that aid with the transmission of impulses across synapses between neurons. They regulate our energy levels and our general sense of well-being and they are fast-acting, inducing a quick reaction. Dopamine, serotonin, and epinephrine are all examples of monoamines (Coan, 2016; Cozolino, 2016).

> *Dopamine.* Dopamine is produced in the ventral tegmental area and substantia nigra, both areas in the midbrain. Known as part of the reward system, dopaminergic activity is related to the experience of pleasure. It can be seen as motivating proximity seeking because one is rewarded with a dopamine surge when feeling close to an attachment figure (Coan, 2016). Thus, the dopaminergic systems instigate "seeking" behaviors such as a baby seeking out a caregiver or a caregiver retrieving a baby. It aids in trust-building because it assuages our fears. It is also seen as instrumental in learning because it reinforces positive, growth-promoting activities, such as eating healthily and being involved in good relationships. Interestingly, when dopamine acts in the brain, it acts as a neurotransmitter. However, when it acts on the adrenal glands, it is acting as a hormone (Cozolino, 2014; Baylin & Hughes, 2016).

Serotonin. In humans, most serotonin is located in cells in the gastro-intestinal tract, the brain, as well as in platelets. It helps us regulate our appetite and sleep patterns as well as our mood. Serotonin is seen as critical to our organizing and regulating our emotions. For instance, low levels of serotonin are associated with depression and aggression, while increased levels aid the body in calming down (Jensen & Nutt, 2015). Romantic love is associated with lower levels of serotonin, as is obsessive compulsive disorder. We may understand this as serotonin levels being involved in maintaining a person's interest in a romantic partner.

Epinephrine. When in distress and needing to react immediately, epi-nephrine is synthesized in the adrenal glands and then discharged into the bloodstream. This prepares the body to act. Heart rate is increased, pupils dilate, and gastrointestinal tracts constrict. At the same time, there is an increase in the supply of oxygen in the blood as well as an increase in glucose that goes to the brain and to muscles needed for action. The full stress response will be described later in this chapter.

Neuropeptides

Neuropeptides are signaling molecules used by neurons to communicate with one another, thereby influencing activity in the brain and the body. They affect pain, pleasure, sexuality, and attachment relationships. Neuro-peptides are a type of neurotransmitter that tend to be slow acting and induce a prolonged reaction. Oxytocin, vasopressin, and endogenous opioids all serve to increase motivation for social bonding by making it more pleasurable. They reinforce nurturing behaviors such as cooing, gently touching, or feeding (Cozolino, 2014).

Oxytocin. Mostly produced in the hypothalamus, oxytocin is released into circulation by the pituitary gland and the limbic system and cortex, in response to cues including giving birth, breast feeding, copulation, and stress. Attachment researchers are particularly interested in oxytocin because it is a critical factor in affiliative behaviors, such as social engagement, cooperation, and empathy. In fact, higher levels of oxytocin in caregivers is related to more affectionate behavior. It makes a mother feel good when interacting with her baby and facilitates positive feelings in the baby as well. Interestingly, female brains produce oxytocin in greater quantities than do male brains. Oxytocin can instigate the release of dopamine with the combined effect being to enhance the reward of relating to our loved ones. Additionally, it interacts with the amygdala and helps to mediate anxiety, fear, and stress (Panksepp & Biven, 2012; Cozolino, 2014; Coan, 2016; Hane & Fox, 2016).

Vasopressin. Also synthesized in the hypothalamus, vasopressin is involved in aiding partner choice. It too forms as a result of social behaviors (Coan, 2016).

Endogenous opioids. Released throughout the central and peripheral nervous systems, endogenous opioids, such as endorphins, can serve two purposes: to relieve pain and to engender a sense of contentment when connecting with others.

Pain relief. As the amygdala has many opioid receptors, it seems that our fear responses can be mediated by endorphins, which helps to calm us. The opioid receptors in both the insula and anterior cingulate aid in the regulation of physical and emotional pain (Cozolino, 2014). Supporting this, it has been shown that genetic variations in the number of opioid receptors in both the insula and anterior cingulate correlate with an individual's level of sensitivity to rejection (Way et al., 2009). Opioids can help with social pain by allowing a child to experience comfort. Another way that opioids relieve pain is by promoting dissociative defenses (Baylin & Hughes, 2016). In fact, with trauma, we see a rise in dissociative defenses that is associated with the release of endogenous opioids and other neurochemicals that change the ways that lower and higher brain structures communicate with one another. This can inhibit horizontal and vertical integration in the brain. In this way, trauma (to be discussed later in the chapter) can impact our overall functioning (Lanius et al., 2014).

Engendering connections. Endogenous opioids also seem to promote attachment. For instance, they are often discharged during childbirth, breast feeding, sexual activity, and times of caregiving. Opioids increase the pleasure associated within human relationships. Just seeing a mother's face prompts the release of large amounts of endogenous opiates in infants and play and laughter do the same. Conversely, a decrease in levels of endorphins has been noted in mothers when separated from their young. Thus, higher levels are associated with feeling happy and safe, while lower levels are associated with feeling anxious, thereby motivating proximity seeking (Cozolino, 2014; Baylin & Hughes, 2016; Coan, 2016).

Stress: how our body reacts when we encounter distress

Most of our clients present with stressors. Generally, our brains and bodies tend towards homeostasis, and thus, when we feel stress, our bodies try to relieve it. Human connection is now seen as critical to the process of stress-relief, and can allow us to decrease both our psychological and our physiological stress reactions. As a clinician, it is important to understand the psychophysiology of stress in order to implement modern attachment theory into practice. What is stress? It can be defined as "a real or interpreted threat to the physiological or psychological integrity of an individual that results in physiological and/or behavior responses" (McEwen, 2000, p. 508). Again, as a rule, we seek to maintain homeostasis. A stressor is something that disrupts a body's homeostasis and the stress-response consists of the actions a body takes to achieve homeostasis again. Stressors come in many forms and last for varying lengths of time. Stressors may not even be actual events. Simply the thought or the anticipation of something stressful can create stress, like having to give a public speech or worrying about future employment opportunities. A certain amount of stress can actually be beneficial to us. It galvanizes us in the short term. It prepares us to act by mobilizing our energy, enhancing our cognition, and dampening any pain we may feel. This is obvious in the animal kingdom. Take a zebra, for example. He is quietly resting in the wild, when he senses the approach of a lion. The zebra's stress system kicks into gear, energizing him to escape the lion. The lion, however, is also stressed. He is hungry and hasn't eaten in a while. His system also goes into high gear. In both cases, stress causes an adaptive response. In sum, a moderate amount of stress can be adaptive in certain situations (Sapolsky, 2004).

Problems in humans begin when we experience prolonged and/or overwhelming stress. Should our stress responses be unable to handle the stressors, the responses can actually incur more harm than the stressor itself. Stress expert Bruce McEwen and his colleague Seeman (1999) provide a model, or way of understanding stress and stress responses. They added two new terms to the stress literature: allostasis and allostatic load. Allostasis means "maintaining stability (or homeostasis) through change" (McEwen & Seeman, 1999, p. 32) and refers to physiological mediators, such as hormones and neurotransmitters, that are released into the body to restore balance. It implies a dynamic process whereby an organism's internal stability is maintained through the interaction and modulation of environmental demands (Evans, 2003). Allostatic load denotes the wear and tear allostasis may cause the body because of repeated adjustments made to manage changing environmental demands. If there is a great deal of exposure to social and physical demands, the body will mobilize to meet these demands. Making allostatic adjustments is critical to survival, but too much activity can incur damage (Gunnar & Vazquez, 2006).

Allostatic load is the result of an interaction of factors, where responses to external demands are moderated by genetic predisposition, prior experiences, and living situations (Evans, 2003). The stress model proposed by McEwen and Seeman (1999) outlines four central characteristics of stress responses. Firstly, behavioral and neuroendocrine stress responses are managed and organized by the brain. It is our brain that triggers the release of the neurochemicals that aid in our "fight or flight" response. Our sympathetic and parasympathetic nervous systems are stimulated by the brain to react to the stressors we encounter (to be discussed further below). Secondly, an individual's genetic make-up, developmental stage, and experience all converge to shape a stress response, which means our responses are not uniform. We all can and often do react differently, sometimes to the same stressor. Thirdly, the ability to adapt to stress and regain homeostasis is intrinsic to the stress response. We naturally want to "come back to normal." A successful stress response involves not only reacting to the stressor and negotiating it, but also deactivating the neuroendocrine response we experience. This is critical to our physiological and psychological well-being. And lastly, if either too much stress is experienced or an individual does not respond efficiently (i.e., not turning on the stress response or not turning off the stress response at the appropriate time) to a stressor, the body suffers. It is important to note that allostatic load is incurred not only by chronic stress, but also by maladaptive responses to stress.

The stress reaction

Stress is both a psychological as well as a biological reaction (Gunnar & Quevedo, 2007). When an individual appraises or anticipates a stressor, a physiological response begins. The thalamus perceives the threat and sends the signal in one of two directions: to the amygdala or to the cortex. The amygdala acts as a screening process by evaluating the level of threat the incoming signal poses. It can either directly trigger a reaction or send the signal to the cortex. In the first case, the body reacts without necessarily making sense of the incoming signals. Take for instance seeing a snake. In a split second or less, the amygdala assesses if the threat is dangerous and then, if it concludes it is, it triggers a bodily response without ever involving the cortex. Researchers posit the existence of the "cognitive unconscious," or the unconscious ability to both perceive a signal and then decide its emotional valence. This ability is attributed to our emotional memory, or memories that are stored by the amygdala. In other words, the amygdala often draws conclusions based on memories of past experiences. This can be very helpful, allowing our bodies to react much more quickly to danger. However, it can also result in the amygdala misperceiving the current level of threat because of past experiences. For instance, an adult individual who was bullied in middle school for being overweight gets into a rage when a waitress asks him if he'd like the salad of the day because he assumes she is mocking his food choice. Daniel Goleman, an internationally known psychologist and science journalist (1995), coined the term "emotional hijacking" to describe reacting emotionally without thinking, a process that occurs when our amygdala reacts without us being aware of why we are reacting in the way we are. Hijacking occurs when our feelings bypass cognitive understanding. Verbally exploding at a partner when he is home late from work because it is similar to an experience with a previous partner who was unfaithful is an example of being emotionally hijacked. The fear of being abandoned again may not be conscious, but the amygdala picks up on the potential threat. When the signal does go to the cortex, the cortex can make sense of it. It has a much slower response time and the ensuing reaction is better planned and more coordinated (Goleman, 1995). The body's immediate response is crucial to survival. Just as important is the body's return to normality after the threat has been negotiated. If all works well, we respond immediately and adaptively and we then return to our homeostasis.

There are actually two separate but interconnected stress systems in our bodies: the sympathetic-adrenomedullary (SAM) system and the hypothalamic-pituitary-adrenocortical (HPA) system. When stressors are seen as challenges that are manageable, the SAM system kicks in. However, when stressors are evaluated as threats and not manageable with our current resources, our bodies need to step it up a notch. This is when the HPA system is activated (Diamond, 2015).

The SAM system. The brain is connected to the rest of the human body by the central nervous system and the peripheral nervous system. The brain and spinal cord are part of the central nervous system, while the peripheral nervous system is made up of the autonomic nervous system and the somatic nervous system. The autonomic system is composed of two systems; the sympathetic and parasympathetic systems. The sympathetic-adrenomedullary system, composed of the sympathetic and the parasympathetic autonomic nervous systems, supports a fight-or-flight response to stress. As a stressor is perceived, cells in the intermediolateral gray matter of the spinal cord are activated. Once stimulated, these cells, part of the sympathetic division, release catecholamines from the adrenal gland, located just above the kidneys, into the body. The catecholamines involved are mostly epinephrine (an American term), or adrenaline (a British term), but norepinephrine is also activated. These hormones mediate arousal and mobilization by ensuring that the body has enough energy to negotiate the stressor. Memory formation is enhanced (McEwen & Seeman, 1999; Sapolsky, 2004; Gunnar & Quevedo, 2007; Cozolino, 2014). There is an increase in blood supply to muscles and the brain, raising the individual's heart rate, and stimulating glucose production in the liver. Neither epinephrine nor norepinephrine crosses the blood–brain barrier (Gunnar & Quevedo, 2007). While epinephrine and norepinephrine course through the body, kicking it into action, they also stimulate the vagus nerve. The vagus nerve triggers the parasympathetic system, a system that has an antagonistic effect on autonomic operations, to act. Thus, the arousal of the sympathetic system fades quickly due to the rapid activation of the parasympathetic system, which orchestrates recovery after stimulation. The heartbeat slows, digestion begins to function properly again, and in a well-functioning system, the body returns to homeostasis (Goleman, 1995; Diamond & Fagundes, 2008; Ulrich-Lai & Herman, 2009).

The HPA system. While the SAM system is the body's first response to a stressor, the HPA system may also kick into gear. This system is initiated when the hypothalamus discharges many releasing hormones into the hypothalamic-pituitary circulatory system. The main releasers are corticotropin-releasing hormone (CRH) and arginine vasopressin (AVP), secreted from the paraventricular nucleus of the hypothalamus. The secretion of CRH and AVP stimulates the pituitary to synthesize and discharge adrenocorticotrophic hormone (ACTH) into the bloodstream. ACTH travels to the adrenal glands and binds to the receptors in the cortex of the adrenal glands, which triggers the secretion of glucocorticoids, or steroid hormones, the most important of which is cortisol. Cortisol circulates throughout the brain and the body and binds to receptors in both locations. Cortisol acts in analogous ways to epinephrine, mobilizing energy, increasing blood pressure, regulating glucose metabolism, acting upon immune activity, and regulating cognitive alertness, learning, and memory (Flinn & Egeland, 1995; Sapolsky, 2004; Ulrich-Lai & Herman, 2009; Anacker, O'Donnell, & Meaney,

2014). Yet, while epinephrine acts quickly, often within seconds, cortisol levels take longer to reach peak (often 25 minutes or more) and the effects of the cortisol take longer to activate, from minutes to hours. Additionally, while epinephrine and norepinephrine do not cross the blood–brain barrier, glucocorticoids do. Cortisol can impact gene expression, while catecholamines cannot. Thus, cortisol takes longer to infiltrate a body's system and its effects remain active for longer periods of time (Sapolsky, 2004; Gunnar & Quevedo, 2007).

In order to re-establish homeostasis once cortisol is released into the body, it must be reabsorbed. A negative feedback process of the HPA axis reinstitutes homeostasis (Ulrich-Lai & Herman, 2009). Cortisol is released into the body and then binds to receptors located on the outside of our cells. This suppresses the HPA axis and leads to a rebalancing of basal cortisol levels (de Bellis, 2001). Ultimately, emotional reactivity is hypothesized to be related to the negative feedback that exists between the hippocampal corticoid receptors (Oitz, van Haarst, & de Kloet, 1997; Gunnar & Vazquez, 2006). The efficiency of the SAM and the HPA axes rely on both systems turning on and turning off at the appropriate moment. Problems occur when either system does not function efficiently. A well-orchestrated response by both systems is adaptive, but chronic stress and prolonged activation of these systems can be detrimental to both physical and mental well-being (Gunnar & Quevedo, 2007).

It is important to note that not only is cortisol produced when under duress; it is produced in our bodies all the time. Research shows that, barring illness or large amounts of stress and trauma, we all have a natural "stress" daily circadian rhythm, where our cortisol levels are at their lowest at midnight and build up during the night hours so that they are at peak levels when we wake. The levels decrease slowly over the course of the day (Chan & Debono, 2010). This rhythm can change at various developmental points. For instance, cortisol levels tend to be higher during adolescence than adulthood, especially for adolescent girls (Jensen & Nutt, 2015). And with prolonged or chronic stress, cortisol stays in a system for long periods of time, changing the diurnal rhythm. The feedback system may become altered and this can affect the body's production of cortisol in one of two ways; either by increasing *or* decreasing it, meaning chronic stress can lead to a hyperactivated or a blunted cortisol diurnal rhythm (Diamond, 2015).

Chronic stress

A broad array of adverse life experiences can affect the hypothalamic-pituitary-adrenal (HPA) axis, including socioeconomic disadvantage, lack of social support, mental illness, community violence, and family dysfunction. All of these may increase an individual's "allostatic load." In the model formulated by McEwen and Seeman (1999), they delineated four types of "allostatic load." The first is when a stressor occurs repeatedly and over time. For example, a child living with an abusive parent has an increased allostatic load. A second type occurs when an individual is unable to habituate to that stressor. The body becomes flooded by stress mediators because it cannot quieten the stress response. This often happens with trauma (described in more detail later in this chapter). A third type of allostatic load occurs when the body cannot shut off a stress response or when a body displays dysregulated diurnal rhythms of cortisol production. Trauma can induce this and can lead to feeling agitated and on edge. Lastly, a fourth type occurs when other physiological systems are disrupted because of an insufficient stress response. Increased allostatic load can be deleterious to an individual's ultimate outcome. It can lead to increased blood pressure, heart disease, strokes, ulcers, or to overall problems with the immune system, as well as depression, anxiety, trouble sleeping, and general psychological stress.

Neurobiology of chronic stress and trauma

Research documents that experiences can change the neurobiology of the HPA axis and of our brains. In particular, prolonged stress and/or trauma, defined as stress that overwhelms an individual (Van der Kolk, 2003), can induce physiological and structural changes in our brains and our neurons. There are two different processes shown to be influenced by chronic stress. Firstly, protein production is inhibited leading to increased rates of metabolism. This has the unfortunate consequence of affecting our body's ability to fight disease and partially explains why chronic stress causes illness and disease. Secondly, with increased rates of metabolism, sodium continues to be pumped into neurons. Too much sodium with no way to process it all can cause eventual cell death. Cells in the hippocampus seem to be particularly negatively affected, which can result in problems with memory and learning (Cozolino, 2014). Indeed, studies have related high levels of stress to differences in the physical structure of the hippocampus and of the amygdala (Gunnar & Barr, 1998), and both of these structures are associated with a variety of psychopathological and neurodevelopmental disorders (Buss et al., 2012). Dendrites shrink and with this, the loss of synaptic connections occur, leading to apoptosis, or cell death. Chronic stress has been shown to affect the overall functioning of neurons, to cause neural networks to disconnect, to inhibit neurogenesis or the birth of new neurons, and to either endanger the well-being of neurons or cause cell death (Sapolsky, 2004).

The changes in neurons and in the brain can perpetuate the poor negotiation of stressors. Epigenetic modifications and structural differences tend to sensitize an individual's HPA axis to the effects of stress, potentially increasing vulnerability to stressors (Gunnar & Vazquez, 2006). As previously mentioned, chronic stress has been associated with either exceedingly high or chronically low levels of cortisol, depending on the situation (Diamond & Fagundes, 2008), which often leads to various health problems as well as psychopathologies. For instance, depression has been linked with elevated levels of cortisol (Anacker et al., 2014) and the hyperactivity of CRH is associated with chronic stress, posttraumatic stress disorder (PTSD) and depression (Gunnar & Quevedo, 2007; Ulrich-Lai & Herman, 2009). Further, serotonin levels, involved in the regulation of mood and behaviors such as impulsivity and aggression as well as compulsive behaviors, have been shown to be affected by stress, where decreased levels of serotonin are evidenced in studies of animals experiencing uncontrollable stress (de Bellis, 2001). Studies show that individuals with PTSD often hyposecrete cortisol, leading to a blunted response to stress, whereas those diagnosed with depression frequently hypersecrete cortisol, potentially leading to a highly sensitized response to stress. Changes in the diurnal rhythm of cortisol secretion have been found in children living in orphanages, places where children are often neglected (Gunnar & Quevedo, 2007), as well as in abused children suffering from major depression (de Bellis, 2001). Experiencing trauma has been shown to affect the brain's reactivity. For example, research shows that early exposure to family violence is correlated with a child's increased amygdala reactivity in response to angry, not sad, faces (McCroy et al., 2011). Adults with PTSD have been found to have hyperactive amygdala responses while concurrently having hypoactive areas of the ventromedial prefrontal cortex, meaning the amygdala is not well-regulated (Scott et al., 2015). All of these factors can contribute to regulation difficulties. Thus, as clinicians it is imperative that we understand the potential tremendously negative physiological and psychological effects of stress on our brains, bodies, and emotions.

Attachment and stress

Where does attachment fit in with our experiences of stress? It turns out that the attachment bond is critically related to how an individual copes with stress. Studies have shown that the dyadic relationship can serve as a buffer against the terrible consequences of overwhelming stress (Coan, Schaefer, & Davidson, 2007). To reiterate what was said in Chapter 1, a secure attachment bond offers safety and security in times of distress. Simply knowing an attachment figure is available and responsive can provide enormous comfort to a child. With repeated positive experiences, attachment theory hypothesizes a child to develop a secure internal working model, or a "secure-base script," meaning the child trusts that it is possible for his or her stress to be reduced. He also develops confidence that he can ask for help because others have proven helpful in the past. Securely attached individuals do tend to use others to help negotiate their stress and amazingly, may not even produce an adrenocortical response when stressed while in the presence of an available attachment figure.

On the flip side, we suffer when we don't have proper care and this suffering can cause us significant stress. Sapolsky (2004), a prominent stress researcher, concluded "[s]omething roughly akin to love is needed for proper biological development, and its absence is among the most aching, distorting stressors that we can suffer" (p. 116). An unavailable caregiver can be doubly damaging in that not only does the child experience the initial stressor, but then has no help with reducing the ensuing stress. This results in psychological pain and can cause biological changes as well. There is evidence to suggest that the SAM and HPA systems can endure permanent physiological changes, thereby changing how an individual responds to stress. Thus, on a psychological level, there is the ache caused by not being comforted by an attachment figure and the feelings of helplessness that often occur when having to deal with stressors alone, but at a developmental stage when one is not ready to do so. Here, a child is forced to adopt his or her own coping mechanisms, or secondary attachment strategies (hyperactivating or deactivating strategies), that often are not adequate in dealing with the situation at hand (Mikulincer & Shaver, 2007). These secondary attachment strategies may become codified as insecure attachment patterns. Researchers suggest that insecure attachment patterns may simply be "failed coping", or responses to stress, while secure attachment patterns may represent adaptive coping responses to stress (Spangler and Grossman, 1993; Gunnar et al., 1996). In these ways, lack of adequate care can induce stress. However, having a positive attachment bond can moderate the negative effects of stress. Our brains are plastic. Attachment bonds can ameliorate the damage incurred by chronic stress. The next sections will show how research supports this dual role of the attachment system.

Caregiving and stress

Animal research

Much of the research into maternal moderation of the effects of early stress on reactivity has been conducted on rodents. Michael Meaney, a psychobiologist at McGill University, has spent his career examining the impact of maternal care on the developmental course of rats. In rats, maternal care is defined by how much mothers (dams) lick and groom their babies (pups). His findings have supported that having attentive mothering can very much affect how stressed a baby feels. In comparison to pups of low-licking and -grooming (LG) dams, pups of high-licking and -grooming (HG) mothers grow up to be less fearful and better able to negotiate stress. In fact, evidence suggests that licking and grooming can actually increase the expression of hippocampal glucocorticoid receptors (GR), suggesting that grooming behavior may be as influential, if not more so than genetic inheritance. As mentioned, GR are part of ending the stress responses of the HPA system, where having more receptors is correlated with increased efficiency of the stress response (Weaver et al., 2004; Levine, 2005; Gunnar & Quevedo, 2007). Additionally, rats that receive more maternal care are able to learn more quickly and have better memory abilities (Cozolino, 2014). On the other hand, it has been shown that inadequate maternal care in rats can negatively impact the development of HPA responses to stress by affecting gene transcription and decreasing GR expression. Again, when GR are activated, HPA activity is inhibited; therefore, the pruning of these receptors in rats is associated with increased HPA activity under stressful conditions (McGowan et al., 2009). In sum, variations in maternal care in rats have proven to affect the neurobiological development of the HPA system. Though we have a good deal of studies documenting the effects of maternal deprivation in rats, our understanding of the physiological effects of maternal deprivation on the human HPA system is still in its early stages of development.

Human research

In humans, research has supported that the attachment relationship can be soothing and stress-reducing. It has been shown that from a functional perspective, a sensitive and available caregiver can enable an effective stress response in children without increasing the production of cortisol. One study (Nachmias et al., 1996) examined how attachment security or insecurity interacts with behavioral inhibition during the Strange Situation. Behavioral inhibition was defined as a facet of temperament where a child has the tendency to be reticent or reserved with new people and in new situations. They found that during the Strange Situation, insecurely attached and behaviorally inhibited toddlers exhibited elevations in cortisol, while securely attached behaviorally inhibited toddlers did not show this reaction. Attachment security served as a buffer to those with an inhibited temperament. In another study, infants were given two injections in the presence of their caregivers. Again, it was found that attachment security buffered those with inhibited temperaments. In comparison to highly fearful (temperamentally inhibited) children with secure attachments who did not have elevations in cortisol, highly fearful children with insecure attachments were more likely to have surges in cortisol when receiving the injections (Gunnar et al., 1996; Nachmias et al., 1996; Sroufe et al., 2005a; Blair, 2010). Additional evidence points to the presence of an attachment figure serving to buffer against increases in cortisol activity in situations such as being approached by a stranger, meeting a live clown (a novel stimuli), or receiving medical exams after inoculations. In all of these situations, those with secure attachments to their caregivers do not experience as sharp an increase in cortisol production in comparison to those who are insecurely attached (Gunnar & Barr, 1998).

Physical touch is a powerful way attachment figures can engender feelings of safety. It has been shown to actually reduce cortisol levels. For instance, infants whose mothers physically touched them during the still-face paradigm had lower cortisol levels afterwards in comparison to infants who weren't touched (Feldman, Singer, & Zagoory, 2010). The sound of a mother's voice has also been shown to be soothing. Following a stressful procedure where children had to do public speaking and perform math tasks, these children were randomly assigned to one of three groups; a group that had direct contact with comforting mothers, a group who received a telephone call from their mothers, and a group who watched a neutral film and had no interaction with their mothers. All three groups of children exhibited elevated cortisol levels when performing the task. Physical contact *and* just vocal contact was shown to reduce cortisol levels an hour after the task. Simply hearing a mother's voice was enough to quell stress (Seltzer, Ziegler, & Pollak, 2010).

In adults, the presence of a supportive partner can be enormously stress-alleviating. James Coan, a Professor of Psychology at the University of Virginia and Director of the Virginia Affective Neuroscience Laboratory, has conducted research on how an attachment relationship may help individuals deal with stressors. In one study, he and his colleagues observed married women in an MRI scanner while they were threatened with a mild electric shock. The subjects were either alone, holding the hand of a stranger, or were holding their partner's hand. The researchers found that a secure relationship can greatly ameliorate a person's distress. There was the least amount of threat-activation in the brains of women who were in the more secure relationships, while there was a great deal of threat activation in the brains of those in poorer quality relationships. Holding the hand of a stranger was not nearly as soothing as holding the hand of a secure partner, but was still more effective than simply negotiating the threat alone (Coan, Shaefer, & Davidson, 2007; Coan, 2016).

In addition to reducing cortisol levels, a supportive presence has been shown to decrease other physiological signs of stress as well. In a study where researchers measured blood pressure in married and cohabitating couples over the course of a week, they found that participants had much lower blood pressure when interacting with their partners as opposed to socially interacting with anyone else or to when not engaged with anyone. Not only that, the quality of the relationship had no bearing on the observed effect. The bottom line was an individual's blood pressure was lower when a romantic partner was present. This indicates that a partner's presence can positively affect our cardiovascular activity, thereby aiding our bodies negotiate stress (Gump, Polk, Kamarck, & Schiffman, 2001). Even physical pain can be reduced when an individual feels supported. Female participants in a study underwent functional MRI (fMRI) scans while being subjected to painful heat stimuli. One group of women were shown photos of their significant others while being scanned and another group was presented with a picture of a stranger or of an object. Results showed that just seeing an image of an attachment figure reduced activity in the dorsal anterior cingulate cortex and bilateral anterior insula, the areas of the brain that register pain. This was different to those who saw an image of a stranger or an object. Their pain was not reduced. Additionally, seeing a photograph of a significant other led to more activity in the ventromedial prefrontal cortex, an area of the brain involved with feeling safe. These results indicate that an attachment figure can signal safety when feeling threatened (Eisenberger et al., 2011).

While a secure attachment can buffer an individual against stress, the lack of a secure attachment may make him more vulnerable to feeling stress. Spangler and Grossman (1993) examined cortisol levels in infants during separation in the Strange Situation paradigm and found that compared to secure infants, insecure and disorganized infants had significant cortisol increases even 15 to 30 minutes after the procedure had ended. They attributed this to the fact that secure infants seem better able to manage the stress of separating from a caregiver. It seems that a child who is secure in his or her attachment relationship can better weather perceived stress and may suffer less deleterious effects on his or her regulatory abilities, while a child who is insecurely attached may be less able to negotiate environmental as well as internal stress and may be less likely to possess the skills necessary to persist in meeting long-term goals.

Secure individuals have been found to perceive stressors as less stressful, presumably because they are confident that either they can manage on their own or that they will benefit from the support of others. Studies show that in comparison to insecure individuals, those who are securely attached appraise a variety of stressors in less menacing terms and additionally feel more confident in their ability to cope with the stressors they encounter (Shaver & Mikulincer, 2002). Conversely, those with insecure attachment patterns may find stressors more stressful and can actually feel threatened by others offering support. In one study (Mikulincer & Florian, 1997), secure, avoidant, and anxiously attached individuals were asked to handle a poisonous snake, presumably a stressful experience. The researchers found that the stress level of securely attached subjects decreased after talking to another person about their feelings, but the stress levels of avoidant subjects increased following a conversation that was emotion-focused. Those who were classified as anxiously attached did not have any reaction, either negative or positive, to venting their feelings, but their stress levels heightened with attempts to problem-solve their distress. And in another study (Feeney & Kirkpatrick, 1996), 35 female college students had to complete a challenging mental arithmetic task twice, once in the presence of a romantic partner and again without the partner's presence. Participants' heart rates and blood pressures were measured in both conditions. Results showed that secure women tended to have less of a physiological stress response in comparison to anxious and avoidant women, meaning a secure attachment bond buffered the effects of stress. On the opposite side of the coin, not only was physiological arousal evident for anxious and avoidant women when their partners were absent, but the physiological arousal heightened when the partner was present. This indicates that offers of support may not help insecure individuals and, in fact, can sometimes feel *more* stressful. Clinicians should note that direct offers of support can sometimes increase stress levels and can use this to more sensitively intervene with an insecurely attached client.

In sum, a secure attachment bond can serve as a buffer against the negative effects of stress and an insecure attachment bond can render an individual more vulnerable to stress. As clinicians, it behooves us to understand the confluence of factors that impact our ability to negotiate stressors. In particular, our clients may benefit greatly from the therapeutic relationship which ultimately becomes an attachment bond.

Polyvagal Theory

How exactly do the fear system and the attachment system interact from a psychophysiological perspective? On October 8, 1994, Dr. Stephen Porges, a Professor of Psychiatry at the University of Illinois and Professor of Human Development at the University of Maryland, first described the theory that explores the connection between these two systems: the Polyvagal Theory. Talking to the Society for Psychophysiological Research, he detailed his hypotheses on the relationship between attachment and the body, a theory that has come to be critical to our understanding of stress, trauma, and human bonds. The Polyvagal Theory, referring to the many branches of the vagus nerve, describes the way that we can respond to stress in an adaptive, hierarchical, and systematic way, utilizing our attachment systems to serve as a buffer to distress. Feeling safe is viewed as essential to our well-being and is understood as the byproduct of socially engaging. Safety is not seen as purely the result of removing the stressor. It is a theory that fits nicely with clinical practice, allowing clinicians to understand how to use security in relationships to negotiate stress and trauma. In essence, it enables us to reestablish resilience in our clients through the therapeutic bond (Porges, 2017). The next sections describe the theory.

The autonomic nervous system: three divisions

Polyvagal Theory addresses our ability to maintain social connection even when faced with distress. This ability depends on the vagus, a pathway of nerves that regulates our sympathetic arousal during social interactions. Part of the autonomic nervous system, the tenth cranial nerve, or the vagus, modulates digestion, breathing, and cardiac activity, as well as social interaction. Contrary to its singular name, it is not a singular nerve, but a conglomeration of many nerves, leading from the brain stem to many different places in the body, including the lungs, heart, throat, and the digestive system, and then back to the brain. Our facial gestures, expressions, actions, ability to swallow, and voice prosody (the tune and rhythm of our speech), are all part of our vagal system. Thus, a soothing voice or a smiling face can induce feelings of safety. In contrast, a raspy voice or someone who uses short sentences with a frowning face can convey a lack of safety. All of these nerves work together to form a communication system, enabling the coordination of the brain and the body, and encouraging the maintenance of the body's emotional and physical homeostasis and regulation. The vagal system can be seen as a modification of the autonomic nervous system, giving us the ability to modulate the level of our arousal when distress occurs. Without the vagus, fight-or-flight is an all or nothing response. The vagus enables different degrees of response. It allows us to decrease our heightened experiences by social contact, rather than fighting or fleeing. (Cozolino, 2014; Hane & Fox, 2016; Porges, 2017).

Similar to MacLean's concept of the triune brain that develops phylogeneti-cally, Porges hypothesizes that our autonomic functioning develops sequentially in three steps. First to form is our *vegetative vagus*, a system, seen in reptiles, that controls our body's ability to shut down and immobilize. It can potentially be lethal. The activation of this depends on the "oldest" parts of our para-sympathetic nervous system, the unmyelinated vagal pathway, or the dorsal vagal complex, that leads to organs below the diaphragm. The next system to mobilize is the *fight-or-flight system*. This system increases heart rate, rate of breathing, and other functions designed to kick the body into gear. It is the sympathetic nervous system that is responsible for this system's activation. Lastly, the third system to initiate is the *social engagement system*, a system that relies on the myelinated branch of the vagal system, the ventral vagal, which is a newer part of the parasympathetic system which leads to organs above the diaphragm. It allows us to inhibit, regulate, or calm our sympathetic nervous system. The systems function hierarchically, where newer systems can suppress or deactivate older ones (Porges, 1998; 2017).

Porges suggests that it is the last system, which is unique to human beings, that enables us to maintain our social connections even in times of stress. He believes we are wired to connect because this is advantageous from an evolu-tionary point of view. Our social engagement system helps us to join with others in order to keep our fight-or-flight responses deactivated. When there are no environmental challenges and our fight-or-flight system is dormant, our body can grow and change. During manageable levels of distress, there is a decrease in vagal stimulation. This allows the sympathetic system to kick into gear and engage the fight-or-flight response system. We can effectively combat the stressor, but at the expense of our exploration and growth. It is only when the "smart" vagus regulates our sympathetic nervous system and instigates our social engagement system, that we become able to effectively negotiate stress as well as engaging with others and with the environment.

Rather than a cognitive understanding of safety, Porges hypothesizes that safety is a visceral sense, an evaluation conducted by our bodies, oftentimes without our awareness. He terms the unconscious neural activity required to assess danger in our environment neuroception. Cues for safety are assessed by signals such as tone of voice, others' smiles, or gestures. Upon *feeling* safe, the "vagal brake," together with oxytocin and vasopressin, decelerates our heart rate and disables our fight-or-flight response. When we feel safe, we can signal to others that we want to interact. Our facial muscles relax and we smile at others. We widen our eyes in sympathy when others share misfortune with us. By staying engaged with others, and by not acti-vating our sympathetic nervous systems, we don't become defensive or go on the attack. We can cooperate and be nurtured, all the while reaping the benefits that social connections have to offer (Cozolino, 2014; Baylin & Hughes, 2016; Porges, 2017). Taking this a step further, we can conclude that feeling safe is crucial to our overall well-being. In this way, the smart vagus is a foundation upon which the attachment relationship forms.

Polyvagal Theory and attachment

We can understand the Polyvagal system in attachment system terms. When we feel safe, or when we have a secure base, we can engage with others. We can interact with a secure attachment figure. We can learn and explore our environment and ourselves. However, in times of distress, when we don't feel safe, our exploration system deactivates and we must do what we can to ensure our own safety. This means all of our bodily resources go towards self-protection. According to Porges, safety is vital to our being able to connect with another being. He suggests that attachment theory is missing a "preamble to attachment … [which] is dependent on the signals of safety" (Porges, 2017, p. 123). Only with safety can attachment bonds adaptively develop. Thus, Porges has built on attachment theory, proposing two sequential processes involved in forming a secure social bond: social engagement and the creation of the social bond.

The social engagement system

Our social engagement system relies on facial expressions, vocalization, voice prosody, and gestures to create feelings of safety. Feeding is also part of the social engagement system. For example, when a mother nurses her baby, she is also nurturing him. As with most physiological systems, our social engagement system is thought to be shaped by genes and our environment. Our underlying temperament interacts with the quality of our attachment relationships to mold our "vagal tone," or our vagal system's capacity for regulating many organs, including our heart, lungs, and digestive tract. Quality of care (environment) is assumed to be critical to the quality of vagal tone and, to a lesser degree, an infant's temperament (genes) is seen as affecting the care that is given. Thus, a baby who is easily soothed may encourage his caregiver to maintain attunement. The more positive the interactions, the more mutually rewarding they become and thus, the baby and the caregiver both enjoy the social connection. The baby learns from the experience of the mutual attunement and his vagal tone increases with each constructive experience. This cycle of relating is the underpinning of the development of a secure attachment bond. Higher vagal tone indicates a greater ability to self-regulate. In contrast, poor vagal tone indicates the opposite. Those with poor vagal tone have trouble quelling their feelings when they need to and this can prevent them from engaging with others. They may misinterpret the expressions of others or may have flattened affect themselves. This can become a negative cycle of interaction, where poor vagal tone begets poor vagal tone. Those with insecure and disorganized attachment styles can be assumed to have decreased vagal tone (Cozolino, 2014).

Attachment

A securely attached person generally possesses higher vagal tone. An individual who can regulate various levels of arousal and who can connect with others even in stressful situations is most likely securely attached. This is someone who has been successful in engaging with others and who has the confidence that should he need to call on others for help, he'll be able to do so. An avoidantly attached individual has a bias toward parasympathetic control, with low social engagement and flatter affect. He withdraws as a defense, rather than using his social engagement system. Because of this, it is more difficult for him to feel safe and therefore, he is limited in how much he explores. Those who are avoidantly attached may seem depressed or unmotivated. An anxiously attached individual often has a predisposition to being sympathetically aroused, meaning he tends to have high levels of arousal, which can prevent him from activating his social engagement system and make it difficult for him to feel calm and safe. He may present as irritable, "stressed out," dependent, impulsive, or aggressive and may be overly involved with those around him, without being able to effectively engage socially. A disorganized individual may have had a hyper-activated sympathetic nervous system, one that is constantly "on." Most likely, this is someone who has been exposed to overwhelming fear and has not developed the capacity to use the social engagement system to quell this fear. Relationships are not seen as sources of comfort (Cozolino, 2014). The next section will examine how exposure to trauma impacts the polyvagal system.

Polyvagal system and trauma

Situations and experiences that overwhelm our coping strategies can be trau-matic. Our cortisol levels may become persistently elevated and our systems may be primed to react at even the slightest provocation. Porges was fascinated by our body's dual reaction to fear. During his early research, he noted that newborn babies reacted to stress in two conflicting ways; either they had an elevated heart rate or they had massive drops in heart rate. He set to work to explain these opposing responses. In this way, his theory became more con-cretized. He noted that at first, when we perceive a threat, we attempt to engage others to help us. We use our tone of voice and our facial expressions to do so. If this doesn't work, we must negotiate the stressor on our own. It is then that our sympathetic nervous system initiates. Our heart rate accelerates and our breathing quickens. We are ready for fight or flight. What happens though if the fight-or-flight response doesn't work? It was this question that spurred Porges on. He ultimately named a second line of defense. Following the failure of fight-or-flight and if all else fails, then and only then does the body pull out all stops. The dorsal vagal complex activates, we immobilize, and our heart rate drops precipitously; we freeze and we may feign death. Our breath becomes shallow and our intestines begin to shut down. Porges stated that we not only fight or flee, but, if that fails, we freeze. The response has come to be known as the fight-flight-or-freeze response. It is not a conscious choice to use the sympathetic nervous system or the parasympathetic nervous system. In cases of overwhelming and inescapable traumatic situations, when nothing else works, the body can become immobilized. From a clinical perspective, this is the reaction that may be associated with dissociation (Van der Kolk, 2014; Porges, 2017).

What happens when a child is exposed to stress without having a caregiver to soothe him or her? The child cannot learn that stress can be alleviated by social contact. Relationships aren't seen as comforting or safe. The child may even develop a bias toward perceiving threat when there isn't one and may have "safety blindness," where he can't find signs of safety even when they're present (Baylin & Hughes, 2016).

Summary

We are not only a product of our mind. We are the sum of our mind and our bodies and our emotions. Should we undergo stress, our brains and our bodies respond. If that stress is prolonged or worse, if we experience trauma, there can be dramatic ramifications. Our bodies can become overwhelmed and our actual physiologies can change. This feeds on itself and can become a destructive cycle of being unable to manage stress. It is now known that the attachment bond can serve as a protective factor, buffering an individual against the negative effects of prolonged stress. According to Porges' Polyvagal Theory, if we can instigate our social engagement systems, we can override our fight-flight-freeze sympathetic responses and adaptively negotiate stressors. Those who are securely attached are more likely to be able to initiate their social engagement systems when under duress. Thus, a secure attachment bond can be critical to our optimal functioning.

Chapter 8

Emotions and attachment

Another area of study has resurfaced in the science world over the past few decades, one that has greatly impacted the clinical application of attachment theory. The study of emotion has once again come to the forefront of psychological and neurobiological research. Ironically, though therapists have been known to ask "how are you feeling?," up until recently, cognitive insight and not feelings was seen as the fundamental change vehicle. Feelings and emotions, seen as separate from reasoning and cognition, were viewed as invalid areas of inquiry by the scientific world. As with Ainsworth and Bowlby, for years, scientists placed an emphasis only on what was externally measurable. And in the therapy arena, Freudian analysts paved the way for behaviorists, who tended to have a singular focus on modifying maladaptive, external behaviors. Some even believed emotions to be fictional constructs! In the 1970s, with the development of computers, the "cognitive revolution" occurred. The mind was likened to computers and therapists increasingly emphasized logical thought patterns. Thus, cognitive-behavioral therapy achieved great popularity (LeDoux, 1996; Panksepp & Biven, 2012), and top-down interventions were seen as primary in promoting change (Greenberg & Johnson, 1988; Fosha, Siegel, & Solomon, 2009).

But the tide has turned. With improved technology, circuits in the brain have been linked to feelings. No longer are emotions seen as just ideas, but now they are viewed as concrete functions of the brain. With this, emotion has become a serious, scientific focus of study, launching what has been called the "emotional revolution" (Hill, 2015). In fact, whereas a search of a medical website of citations in the 1960s accessed just 100 articles mentioning "emotion" in the title, in the last ten years, more than 2,000 papers had emotion titles (LeDoux, 2012). And in the clinical world, many treatments have been developed with a "bottom-up" approach, whereby cognitive insight and behavioral shifts are seen as resulting from, not causing, change. Emotions are thus understood to be essential to human experience and as key agents of change (Fosha et al., 2009; Schore, 2009). Indeed, some now say that psychotherapy is "the affect communicating cure" as opposed to the "talking cure" (Schore & Schore, 2008).

What is emotion?

The literature is crowded with terms for and definitions of emotion, sometimes making it difficult to know exactly what emotion is (Gross, 2015). To better understand, it may help to begin by differentiating "emotion" from "affect" and "feeling." Though the words "emotion" "affect" and "feeling" are often used interchangeably, they are not one and the same thing. While "affect" connotes an unconscious response to a stimulus, tending to be more automatic than thought out, "feelings" and "emotions" are both conscious results of processes that were unconscious. "Feelings" are seen as the conscious registering of fundamental sensations and "emotions" are more than simply being aware of an affect. They involve consciously experiencing and integrating feeling states, as well as acting on these states (Greenberg & Paivio, 1997). Examining its roots, the term emotion is derived from the Latin word emovere meaning "to move out," "to stir," or "to agitate" (Van Der Kolk, 2014). By definition, the term implies movement, motivation, and action. In fact, many emotion theorists feel an emotion is a process in and of itself. Ekman, a leading emotion researcher, writes that emotion is the process by which we first evaluate and then act on our perception that something is occurring, where we induce physical actions and emotional reactions in order to negotiate our circumstances. Though we can use language as one way to manage emotion, language does not equate with emotion. Emotions are not synonymous with words (Ekman, 2003). Nor are they the same as our inner drives. They may inspire some sort of action, but not any specific action. Individuals tailor their responses to their emotional experiences to meet their specific needs (Greenberg & Johnson, 1988).

Each experienced emotion has two different dimensions: a valence that is either positive or negative and a certain level of arousal, such as, for example, calm or excited (Schore, 2019). In addition to the various dimensions, an emotion encompasses many components. Firstly, there is the unconscious appraisal or evaluation of a signal. Next, a physiological reaction occurs to this signal, most of the time happening before a cognitive understanding takes place. At this point a cognitive interpretation may occur and meaning is assigned to the various emotion perceptions. Lastly, the emotion can instigate action. For example, as seen in the previous chapter, fear may induce a fight or flight response (Johnson, 2009). Overall, it can be said that emotion is "an expression of the body read by the mind" (Hill, 2015, p. 6). The following sections will explore the evolution of scientific understanding about emotions with a focus on how we've come to our current understanding.

Are emotions universal or culturally constructed?

Do we all feel the same emotions? Does our culture influence the emotions we feel? These are questions that date back to the days of Charles Darwin, the world-renowned biologist who transformed the theory of evolution in the 1800s.

Darwin (1872) proposed there to be seven categorical universal emotions: shame, sadness, anger, surprise, joy, fear, and disgust. The idea of universal emotions became controversial, with many doubting its existence. Paul Ekman was one of those naysayers. It was purely by chance that in 1965, Ekman, who had been studying hand movement, switched tacks and began studying facial expression and emotion, a turn of events that was to greatly impact the field. He happened upon funding to study differences in nonverbal communication in Thailand, with an emphasis on distinguishing between what was universal and what was culturally defined. At the time, he strongly believed that everything, from emotion to emotional expression, was learned and therefore culturally dependent. He vehemently disagreed with Darwin's claim that some emotions were universal and, in fact, felt so certain of his position that he didn't even read Darwin's book on the subject. However, his views soon were to change.

Ekman conducted his first study, showing photographs of facial expressions to people from different cultures. There was a great deal of agreement, pointing to the universality of certain expressions (Ekman, 2003). What often differed between cultures was not how people felt but how people expressed their emotions. He termed these rules of expressions "display rules" and came to believe that rather than the emotions themselves, it was the rules that were socially constructed. To prove his point, he conducted an experiment where he showed Americans and Japanese subjects a film about surgery and accidents. Americans did not moderate their expressions, whether watching on their own or with others. However, Japanese subjects hid their negative expressions, smiling instead, when they watched the film with others. When alone, they displayed the exact same expressions as did the American subjects. Ekman furthered his study of emotion, journeying to New Guinea to support his newfound theory; that some facial expressions are universal. Though it seems there are more than ten thousand different facial expressions, he concluded that there are only six core emotions, each of which is connected to certain, distinct facial expressions. These six emotions are: fear, anger, disgust, sadness, happiness, and surprise, similar to what Darwin had concluded all those years before. In sum, Ekman's research contributed a great deal to the overall study of nonverbal communication, facial cues, and the universality of our emotional experiences.

How are the mind, the body, and emotion related?

In 1884, William James published an article asking the following question: "Do we run from a bear because we are afraid or are we afraid because we run?" (LeDoux, 1996, p. 43). He concluded that emotion is the result of our physiological responses, that our brain cognitively reads our body's response and then feels, which implies, for instance, that we *feel* upset because we cry. Termed the "stimulus to feeling sequence," it has been the subject of major debate over the years. Researchers have argued over how we appraise emotions, how emotions are influenced by context, and if cognition is a necessary and/or sufficient component of our bodily and emotional response.

More recently, Jaak Panksepp, a neuroscientist and psychobiologist, addressed these questions. During his quest to understand emotion, he coined the term "affective neuroscience" to denote the field of study of the interaction of emotion with the mind and the body. He theorized there to be seven basic affective *systems* and referred to them as SEEKING, RAGE, FEAR, LUST, CARE, PANIC/GRIEF, and PLAY. Panksepp linked each of these systems to particular kinds of behavior as well as physiological changes in the body. Additionally, he suggested that the systems are associated with specific modes of affective consciousness as they are each connected with distinct neural substrates. Each raw emotion, Panksepp stated, is produced from particular brain tissues and these emotions then interact with the body. The SEEKING system promotes exploratory behavior, such as moving toward an interesting object. It also encourages proximity-seeking in times of trouble. The seeking generally engenders positive feeling, either as a joyful encounter with something interesting or a soothing relief from danger. The RAGE system promotes aggressive behavior toward the transgressor. It is usually associated with negative emotion. The FEAR system engenders escape behavior, while the LUST system encourages approach and courting behavior. The CARE system enables nurturing behavior and feels positive while the PANIC/GRIEF system is associated with pain and behaviors designed to reengage a caregiver. Lastly, the PLAY system evokes lightness and bouncy movements and brings about positive feelings. Panksepp is known for his unusual experiments where he tickled rats. Surprisingly, rats have a hearty giggle that can be brought on just by tickling. The animals that chirped more were deemed happier by far in comparison to those that didn't chirp as much, proof that play brings happy feelings (Panksepp & Biven, 2012). Thus, in answer to the question William James posed all those years ago, we can conclude from Panksepp's suppositions that we run from the bear because our fear system is activated; we run because, based on an interaction of the mind, the body, and our emotions, we feel afraid of the bear.

As researchers grappled with the question of how cognition, the body, and emotion are related, they had an even more fundamental question. Are emotions always a conscious experience? The more this question was examined, the more it seemed undeniable that we can feel without being aware of the fact that we are feeling. Going back to the bear example, a person walking in the wild may kick into action and run away from a bear even before cognitively registering that a bear is lurking behind a bush. To wait around while the mind processes the image and then feel fear is counterintuitive to survival. That person must run quickly! Too, babies feel emotion long before they can verbalize their feelings and maybe long before they "know" that they are feeling. In fact, some theorists claim that the conscious emotions we recognize can sometimes be distractions or detours from our primary, or "real" feelings (LeDoux, 1996).

It is becoming increasingly apparent that emotion, biology, and cognition are not separate entities; they are inextricably intertwined. Overall, researchers today promote the notion that emotions are a synthesis of cognitive, physiological, sensorimotor, and affective processes. Both conscious and nonconscious as well as cognitive and noncognitive causes stimulate an emotional response, which is then synthesized. Following this, often, there is further integration of emotion and cognition, bringing emotions into conscious awareness. This synthesis and integration connects emotion with meaning (Greenberg & Paivio, 1997). At the end of it all, the neuroscientist Jill Bolte Taylor (2006) crystalized the latest thinking when she said "[a]lthough many of us think of ourselves as *thinking creatures that feel*, biologically we are *feeling creatures that think*" (p. 19, empasis in the original).

What is the basic neurobiology of emotional responses?

Because of the huge effort to expand our understanding of the neurobiological mechanisms of emotion, more and more evidence has accumulated that we are indeed feeling creatures that think. As was mentioned in Chapter 6, the brain has evolved over millions of years, from the bottom up. Our brain stem, the most primitive area of our brain, emerged first. Next, our "emotional" center, or the limbic system, came online, and only more recently, did the neocortex develop. The way the brain has evolved points to the notion that we felt long before we could think complex thoughts. With the growth of the neocortex, emotional life became more complex. In very simplistic terms, it seems there are two paths for emotional experience in the brain: one where the "emotional system" is activated without involvement of the "thinking system" and one where the "thinking system" creates meaning from our emotional responses.

Oftentimes, our brain reacts without the neocortex's involvement. In rats, the amygdala can respond in as little time as 12 milliseconds, while it takes twice as long for a signal to traverse from the thalamus to the neocortex to the amygdala. Thus, when the amygdala, part of the limbic system, is aroused, the emotional memory of this arousal is encoded without necessarily encoding a cognitive understanding. This emotional sense of what happened may lie dormant in the amygdala and may be triggered by the association of something that happens in the present that is reminiscent of past situations (Goleman, 1995). Interestingly, scientists note that our limbic system remains the same from childhood through adulthood. It does not mature. Thus, our current emotional reactions are often a result of past occurrences. In some cases, these responses may be adaptive (Taylor, 2006). For instance, a woman who was once mugged by a man running past her and grabbing her handbag may react quickly to the sound of footsteps coming close to her body. She may pull her handbag towards her and grip it tightly. The amygdala is presumably triggered and her stress response becomes activated. This engages the body's autonomic nervous system so that this woman can better protect herself. However, sometimes skirting the neocortex can be maladaptive. For instance, a war veteran, upon hearing the siren of a firetruck giving a demonstration at his child's birthday party, may suddenly experience severe panic and have difficulty catching his breath. In this case, he may be "emotionally hijacked" (Goleman, 1995), where the brain becomes flooded with emotion (in this case fear) and he fails to recruit the neocortex. He may respond as he would have during the war, by covering his ears, running for cover, and bolting from the birthday party. This response would be based on his brain's memory of what was adaptive in the past, but is no longer adaptive. It may all occur without the neocortex's involvement, which usually serves to modulate and moderate our emotions, as well as to impose a level of awareness on our reactions. As previously mentioned in Chapter 6, it is the pre-frontal lobes in the neocortex that help us make decisions on the best course of action in a given situation (Goleman, 1995). The kinds of situations that are pre-sented in therapy may be the result of an "emotional hijacking." A wife presents her husband with a gift of a green tie. Unbeknownst to her, his father had received a green tie from his mother right before his mother walked out on the family; a consolation prize of sorts. Her husband is emotionally hijacked, his emotional system is overwhelmed preventing him from recruiting his ability to reason, and he yells at his wife, saying it was the worst gift ever. Exploring the emotional reaction from a neurological perspective and reframing it as an emotional reaction based on past experiences can be enormously helpful.

The purpose of emotion

According to the theory of evolution, our fundamental goal is survival and all of our neurobiological and bodily systems work toward that purpose. Emotions are part of our survival in the following ways. Firstly, they are often *motivational*, driving us to act. Positive emotions tend to reinforce appetitive states (i.e., food or sex), connec-tion with others, and the exploration of the environment, while negative emotions propel us to defend ourselves and/or protect our loved ones. For example, happi-ness promotes cooperation, sadness may instigate proximity seeking, and anger compels us to set boundaries. It can be said that emotions motivate us to act in ways that render the original emotion unnecessary, so that when the inspired action occurs, a situation resolves or, even more simply, the sought-out emotion feels good. Secondly, emotions can be *adaptive*, organizing our thoughts and actions so that we meet our goals and can manage what we encounter. Because our emotions often occur outside of our awareness, they can organize us without cognitive pro-cesses being involved. For instance, our autonomic nervous system may be trig-gered, our facial expressions may change to engage another, or the tone of our voice may be altered, all of which can aid us in meeting our goals, often without any cognitive analysis. Lastly, emotions can be *communicative*, conveying information in social interactions (Greenberg & Johnson, 1988; Greenberg & Paivio, 1997; Van Der Kolk, 2014). Emotions serve as signals and ultimately, we function best when we "listen" to our own emotions and to the emotions of others.

The relationship between emotion and attachment

Emotions are intricately connected with an attachment bond. Bowlby (1969, 1982; 1980) stated that our attachment relationships inspire some of our most intense emotions. Forming an attachment bond, positively interacting with a loved one, or even just feeling safe and secure in the presence of another, feels really good. As Schore (1994) writes, sharing affective states and experiencing resonance with another is both energizing and satisfying. "Feeling felt" (Siegel, 1999), or feeling "gotten," accepted, and known by another, is inordinately pleasurable. On the other hand, losing a loved one or even experiencing the threat of loss of an attachment figure can engender anxiety, fear, or sadness. Bowlby viewed emotions as part of our appraisal processes where we appraise the environment and our own internal states so that we can behave adaptively. Emotions are seen as motivators in maintaining the attachment bond, where, in a well-functioning attachment dyad, both caregiver and child actively seek out the joyful feeling of connection and avoid overwhelming negative feelings of relationship turbulence or rejection. Additionally, emotions promote exploration of the environment, where a child may feel joy in learning and exploring and pride in mastering new tasks.

In addition to seeing emotions as forms of motivation towards meeting goals, Bowlby (1969, 1982) also viewed emotions as a means of communication between child and caregiver. From birth, human beings are able to express emotion, thereby communicating needs and feelings of distress to another. Emotional expression is transactional, meaning it occurs between people, and as an infant, within an attachment dyad. It serves a purpose. So, for instance, when a baby cries, he is not crying so that he'll feel better on his own. The baby's cry is to enlist the help of his caregiver so that his caregiver can make him feel better (Greenberg & Johnson, 1988). Anger can be a form of protest against unresponsiveness or impending separation. A toddler screams until she is red in the face when her mother is on the phone. "Notice me," she seems to be saying. Luckily for her, her mother is sensitive to her emotional cues and ends the phone call, smiles at her child, and pulls her closer for a hug. The child visibly relaxes into her mother's arms. Her anger has worked to reengage her mother and she feels safe once more.

According to attachment theory, we may all share similar feelings, but the way in which we feel, how we act on what we feel, and how we express those feelings is shaped by our attachment-related experiences. If a caregiver is sensitive to her child's cues, she will respond appropriately to his cries for help. That child learns that his cries are effective and that he can successfully ask for help. He may be rewarded by a dopamine release when his caregiver gives him a cuddle and his cries will be positively reinforced. What is more, this child will feel free to explore and will reap the benefits of the rush of good feelings associated with exploring novel and interesting surroundings. He will also feel the calmness associated with the knowledge that he will be taken care of should he need help. In contrast, a child who cries and is ignored or rejected by his caregiver will learn to silence his cries. He is more likely to get the help he needs if he does not express his emotional needs. He will seldom feel that rush of joy that adoration from an attachment figure inspires. This child is not free to explore his environment as he has to maintain proximity to his caregiver of his own accord. He can't trust that she will be there for him. He therefore does not often feel the rush of positive emotions that exploration of the environment engenders. Too, he may often feel fearful and overwhelmed, as he is negotiating life on his own without much needed scaffolding. His emotions are most likely more negatively tinged compared to the child who has a sensitive and responsive caregiver. In this way, it can be said that secure attachments encourage positive emotions while insecure attachments foster negative emotions.

In a functional attachment dyad, a child elicits a caregiver's care and a caregiver is motivated to provide that care. Emotion plays a part in reinforcing the workings of a caregiving system, where the caregiver's sensitivity is shaped and reinforced by various emotional responses. Our biology ensures that, in typical circumstances, parenting is pleasurable. A caregiver feels joy when her baby smiles at her and will be motivated to achieve this state again. Dopamine is also released during certain stressful times, such as when a mother cares for a child who is distressed. In these ways, emotions reinforce positive interactions as well as adaptive parenting moments that may not be as positive. Should the caregiving system not function optimally, the caregiver will miss out on the joy of connecting with her child. In fact, in some cases, interactions with a child may actually have the opposite effect, incurring rather than relieving the stress of a caregiver. For instance, it has been shown that chronic substance abusing mothers actually have less of a dopaminergic response when caring for their distressed children. In such cases, interacting with a child may not only lack feelings of pleasure, but may actually induce more stress and the caregiving system may become maladaptive (Suchman, Decost, McMahon, Rousaville, & Mayes, 2011).

Categorical emotions

As mentioned, emotion theorists delineate between five and seven universal, or categorical, emotions. Most often used is Ekman's (2003) list which includes anger, fear, sadness, happiness, disgust, contempt and surprise. Sylvan Tomkins, Ekman's teacher who has been called the founder of modern affect theory, included shame as well (LeDoux, 1996). Each emotion has a positive or negative valence. From an evolutionary standpoint, negative emotions are more primitive, inciting fight-or-flight responses, while positive emotions are more developed and tend to relate to social interaction (Cozolino, 2014). Listed below are the categorical emotions and their relationship to attachment. Each can be viewed as a conglomeration of emotions that vary in intensity. As a clinician, it is helpful to recognize the physiological signs of each emotion and thus, these signs have been included in the following section as a general guide.

Anger

Definition. There are a variety of feelings associated with the word anger, such as annoyance, irritation, or rage. When one feels any of these emotions, one is angry. If we are threatened by emotional or physical harm, anger can be an adaptive response. It communicates a need for change.

Attachment. Within an attachment relationship, anger can be seen as a "protest" emotion, designed to reengage a loved one. It often occurs when feeling threatened by abandonment or rejection. When providing protection, a caregiver can use anger to warn others to retreat. Additionally, rage can set in when someone's physical needs haven't been met, such as when one is extremely hungry, thirsty, or frustrated sexually. This is another way of signaling to a caregiver or a partner that there is a need to be met (Panksepp & Biven, 2012). Expressing anger can lead to distancing if the underlying need being expressed is not accurately read, but can also lead to setting healthy boundaries (Greenberg & Johnson, 1988). A therapist often must reframe anger as really being an expression of vulnerability, which is a more approachable emotion. Dan came into session yelling at his wife, Susan, that she had served pasta for dinner, knowing that he had high blood sugar levels. She yelled back, saying that she shouldn't have to always make dinner and that she had a long day and pasta was all she could manage. With the therapist's help, Dan was able to understand that his anger was more about his hurt that Susan didn't care enough about him to make a dinner he could eat and be healthy. It brought up his fear that she was tired of all of his physical ailments, of which he had many, and that she would one day leave him. His anger was really a protest against feeling rejected. Once Susan understood this, she could respond to his underlying fear much more easily than to the anger he had expressed. She could reassure him that she loved him and was not planning to leave.

Physiology. When anger occurs, there can be surges of testosterone, norepinephrine, glutamate, acetylcholine, and nitric oxide. The autonomic nervous system is activated, increasing the heart rate, and promoting blood flow to the hands, which prepares a person to act. An angry person perspires more and breathes more heavily than when they are calm. Additionally, he may feel a sense of pressure and heat (Ekman, 2003; Panksepp & Biven, 2012). There is also increased sensation in the lower limbs and more of a tendency for forward movement (Nummenmaa, Glerean, Hari, & Hietanen, 2014).

Recognizing in others. Facial expressions of anger as well as angry postures can be threatening. An angry person may get red in the face and if not speaking, he may bite down and push forward his chin (Ekman, 2003; Van Der Kolk, 2014).

Behaviors associated with anger. Considered an approach emotion, anger can initiate assertive or aggressive behavior, either verbal or physical, depending on learned patterns of managing anger (Greenberg & Johnson, 1988).

Fear

Definition. Fear is a feeling aroused by the threat of harm or imminent danger. Worry and anxiety are also ways that fear can manifest, where there is a reaction to an imagined or a symbolic situation, and not to immediate physical danger (Greenberg & Paivio, 1997).

Attachment. In a secure relationship, fear activates the fear system which then activates the attachment system. Expressions of fear tend to display a sense of helplessness or signal danger to others (Van Der Kolk, 2014). A sensitive caregiver responds to a child's fear signals by providing safety and protection. Expressing fear to a partner tends to communicate vulnerability. A sensitive partner responds to his or her partner by consoling and protecting the fearful partner (Greenberg & Johnson, 1988). John spoke to Cathy, his voice trembling. He acknowledged his fear of going for a colonoscopy. His father had died from colon cancer when he was nine and he just couldn't seem to face going for the procedure, though he knew he needed to do so. A lightbulb went off for Cathy as she realized that John's procrastination was really because of his fear. She held his hand and told him she would be there with him. She would not allow him to go through such a scary and worrying procedure by himself. John sighed and agreed to make the appointment.

Physiology. Similar to with anger, the autonomic nervous system is activated and the heart rate increases as does blood flow. However, the blood flow increases to the legs, enabling the person to flee if necessary. Because of this, when we are afraid, our hands may feel cold. A fearful person tends to have an increase in perspiration and respiration increases as well, and may begin to tremble slightly (Ekman, 2003).

Recognizing in others. Upper eyelids and eyebrows are raised when feeling fearful. Jaws drop and lips appear stretched horizontally.

Behaviors associated with fear. Self-protective behaviors, such as flight or freeze behavior, can occur with fear. When fear is incited, all other action ceases so that flight or freeze behavior can take place (Greenberg & Johnson, 1988; Greenberg & Paivio, 1997; Johnson, 2019).

Sadness

Definition. Tending to last longer than other emotions, sadness is the condition of feeling sorrow, loss, grief, or despair (Ekman, 2003).

Attachment. Sadness occurs with separation, loss, or the threat of loss of a loved one. In a secure attachment relationship, expressing sadness solicits caring responses. It can be a call for help to reengage with others (Greenberg & Johnson, 1988). Amanda called her best friend, Shayna, in tears. She rarely spoke of her mother's death, but today was the first anniversary of her passing. Amanda had spent the year isolating herself and had thrown herself into her work. Shayna had been feeling abandoned and was angry at Amanda's retreat, but the minute she heard Amanda's sobs, she softened and was fully present and available to her friend.

Physiology. Eyelids may droop and eyes may moisten. Pupil size may actually decrease and the throat may feel sore and cheeks may lift, as lip corners turn down. There is decreased activity in the lower limbs (Ekman, 2003; Nummenmaa et al., 2014).

Recognizing in others. Expressions include crying. A wrinkle in the inner corners of eyebrows may appear. Speech may be slower and low pitched (Ekman, 2003).

Behaviors associated with sadness. Sadness leads either to reaching out to others for support or to withdrawal or shutting down behaviors (Greenberg & Paivio, 1997).

Happiness

Definition. Happiness or enjoyment can include the pleasure of physical sensations, such as sights of nature, being touched by a loved one, or hearing lyrical music. It also can include excitement, joy, or contentment. Lastly, it can be indicative of our general sense of well-being.

Attachment. Love feels good. We feel joy and other positive emotions. Because we associate love and attachment relationships with positive emotion, we are motivated to seek out these relationships. Our emotion propels us to engage with our attachment figures and this ultimately ensures our survival. It was as if Josh and Miranda were in a bubble when they were together. Josh's face would light up when he saw Miranda across the room and Miranda's expression matched that of Josh. No matter how difficult their days were, it would all fade away when they were with one another. They laughed easily and often. They loved each other and looked forward to being together. Both Josh and Miranda described feeling butterflies when they were in each other's presence.

Physiology. During happy moments, our bodies may release dopamine and/ or serotonin. During moments of connection, oxytocin may be released and when playing, an enjoyable activity, we release endogenous opioids. All of these neurochemicals reinforce our seeking these feelings out. With excitement, or intense moments of pleasure, our face may feel flushed and our heart rate may increase. During relaxing pleasurable times, we may breathe more deeply and our body may physically relax. In general, happiness is linked with enhanced feeling all through the body (Ekman, 2003; Panksepp & Biven, 2012; Nummenmaa et al., 2014).

Recognizing in others. Facial muscles may relax and smiling and laughter frequently occur. Additionally, the muscles around the eyes pull down. An upbeat voice signals enjoyment too.

Behaviors associated with happiness. An approach emotion, it leads us to approach others or situations that make us happy. Interest and excitement, two positive emotions, promote exploratory behavior.

Disgust

Definition. Disgust is a feeling of aversion to something. Paul Rozin, a disgust researcher, found that disgust is usually triggered by something orally offensive or excretions from the body such as mucus, blood, urine, feces, and vomit. Rozin names interpersonal disgust as being triggered by those who are ill, strange, suffering from misfortune, or morally challenged as inspiring the emotion (Ekman, 2003).

Attachment. Ekman (2003) found that when showing a film of an aboriginal circumcision rite and another of an eye surgery to college students, 80% of subjects in America and Japan were disgusted. However, 20% of subjects had a different reaction, feeling pain and sadness for the individuals undergoing surgery. Ekman concluded that though we may be disgusted when seeing the inside of a stranger's body, we feel differently when it is someone we know. We then seem motivated to relieve the individual's suffering. Thus, disgust may be suspended when we really care for the person undergoing a "disgusting" procedure. Not only that, but not finding something disgusting that others do, may actually strengthen a relationship. For instance, when a child is sick with a stomach bug, most mothers are able to overcome their disgust in order to care for their child.

Physiology. Sensations of disgust include sensations in the digestive system, in the throat area such as slight gagging and physical feelings increasing in the nostrils and upper lips (Ekman, 2003; Nummenmaa et al., 2014).

Recognizing in others. Expressions of disgust may include upper and lower lips being raised and protruding, raising of the cheeks and brows lowering, and wrinkling appearing by the eyes.

Behaviors associated with disgust. Feelings of disgust promote moving away from the offending situation.

Contempt

Definition. Contempt is defined as feeling superior or disdainful of others (Ekman, 2003).

Attachment. Contempt is a destructive emotion when expressed within an attachment relationship. In fact, John Gottman, a preeminent researcher on marriage and divorce prediction, has found that contempt is the emotion the most predictive of divorce (Lisitsa, 2013). Jason and Ann came to therapy to address their failing relationship. Jason was a successful business man and Ann was a stay-at-home mother. "What does she do all day?" Jason said, looking at his i-phone as he spoke. "I'm expecting an important call," he announced. Ann looked at the floor, her lips pursed. "I do your laundry. I cook. I clean. Where would you be without me? You can barely boil an egg by yourself." Jason's nostrils flared and he rolled his eyes. From the beginning, the therapist knew this marriage was going to be tough to save. Their contempt for one another was palpable.

Physiology. Feelings increase in nostrils and upper lip. Tightening may occur in the corner of the lips (Ekman, 2003).

Recognizing in others. Expressions of contempt can include rolling of the eyes, sneering, or mocking behavior (Lisitsa, 2013).

Behaviors associated with contempt. Name-calling, mocking, using sarcasm and disdain are all examples of contemptuous behavior.

Surprise

Definition. Surprise is an emotion triggered by an unexpected event that occurs suddenly and catches someone off guard. It is a fleeting emotion that quickly converts to another emotion (Ekman, 2003).

Attachment. In adult attachment relationships, surprises can improve the level of satisfaction with a partner. They indicate caring and challenge patterns that may be maladaptive. It was a tough day for Andy. His boss had reamed him out for a mistake that had cost his company some money. His partner Greg, knowing it had been a hard day for Andy, cooked dinner, dimmed the lights, and placed a Starbucks white chocolate mocha in Andy's place. Andy came home, dejected and weary, but when he saw what Greg had prepared and then when he saw his favorite drink, his mouth opened wide and his bad day quickly faded into the background. "What a nice surprise," he exclaimed.

Physiology. Muscles tense, especially in the neck. There is a release of adrenaline.

Recognizing in others. Eyebrows may become raised and eyes may widen. Jaws may drop and lips and teeth may be parted.

Behaviors associated with surprise. Though not one and the same, surprise behavior can be included in the same category as a startle response. Fight-or-flight behavior can be seen when an individual is startled or surprised.

Shame

Definition. Shame can be defined as painful feelings of lack of worth or feeling exposed. Fear is involved in that shame incorporates the fear of being negatively evaluated by others.

Attachment. Shame only comes online with toddlerhood. The complete attunement of infancy is replaced with moments of misattunement. A toddler explores the environment and may feel elated by new discoveries that he then displays to his caregiver. The discovery can include behavior that is dangerous. For example, a toddler becomes intrigued by the straps on his car seat. He fiddles with them and then miraculously undoes the straps. Excited by his achievement, he exclaims to his mother "Look!" She turns around quickly, taking her eyes off the highway for a brief moment, and then yells loudly for her son to strap himself back in. He feels deflated. Having expected his mother to share his joy, the pair experience a mismatched state. He feels shame and begins to cry. In a secure relationship, these moments are repaired. In this case, the mother who is a sensitive caregiver, reaches her hand back to her child's seat, touches him gently, and tells him she is sorry she yelled. She was just scared that he was unstrapped from his car seat and that it was dangerous for him. She told him it would be okay and pulled over to the side of the road to remedy the situation. Thus, during times of mismatched states between caregiver and child, the child experiences feelings of shame, but if managed well (experienced for just the right amount of time, where the child is neither underaroused nor overwhelmed by feelings of shame), shame can be a positive emotion, functioning to help the child learn boundaries and social behaviors. However, it can quickly become a negative emotion if the repair is inadequate or doesn't occur. The child then can become overwhelmed with negative affect and it can almost feel like a loss of love (Schore, 1994; Hill, 2015).

Physiology. The heart slows as the chest cavity constricts (Hill, 2015).

Recognizing in others. A person feeling shame may become speechless, his head may hang down, and he may avert his gaze from others. He may blush or cry.

Behaviors associated with shame. Shame may instigate withdrawal or hiding behaviors (Johnson, 2019).

Process-experiential psychotherapy

While Ekman was studying emotions in the northern hemisphere, Les Greenberg was studying engineering in the southern hemisphere. During an exam at the University of Witwatersrand in South Africa, Greenberg was to have a realization that was to be the seed for what we now call emotionally-focused therapy (EFT), a therapy that focuses on emotion and, later on together with the work of Sue Johnson, incorporated attachment theory into a way of doing therapy. During this exam, Greenberg solved a problem without knowing *how* he did so. He just intuitively knew what to do. How was it that he could know something without consciously knowing it? The notion that we understand more than we can say drove him into the field of psychology. He began with the fundamental question of what motivates us and creates change and through his studies he concluded that emotion was the key. At the time though, there was hardly anything written about emotion. He delved into the subject with a passion, moved to Canada to study and research further, and eventually, together with one of his students, Sue Johnson, devised EFT, a process-oriented, systemic, experiential therapy that focuses on emotion (Greenberg, 2016).

Greenberg divided emotion into two classes: biologically-based emotions and socially-derived emotions. Biologically-based emotions are more automatic, and are akin to the categorical emotions described above. Socially-derived emotions are biological emotions that have been influenced and shaped by cognition, learning, and culture. For example, sadness and anger are biologically-based responses to loss or threat, while pride and envy are socially-derived emotions that manifest differently depending on cultural influences. Greenberg further divided emotions into four categories: adaptive primary emotions, secondary emotions, instrumental emotions, and maladaptive primary emotions (Greenberg & Johnson, 1988).

Adaptive primary emotions

Biologically-based emotions – these emotions are basic states which directly relate to a trigger. They are irreducible. It is what it seems to be, not a convoluted expression of another emotion. For instance, we feel angry when we are attacked and we feel sad when we suffer a loss. Primary emotions often occur outside of our awareness. Experiencing and being able to express these emotions enables constructive problem-solving and more beneficial interactions (Greenberg & Johnson, 1988; Greenberg & Paivio, 1997).

Secondary emotions

Secondary emotions are emotions that come second, after the primary emotion occurs. They are reactions and/or responses to primary emotions or to cognitive processes, such as expressing anger when really feeling vulnerable or feeling depressed when thinking about a recently experienced loss. Culturally based, they can often interfere with getting one's needs met. Greenberg divides secondary emotions into "bad feelings" and "complex feelings." Bad feelings encompass depression, anxiety, feeling hopeless or helpless, and also fear, rage, or shame. "Complex feelings" are complex secondary reactions to a primary feeling, such as feeling depressed about being depressed. For instance, crying is not always evidence of sadness. As a new therapist just starting out, I once watched a couple and a therapist from behind a one-way mirror. The wife cried every time she opened her mouth to speak, sputtering and wiping her tears with the back of her sleeve. Her husband sat next to her, silent and impenetrable. I felt sorry for the wife and was shocked when the therapist, a structural family therapist, asked the wife mid-cry "Why are you crying?" She continued to sob and the therapist asked once more, in a dispassionate voice "Why are you crying?" This time, she stopped crying abruptly and, following a sigh, was able to realize that she was really frustrated with her husband's lack of involvement. The tears were an expression of a complex secondary emotion, a reaction to her inner frustration.

An example of the difference between a secondary emotion and a primary emotion is the comparison between shame and guilt. Shame, as mentioned above, is a primary emotion, one that concerns one's feelings of worth. It can be understood as internalized disgust and contempt, and tends to inspire hiding so as not to have one's imperfections exposed. Guilt, on the other hand, is a more complex emotion with a cognitive component involving learned views about one's behaviors. It motivates different behavior to shame, such as penitence or a quest for forgiveness (Greenberg & Paivio, 1997).

Instrumental emotions

Culturally based, instrumental emotions serve a function in interpersonal interactions. These emotions are used to make gains or to affect the responses of others. For example, expressing anger may be done in order to defend against acknowledging one's part in a situation (Greenberg & Johnson, 1988). A couple arrived in therapy, with the wife continually lambasting the husband. The husband, a man quick to anger himself, fought back vociferously. He left the chicken out of the fridge for the night. He forgot to pick up his wife's dry cleaning on his way back from work. "Can't he do anything right?" his wife complained. Her husband spewed venom, challenging the details of everything she said and fights ensued. As therapy progressed, it became apparent that the wife felt lesser than her husband. By focusing on her anger at her husband, and creating conflict about minor difficulties, she was able to avoid the inner shame she often felt.

Maladaptive primary emotions

Created from an interaction of biological and cultural factors, certain feelings are negatively reinforced and ultimately become maladaptive responses with this reinforcement. They are primary emotions because they can't be reduced further. It is an initial response to a trigger. Phobias are examples as is the anger experienced when someone attempts to befriend an individual who instead perceives the friendly overtures as a boundary violation. Typically formed in an abusive or neglectful environment, these emotions can be adaptive at the time, such as experiencing fear of being vulnerable with a verbally abusive parent. It is adaptive to fear being too vulnerable and to protect oneself by presenting a strong front. However, it becomes maladaptive when fear is experienced whenever anyone wants to connect (Greenberg & Johnson, 1988; Greenberg & Paivio, 1997). To illustrate: Mike had been depressed for years before he began therapy. He stayed at home playing video games all day long, and felt unable to find a job. He had no actual friends, though occasionally he conversed online with some "buddies" he had never met in person. His parents supported him financially, even though he was 30 years old and had an undergraduate degree from a prestigious university. His mother did his laundry, prepared his meals, and listened to him for hours on end while he talked of his feelings of eternal loneliness. His sadness was maladaptive and rendered him dependent on his parents. Through therapy, he came to understand that he could deal more adaptively with his feelings of loneliness and sadness.

EFT

The primary goal of EFT is to utilize emotion to bring about change. Greenberg proposed that we organize ourselves around emotional schemes, or ways of arranging the emotion learned within the attachment relationship. The schemes develop within a system, and are therefore transactional and socially constructed, often from moment to moment. Thus, they are viewed as processes that are active, and not static. Though not necessarily in our conscious awareness, the schemes can be brought to light through accessing the experiences they induce (Elliot, Watson, Goldman, & Greenberg, 2004). In therapy, EFT views true change as emerging from uncovering the adaptive primary emotions underlying the secondary, instrumental, and primary maladaptive emotions (Greenberg & Johnson, 1988; Greenberg & Paivio, 1997). Once the adaptive primary emotions have been accessed, the therapist can promote optimal regulation of these emotions. However, though enabling adaptive emotion regulation is a key element in this process-oriented model, it is not the sole focus (Elliot et al., 2004). The prime focus of Greenberg's therapy is on emotion and the idea that our emotions, and in particular our adaptive primary emotions, are central to our experiences and to ultimately enabling change (Greenberg, 2016).

Emotionally-focused therapy

How does attachment theory fit in with EFT? This is exactly the question that inspired Les Greenberg's student Sue Johnson. While the psychotherapy Les Greenberg promoted became known as process-experiential (PE) psychotherapy, a specific form of emotion-focused therapy aimed at improving emotional intelligence (Elliot et al., 2004), Sue Johnson came along and further developed the emotionally-focused therapy (EFT) she and Greenberg initiated. She incorporated attachment theory, recognizing that emotions are a critical and fundamental part of the attachment bond. In fact, she promoted the idea that our emotions are shaped and regulated by our attachment bonds and our attachment bonds are organized by emotions. We cannot separate the two constructs as they are inextricably intertwined.

Sue Johnson's childhood played a part in how she came to her ideas. She grew up in Britain, spending a great deal of time in the pub her father ran. It was here that she witnessed the rise and fall of relationships, the fighting and the making up, the talking and the drinking that bonded people to each other. Human relationships fascinated her. But there was no relationship more compelling than that of her parent's marriage. She watched as they fought and disagreed, as their relationship collapsed along with themselves. Though they were very much in love, they were unable to maintain their union. Despite her intentions of never marrying, she fell in love and committed to her now husband. The ups and downs and contradictions and paradoxes of love continued to intrigue her. How could her parents psychologically obliterate each other when they loved each other? How could she fall in love and marry when this commitment made no logical sense to her? She began to study love and ended up getting her doctorate in Vancouver with Les Greenberg as her advisor. And thus began emotionally-focused therapy (Johnson, 2008).

After carefully working with and studying couples for hours, Johnson concluded that romantic love was about being able to rely on and have the support of a loved one. Troubles began when the security of this bond was in question. Intense emotions are part and parcel of this bond and cannot be viewed separately. Johnson set to work on developing a clinical approach to therapy that included working with emotions within an attachment bond. She espoused the view that we are evolutionarily programmed to connect and to be interdependent. This was an idea that was radically unpopular at a time when independence and individuating was valued. Despite this, Johnson pushed on, stating that our dependence on a partner was as critical to survival as was a child's dependence on a caregiver. Without having that safe haven and secure base, we feel a host of emotions, such as sadness, hurt, anger, and fear. Our very survival is threatened (Johnson, 2008).

EFT concentrates on the bond between romantic partners, focusing on engendering attunement and responsivity to one another to create the safety and security we crave and require. It is an experiential, process-oriented therapy where the therapist tracks moment-to-moment interactions. By doing so, the therapist aids with regulating emotion and facilitating connection (Johnson, 2019). Emotion is believed to be the key change agent. Primary-attachment-oriented emotions are accessed through the restructuring of negative interaction cycles based on secondary emotional responses. The underlying primary emotions are presumed to reflect unmet attachment needs. So for instance, anger and blame are seen as secondary maladaptive emotions resulting from the primary fear of being abandoned. Expressing a fear of being vulnerable evokes a different response from a partner than does expressing anger. With this, couples are able to heal and regain trust in one another (Johnson, 2009). And having a secure bond promotes adaptive affect regulation and optimal well-being.

Summary

Emotions are an essential component of an attachment bond. They serve a purpose by compelling an attachment figure to engage in care of another. Emotions are communication signals that must be sensitively interpreted in order to serve the purpose of facilitating connection. It seems there are certain universal emotions experienced by all. Ekman's (2003) list is most often used and it includes anger, fear, sadness, happiness, disgust, contempt, and surprise. Though individuals across the board may feel these emotions, they may be expressed differently, depending on culture and context. Process-oriented therapy and emotionally-focused therapy are therapies based on working with emotions and on the idea that emotions are key in creating change in the therapy room. In the next chapter, we will delve into how we regulate these emotions.

Chapter 9

Affect regulation

"If I allow myself to feel my rage, what will I do with it?" "I'm afraid if I allow myself to be sad, I will never stop being sad. How will I manage this?" These are questions I often hear from clients. We may know what we are feeling in the moment. For instance, our primary emotion of fear may activate when our partner threatens to leave us. We may feel panicky, scared, jittery, and downright traumatized. But then a new fear may take hold. What are we going to do with these overwhelming feelings? Here is where the concept of emotion regulation comes in. As it turns out, being able to regulate our emotions is key to our well-being. And according to attachment theory, our attachment bonds have everything to do with how we ultimately regulate ourselves.

The field of emotion regulation appeared in the mid-1990s and has continued to gather strength in the neurobiological and psychological world ever since (Gross, 2015). A man named Allan Schore became particularly prominent in the research arena. Schore, a psychologist sometimes known as the "American Bowlby" (Schore, 2014), is seen as the founder of an interdisciplinary psycho-neurobiological theory, one that integrates attachment theory and neuroscience. While emotionally-focused therapy incorporates emotion regulation, its primary focus has been on emotion. Schore has furthered the concept of emotion regulation. He proposed that our ability to regulate our affect and ourselves develops within our attachment relationships and that, ultimately, it is these early affective relationships that shape the maturation of our brains. Regulation serves a purpose by ensuring we maintain our attachment relationships, thereby promoting our survival. Schore emphasized the role of our right brain in the regulating of our affect and stated that, often, much that occurs of this regulation is nonconscious, happening outside of our awareness. Not only is the right brain integral to our ability to regulate ourselves, but the whole body is involved in this developmental, experience-dependent process. When we connect fully, our inter-subjective field between one another includes our minds and our bodies. Schore emphasized that the co-created affective communication that happens within an attachment bond is critical to the change process in therapy. Thus, not only is it emotion that is key to inducing change, but also the communication and regulation of both conscious and unconscious emotion. And, in particular, it is the communication and intersubjective understanding that happens within an attachment relationship that makes all the difference. We learn how to be a part of a meaningful relationship through this intersubjective process. So important is our ability to regulate affect that Schore recently suggested that attachment theory has expanded and has become more of a regulation theory. He has called it modern attachment theory (Schore & Schore, 2008; Schore, 2009; Schore, 2019). Overall, this theory addresses the effects of early development within the *attachment relationship* on the developing *right hemisphere* and on the ability to *regulate affect*, something that is believed to be at the core of optimal functioning.

Affect regulation

To understand modern attachment theory, we need a working definition of affect regulation. The following questions arise when we attempt to define regulation. When we have an emotion, how do we know what we are feeling? How do we decide when to put a brake on our impulses or when to indulge ourselves in acting according to our emotions? What meaning do we give to our various levels of arousal and how do we express this meaning? What part of this meaning we assign is innate and what part is learned? And how do our attachment relationships influence our ability to regulate what we feel? The answer to these questions involves us understanding what emotion or affect regulation is. According to James Gross (2014; 2015), a psychologist known for his research on emotion and emotion regulation, emotion regulation is one part of the broader construct of affect regulation. He defines *affect* as the overarching term for states that encompass quick distinctions between positives and negatives. Affective states include emotions, stress responses, and moods and Gross suggests that affect regulation is composed of three facets: (1) emotion regulation, (2) coping, and (3) mood regulation.

Emotion regulation

Once an emotion is triggered, changes occur both within and outside of our awareness. We experience physiological arousal and neurochemicals that flow. Our autonomic nervous system may activate, learned behaviors can be triggered, and memories may reignite. Over time, these patterns of arousal become what we know as feelings and may be symbolized in our awareness by emotions, such as sadness or anger. Two automatic responses occur each time we are aroused; the instigation of an action tendency and the regulation of this tendency. It is the expression of these tendencies that involves emotion regulation. Emotion regulation can be seen as "the ability to choose when to express one's emotions rather than to have one's emotions automatically control one's behavior" (Greenberg & Paivio, 1997, pp. 30–31). When we regulate our emotions, we choose which emotion we have, when we have these experiences, and how we express them. Often our choices are conscious (termed *explicit*), such as actively calming ourselves down when we are nervous. But sometimes the choices we make happen outside of our awareness and may be involuntary (termed *implicit*), such as suddenly retreating from an upsetting stimuli. Whether conscious or not, the choices we make become synthesized reactions, almost like a set of "instructions," that enable us to adaptively respond to our various levels of arousal.

Emotion regulation has the following three characteristics:

> *Goal achievement.* This is an integral part of effective emotion regulation, where the better we regulate ourselves, the more flexibly we respond and are able to meet our goals.
>
> *Strategy.* The second characteristic of emotion regulation is the strategy we use to meet our goals. Of note, emotion regulation strategies involves the suppression of emotions, maintaining, and the amplification of emotions as well. According to Tomkins (1962), most times, humans are motivated to maximize positive affect and to minimize negative affect. Yet, there are times we may need to do the opposite. Thus, effective emotion regulation involves effectively balancing positive and negative arousal, adjusting our strategies according to the needs of the moment. Thus, we use strategies to dampen or heighten our emotions to better achieve our end goals. We can influence the duration of the emotion (such as celebrating an achievement publicly to continue to feel good), the intensity of what we feel (for instance, pretending to others that all is okay when it isn't), or convert the feeling from one to another (such as finding humor in an embarrassing situation).
>
> *Outcome.* The third characteristic of emotion regulation involves the outcome, which is the end result of the strategies we use to regulate ourselves. If we regulate well, we won't become overwhelmed with depression or anxiety. We manage our frustration better and can constructively handle our anger. Too, we can experience joy and pleasure, even when going through a hard time (Cassidy, 1994; Greenberg & Paivio, 1997; Ekman, 2003; Gross, 2014; 2015; Gyurak & Etkin, 2014).

Coping

Coping is a set of conscious, goal-directed, volitional attempts to regulate the self and the environment when stress is encountered. It is specifically related to negotiating stress and tends to relate to situations that are longer lasting than those for which emotion regulation is implemented (Losoya, Eisenberg, & Fabes, 1998; Compas, Connor, Saltzman, Thomsen, & Wadsworth, 2001; Gross, 2014;). Eisenberg and colleagues (Losoya et al., 1998) consider coping to be strongly related to the self-regulation of emotion when faced with stress and suggest three types of emotion regulation relevant to the study of coping and the development of social-emotional health: efforts to regulate emotion, efforts to organize the situation, and attempts to manage behavior that occurs as a reaction to emotion. In general, coping is viewed as just one aspect of the process of self-regulation of emotion, behavior, cognition, physiology, and external surroundings (Compas et al., 2001).

There are several different ways to cope, or self-regulate: situation selection, situation modification, attentional deployment, cognitive change, and response modulation. Situation selection involves adjusting your actions to either avoid or welcome certain situations that you anticipate will impact your emotions. This could mean turning down an invitation to a party because you know you are likely to feel uncomfortable or calling a friend to talk in a time of need. Situation modification is when you directly change a situation in order to modify its emotional effect. For example, after hours of no structured activity at home, your three-year-old child begins to tantrum. You take your child to a playground for a change of scenery. Attentional deployment occurs when you redirect attentional focus in a specific situation to alter your emotions. One of the most oft used forms of this strategy is that of distraction, where, for example, you encourage shifting attention away from certain aspects of a situation or from the entire situation. When a child is receiving a shot at the doctor's office, the doctor begins to ask the child questions about his school year to distract her from the shot. Another example of attentional deployment occurs with the use of mindfulness, an increasingly popular practice that encourages acceptance of one's emotions by promoting awareness of the here and now. Cognitive change happens with the modification of one's evaluations of one's circumstances so as to revise its emotional impact. Cognitive change can be used with external situations, such as viewing a sports tryout as an opportunity to get to know a coach, or an internal situation, such as reframing frustration as part of the learning process and not as being unable to master a math problem. Finally, response modulation involves altering behavioral, experiential, or physiological aspects of an emotional response. Examples are doing meditation or breathing exercises to reduce anxiety feelings or ingesting alcohol to feel less sad (Gross, 2014).

Mood regulation

In comparison to emotions, moods usually last for longer periods of time and tend to be more diffuse, coloring one's perception of cognition more so than impacting action. Mood repair and mood regulation are more related to changing our emotional experiences than our emotion behavior. Affect regulation involves the regulation of moods as well (Gross, 2014).

Autoregulation and co-regulation/interactive regulation

When defining affect regulation, it is important to distinguish between autoregulation and co-regulation. Until recently, autoregulation, or the regulation of the self (as described above), has been more of a focus in the literature on emotion regulation. Recently, the notion of extrinsic emotion regulation has come to the forefront in the developmental literature and especially in the attachment world (Gross, 2015). Schore (2009) refers to *autoregulation*, which happens separately from others versus *interactive regulation*, or "the ability to flexibly regulate psychobiological states of emotions with other humans in interconnected contexts" (p. 117). With interactive regulation, our state of organization is affected by external processes, meaning we don't operate in a vacuum. Our emotions and the regulation of them influences and is influenced by the emotional states of others. Recall that emotions are a way of communicating our needs. For instance, a baby's cry to elicit comfort from a caregiver may induce anxiety in that caregiver until she is able to comfort her baby. Her anxiety will be regulated by her caring for her child and her child's distress will be regulated by the comfort she provides. Not only do caregivers and babies interactively regulate, but so do romantic partners. And it seems that up to 98% of our emotion regulation as adults may in fact occur within social contexts, and not on our own (Levenson, Haase, Bloch, Holley, & Seider, 2014). In fact, the neuroscientist James Coan suggests that interactive regulation is the more efficient strategy for affect regulation and states that the brain seems to bank on us having others to support us (Coan, 2016). Once again, it seems we are wired to connect. Thus, as therapists, we are constantly interactively regulating with our clients. We aim to flexibly shift between autoregulation and interactive regulation, alternating between the two when necessary.

The neurobiology of affect regulation

The prefrontal cortices, and more specifically the dorsolateral and ventrolateral prefrontal cortices, are involved in the conscious regulation of emotion, while the medial prefrontal regions (mPFC), including the ventral portions of the anterior cingulate cortex and ventromedial prefrontal cortex, are associated with emotion regulation that occurs outside of our awareness (Gyurak & Etkin, 2014). Not only is the prefrontal cortex involved in emotion regulation, but so too is the amygdala, the area of the brain that perceives emotion. Evidence points to the fact that as we age, our prefrontal brain regions develop and our regulatory abilities, including attentional modulation, get incrementally better (Johnstone & Walter, 2014). Our amygdala-mPFC connectivity matures as we age. However, the way the amygdala interacts with the mPFC shifts in nature. Children show a positive correlation between the two, where the amygdala and the mPFC are activated similarly. But adolescents and adults have an inverse relationship where, as the activity in the mPFC increases, the activity in the amygdala decreases (Tottenham, 2014). In fact, many studies have shown that during emotion regulation, and in particular during the down-regulation of emotion, activity in certain areas of the prefrontal cortex increases while the amygdala's overall level of activity decreases (Proudfit, Dunning, Foti, & Weingberg, 2014). Thus, negative connectivity is typically associated with decreased anxiety. Counterintuitively, in children with a history of caregiver deprivation there is evidence of increased amygdala-mPFC connectivity, similar to what is seen in adults. However, while in adults this connectivity leads to less anxiety, in children with caregiver deprivation, this increased connectivity seems to lead to higher levels of anxiety. Interestingly though, while overall, there is a higher level of anxiety, these children exhibit lower levels of separation anxiety in comparison to caregiver-deprived children with positive connectivity. It may be that this is a protective adaptation that occurs for caregiver-deprived children and may help them navigate their already over-reactive amygdalae (Tottenham, 2014).

Affect regulation and attachment

According to modern attachment theory, the attachment bond has everything to do with overall affect regulation, particularly the regulation of distress. In fact, attachment theory views self-regulatory abilities as one of the "inner resources" necessary to coping with stress and adversity (Mikulincer & Florian, 1998). To reiterate what has been previously stated, the theory proposes three systems: the exploration system, the fear system, and the attachment system. These three interlocking attachment systems can be conceptualized as arousal regulating mechanisms. When stress occurs, first the fear system and then the attachment system are activated, and the child experiences increased levels of both physical and emotional arousal. When the arousal feels unmanageable, a child will seek a safe haven in order to down-regulate the increased sense of arousal. A sensitive caregiver, or one who provides this safe haven, is seen to enable such down-regulation to occur (Ainsworth et al., 1978) by providing developmentally appropriate interventions to the child in a way that reinstates the child's homeostatic baseline. In this way the attachment dyad can moderate perceived stress, where the child uses a "safe haven" to achieve homeostasis and from there, a "secure base" to launch from and continue with exploration of the environment. Should a child's needs be met often enough, he or she will gain experience in being regulated as well as in learning to regulate. However, should a child's needs for security and reconnection remain unmet, a child will organize his or her behavior in a way that makes the situation tolerable. The child's organization may work in the moment, but can have deleterious effects later on in development.

Attachment classifications can be seen as patterns of affective, physiological, and behavioral regulation of emotions (Enlow, Egeland, Carlson, Blood, & Wright, 2014). The three characteristics of emotion regulation, that of having a goal, a strategy, and an outcome, can be used as a framework in understanding the attachment strategies involved in the regulation of emotion. The over-arching goal of the attachment bond is for a child to maintain proximity to an attachment figure so that the attachment figure will provide the best care possible. The child develops a strategy to make certain proximity is maintained.

The outcome is that the bond continues, no matter the quality of that bond. Recall, Cassidy (1994) proposed that emotion regulation is one mechanism a child uses to maintain a relationship with an attachment figure. She spoke of "strategies," or adaptive ways in which a child deals with the varying levels of availability of a caregiver. A child therefore has two nonconscious choices in his relationship with his caregiver. The first choice is to stay safe by meeting his parent's expectations. The second choice is to chance being rejected or abandoned if he does not meet his caregiver's expectations. The most adaptive way to survive, of course, is to make sure to meet a caregiver's expectations (Ogden & Fisher, 2015). A securely attached child has a history of receiving responsive caregiving and has internalized a level of confidence in the ability of his or her caregiver to reintroduce calm should he or she become overly aroused (Gilliom, Shaw, Beck, Schonberg, & Lukon, 2002). He learns that he can use *primary attachment strategies* to stay engaged with a sensitive caregiver and can easily meet this caregiver's expectations. Insecurely attached children (avoidant or ambivalent), on the other hand, are far from certain that they can enlist the help of others when feeling aroused or threatened in any way. With a history of unavailable or inconsistent caregiving, they tailor their behavior accordingly and employ *secondary attachment strategies* to negotiate the distress they feel. The main purpose of these strategies is to increase the likelihood of maintaining a relationship with the caregiver. They do not want to demand too much from a caregiver as they are afraid that this will cause them to be rejected. They meet their caregivers' expectations by avoiding behavior that overwhelms their caregivers (Cassidy, 1994). They will do what it takes to stay close, even if they employ less than optimal means to do so. Importantly, though less than optimal, secondary attachment strategies are indeed adaptive for the time. As mentioned in Chapter 2, secondary attachment strategies include hyperactivation and deactivation of the attachment system in the service of defending against an unavailable secure base (Mikulincer & Shaver, 2007).

The following sections detail the different types of affect regulatory strategies with respect to attachment.

Primary attachment strategies

Secure individuals have a flexible style of affect regulation. They are able to express a range of different emotions and can tailor their responses to suit their situational needs. They maintain emotional balance, are triggered less easily, and tend to manage ambiguity well, staying away from most cognitive distortions. They exhibit an ability to tolerate "negative" emotions and they deal effectively with stress and frustration. In other words, distress does not completely dysregulate them. They usually seek support in times of need, repair relationships should there be a rupture, and in general, practice open communication as a way to regulate themselves. Those who use primary attachment strategies more often than not are securely attached (Mikulincer & Shaver, 2007; Johnson, 2019).

Therapy with clients using primary attachment strategies

In the therapy room, these are the clients who are emotive. They express their positive and negative feelings. They make eye contact. They engage. They tolerate a therapist's interventions and if they have concerns, they voice them. Their affect regulatory strategies are flexible and adaptive. While they may present with life issues, they are typically high-functioning overall.

Example

Melissa was in therapy to address her parenting issues. Her daughter Annie was extremely reactive and Melissa found she reacted alongside Annie, often unable to maintain her objectivity. One day Melissa came to her session seeming particularly agitated. Annie had been excluded from a classmate's get-together. Melissa was triggered, worrying that Annie would go over the deep-end, that Annie had no friends, that Annie would never have friends. The more we talked it through though, the less agitated Melissa seemed. Eventually, she came to realize that Annie was not upset about this exclusion. In fact, she had come home from school saying that she hadn't been included because her friend assumed she didn't enjoy the activity they were doing. It wasn't personal. Through discussion, Melissa recognized that her agitation was due to her own feelings and not Annie's. She herself had often been excluded during her school years. The session turned into a productive exploration of Melissa's past.

Hyperactivating strategies

Hyperactivating strategies consist of heightening emotion and increasing efforts to elicit attention (Cassidy, 1994). The primary purpose of hyperactivating strategies is to solicit support and care from an unreliable or inconsistently available caregiver. An anxiously attached child walks a line between making a bid for attention, but a bid that won't overwhelm his caregiver. The child cannot risk demanding care from a fragile, inadequate caregiver because he knows that his caregiver can't handle anyone needing anything from her and will choose to reject him rather than feel she is inadequate in meeting his needs. However, by heightening demanding emotions, the child gets negative attention, a safe way to maintain proximity to an inconsistently available caregiver. Negative attention is better than no attention at all. Jealousy and anger are safe emotions to express, as are emotions that highlight a child's neediness, such as fear, anxiety, sadness, or shame. Problems are exaggerated and incompetence is highlighted, all to show the caregiver she is needed. However, the bids for attention are rarely direct, as the child feels uncertain that his caregiver will actually be supportive. Paradoxically, heightening negative feelings becomes a way of managing negative feelings. It feels more secure. Importantly, these hyperactivating strategies may be adaptive in childhood, but can quickly become maladaptive in later years. Thus, hyperactivating strategies, should they occur often enough, can become internalized as general ways of negotiating the regulation of affect and can lead to what is termed preoccupied states of mind with respect to attachment or to anxious attachment patterns (Mikulincer & Shaver, 2007; Shaver & Mikulincer, 2014).

Therapy with hyperactivating clients

In therapy, these individuals may sit close to the therapist. Because they heighten their attachment needs, they often tend to seem clingy. At any sign of possible rejection by the therapist, they may become agitated, both physically and affect-wise. In fact, they may become aroused with any minor stimulus. Their expressions are sometimes exaggerated and they show a great deal of emotion much of the time. They are using affect regulatory strategies that were adaptive in the past, in that they served to keep a caregiver engaged. However, they have become maladaptive at present. These individuals may feel lonely despite their intense need and push for interaction. They often unwittingly push others away.

Example

After two years of working together in therapy, Chloe seemed to be doing well. The self-doubt she had expressed at the beginning of therapy had dissipated. She was thriving at work. Her irritable bowel syndrome was under control. She felt secure in her relationship with her boyfriend, or so she said. I initiated a discussion of how she would know when she was able to terminate therapy, saying that though we wouldn't end now, we could begin thinking about it. Chloe arrived at the next session in tears. She sobbed as she told me that she was disappointed in her boyfriend, that he wasn't meeting her emotional needs, and that despite his declarations of love for her, she was thinking of ending the relationship. I was taken aback. Chloe had been doing so well. And then it slowly dawned on me what may be happening. Chloe grew up with a depressed, single mother who hid out at work and was hardly home. When she was home, she lay in front of the television, while Chloe took care of the house. The only times that Chloe was able to get her mother's attention was when her friends let her down. Suddenly, Chloe's mother then came to the rescue, believing that she and Chloe were together against the rest of the world. Chloe learned that appearing to be competent, taking care of the house and not bothering her mother, allowed her to be close to her mother. She also unconsciously learned that she would get the attention she craved from her mother if she exaggerated her woes with her friends. Thus, I had unwittingly made Chloe feel rejected for being too competent, just as her mother had made her feel. She had responded by heightening her negative feelings about her boyfriend, telling me without words that she needed me. I talked in a soothing voice, telling Chloe that my suggesting she was ready to end therapy must have felt overwhelming. She was so used to going through life alone, without getting the support she really needed, and my suggestion just made her feel all the more lonely, all the more misunderstood. I validated her feelings about ending therapy and talked of how she found it easier to find fault with her boyfriend rather than directly expressing what she felt about me. I also pointed out how she was showing me that she was not ready to end therapy and I reinforced that I was always there for her and questioned her feelings about her boyfriend, who up until this point, had really met her needs. She acknowledged that he usually did and somehow only in the past week, had seemed inaccessible to her. I gently suggested that she may have exaggerated her disappointment in him to get my attention. When she agreed, I apologized for my suggesting she think of terminating therapy and said that I trusted that she would tell me when she was ready to end. The ball was in her court. She stopped crying and visibly relaxed.

Deactivating strategies

The main goal of deactivating strategies is to shut down the attachment system so as to avoid rejection or punishment by an attachment figure (Mikulincer, Shaver & Berant, 2013). It is too risky to express any attachment needs as doing so may actually push this caregiver away. It is much safer to minimize emotion and to dampen attachment needs. Paradoxically, this is more likely to ensure a caregiver's continual engagement, and therefore it gives the child a better chance for survival. A child quickly learns that asking a rejecting caregiver for attention may cause him further alienation and that an adaptive strategy to maintain proximity is to shut down emotion. This is true for all emotions. Anger can be engaging, so it is in the child's best interest to quell his anger. Even joy can become problematic because it may show some need to connect with the caregiver. An avoidant child learns to stifle joy too. And fear is the most problematic, indicating the child needs help from the caregiver. Again, the child adjusts any expression of need, learning to exhibit little emotion (Cassidy, 1994). Should this suppression of emotion or dissociation from feeling occur often enough, it can become an overall strategy to deal with all emotion. Bowlby (1980) referred to this strategy of avoiding the experience and expression of emotions as "defensive exclusion." Because of this mechanism, the integration of emotional experiences into memory or the processing of these experiences may be stunted. In this way, deactivating strategies may become internalized as general ways of regulating affect and can lead to dismissing states of mind with respect to attachment or to avoidant attachment patterns (Mikulincer & Shaver, 2007; Shaver & Mikulincer, 2014).

Therapy with deactivating clients

These individuals may sit as far from the therapist as they can during sessions. Withdrawal is a tried and true tactic, often preferred over initiating interaction with others. Shutting down emotional expression is another way of implementing a deactivating strategy. Clients with such strategies may appear stone-faced, blank, or unemotional. They may often avoid eye contact, finding it too overwhelming or dysregulating. It is important to remember that these are affect regulating strategies, and ones that have served these individuals well. It is only now, that they are seeking help, that the strategies may have become maladaptive. These individuals may be lonely and feel alienated and disconnected. They may not have the tools to connect and may actually find it overwhelming to do so. Their ability to regulate their affect is dependent upon them shutting it down. Any emotion may feel dysregulating.

Example

During one session in therapy, I had just given Ryan a compliment. I had praised him for a recent accomplishment, saying how impressive it was, and he sat there looking at me without any discernible expression. I quickly realized I had dysregulated him. After three years of working together, Ryan rarely smiled. In fact, he rarely expressed any emotion. I waited a few minutes, knowing that I couldn't wait too long. It would be too overwhelming for him. Then I asked him what it was like for me to compliment him. "I don't know," he replied, pulling further back into the couch across from me. If he could have gone through the couch or even the wall behind the couch, he would have. "I almost feel embarrassed," he said. Ryan had grown up with an extremely rejecting single mother. He had been abandoned by his father at an early age, so it had just been him and his rejecting mother. He had learned to shut down any emotion as his mother seemed unable to handle anything coming from him. The two had coexisted, with Ryan silently getting through his schooling days, just waiting to leave for college. He had struggled with loneliness his whole life and now was no different. I pressed on gently, saying how he could be proud of himself. I wouldn't have dared say I was proud of him. I knew that would be difficult for him. It would have felt like too much of a connection, too much of what he actually craved from me, but felt terrified to receive. Connection meant abandonment in Ryan's world. He looked up at me, maintained eye contact for just a bit, smiled weakly, and nodded. I knew he had let himself feel just a little bit of pride. And he had very slightly allowed me to approach him.

Disorganized/unresolved strategies

In infancy, while avoidant and anxious infants have organized, albeit maladaptive strategies for negotiating arousing situations, disorganized infants do not possess a coherent behavior pattern to deal with dysregulation. In fact, Main (1995) has argued that, in the case of disorganized attachment, it may be the caregiver herself who is causing dysregulation in the infant. Thus, the infant experiences an irremediable bind when seeking proximity with a caregiver who is causing distress. The result can be a lack of coherent strategy in negotiating ensuing arousal. Adults who are unresolved with respect to attachment also display a lack a coherent strategies.

Therapy with disorganized/unresolved clients

These individuals display a lack of a coherent strategy in regulating their affect. They may sit very close to you in session and then pull all the way back. They may vacillate between extreme emotions, such as anger or anxiety or sadness, and then appear stone-faced. These are the clients that may display dissociative tendencies, zoning out mid-sentence or becoming incoherent.

Example

Ruth came to therapy to address her feelings of isolation. At 40 years old, she lived alone and couldn't seem to maintain any relationships in her life. At first therapy was smooth sailing. She talked and I listened. Trouble began during the third session, when I dared to suggest she had played a part in alienating her most recent romantic partner. She hovered over me, yelling that she was so angry, that she had wasted her time with me, that I was unprofessional, undereducated, and that she had been foolish to think I could help her. She suddenly sat down and her body became limp. She broke eye contact with me and stared into the distance blankly. She seemed to be unable to hear me asking her what was happening. A few seconds later, she blinked, seemed to come to, took her bag, and got up to leave. I gently asked her to stay. I said that I recognized that she felt misunderstood, that it must have felt awful for me, her therapist who she had trusted, to have seemed so far from understanding her. I spoke slowly, saying that I now saw how lonely I had made her feel, even more lonely than she usually feels and that it must have been really scary for her. As I talked, Ruth seemed to calm down. I kept my voice soft and even, breathing regularly. I asked Ruth to put her hand on her heart, a way to self-soothe and I continued to speak, saying that I hoped that Ruth would be able to continue to work with me, that I really cared, and wanted to better understand her deep feelings of betrayal that she was experiencing because of her partner's actions. We sat silently for a few minutes while Ruth breathed deeply. She arrived at her next session seemingly more engaged than before.

The development of affect regulation

The definition of affect regulation is only part of modern attachment theory's story. The rest has to do with the amazing advances that have occurred in the field of neuroscience together with the renewed interest in emotion. There now is a great deal of evidence to show that while for most people, our conscious, verbal processing occurs in the left hemisphere, it is the right hemisphere that features more prominently when it comes to nonverbal and emotional processing. And this unconscious and nonverbal information processing happens across the life cycle, but particularly so before we learn to speak, during our early years. And because of this, our early attachment relationships are critical to our emotional development. These experiences are internalized as our internal working models of our attachment relationships. It is these models, or lenses, that guide us in regulating our affect across our lifespan. Ultimately, our attachment relationships, if secure, shepherd us through life. They facilitate affect regulation and enable optimal functioning.

Right hemisphere

According to modern attachment theory, the right hemisphere is critical to our regulating our affect. It is therefore essential that we have a deep understanding of the workings of the right hemisphere that underlie our non-verbal, subconscious communications. Indeed, scientists have made great inroads in better understanding the workings of this hemisphere which, up until recently, has been overshadowed by the left hemisphere. To understand the right hemisphere's role in affect regulation, we need a general overview of the hemispheres of the brain. The human brain has two hemispheres: the right hemisphere and the left hemisphere (see Figure 9.1). The hemispheres are connected by neural fibers that make up what is called the corpus callosum.

   The right hemisphere tends to grow quickly during the first two to three years after birth, the same time as we are forming our first attachment relationships. Generally, it is responsible for emotional perception, emotion

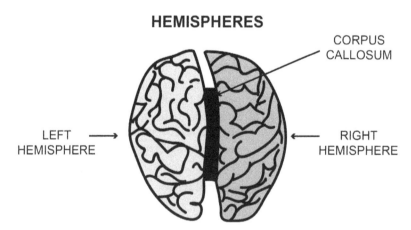

Figure 9.1 Hemispheres, drawn by Toni Mandelbaum (2020), digitized by Chloe Amen
© Toni Mandelbaum

regulation, and for social cognition. It is holistic in its approach to negotiating input, tending to the big picture. No rules or regulations apply. It is intuitive and creative, spontaneous and uninhibited. It also is very present-time oriented.

The right hemisphere is associated with unconscious, implicit processes. It is here that implicit memory, cognition, and communications of emotion occur. Too, this is where nonverbal communication, such as tone of voice or prosody, facial expressions and bodily gestures, originate. Not only does the right hemisphere process nonverbal, emotion signals, but it processes them very quickly, in some cases in less than 50 milliseconds. As stated in Chapter 7, Porges (2017), the creator of the Polyvagal Theory, terms this rapid, nonconscious processing "neuroception," which differs from the conscious process of perception. The right hemisphere is involved with the regulation of autonomic states, assessing the environment for danger and responding quickly to negative emotion, often before it enters conscious awareness. It is linked with states of panic and physiological symptoms such as pounding heart, sweating, shortness of breath, feeling dizzy, and choking feelings. Of note to attachment theorists, it is thought that the right hemisphere mediates the accessing of autobiographical memory and the maintaining of the coherence evaluated in the Adult Attachment Interview (see Chapter 3). And it is where Schore (Schore & Schore, 2008) suggests clinicians focus in their work towards enabling change in their clients.

Jill Bolte Taylor

On December 10, 1996 Jill Bolte Taylor, a neuroscientist, had an experience that was to show just how much the right hemisphere is involved with emotion, with connection, and with feeling whole. That morning, Bolte Taylor, at the age of 37, awoke to find she was having a massive stroke in the left side of her brain. In her book *My Stroke of Insight*, she describes watching herself have the stroke and within four hours, losing the ability to speak, read, write, walk, and remember. Because of her training, she writes with amazing insight and because of her incredible tenacity, she writes with great humanity about her journey and her ultimate full recovery after eight long years. Bolte Taylor (2006) describes how her right hemisphere showed her that her body and emotions were inextricably linked, saying

> One of the greatest lessons I learned was how to feel the physical component of emotion. Joy was a feeling in my body. Peace was a feeling in my body. I thought it was interesting that I could feel when a new emotion was triggered. I could feel new emotions flood through me and then release me.
>
> (p. 120)

And she details how, without her left hemisphere's functioning, she suddenly felt connected, or attached, to others in a profound way. It was as if she were having a spiritual awakening.

> When my left language centers were silenced and my left orientation association area was interrupted from its normal sensory input, my consciousness shifted away from feeling like a solid, to a perception of myself as a fluid - at *one* with the universe.
>
> (p. 136)

It seems that our right hemispheres are the seats of connection, of joining with others, of attaching. It is with right-brain to right-brain communication that intersubjectivity occurs.

Left hemisphere

While it is becoming increasingly apparent that the right hemisphere is intimately involved in our attachment relationships, the left hemisphere is integral as well. The left hemisphere tends to develop later than the right hemisphere and mediates explicit, conscious processes, such as language. It is known to process information more slowly than the right hemisphere. For instance, it can take up to 300 milliseconds to consciously process a facial image or language, as opposed to the 50 milliseconds it takes the right hemisphere to process nonverbal, emotional cues. The left hemisphere is involved with "the three L's - linear, logical, linguistic!" (Siegel, 2003, p. 15), meaning linear processing, including causal reasoning, language use, and logical thinking. It is very detail-focused. It examines, explores, and judges. It is the left hemisphere that aids us in analyzing situations and in gaining conscious insight into our emotions. It helps us to label what we are feeling. In most adults, the left hemisphere is involved with language functioning, conscious coping, and problem solving. It tends to be biased toward positive emotion, with one exception; anger. The left hemisphere seems to be very connected to anger. In terms of emotional expression, the left hemisphere is involved with worry, verbal rumination, and cognitive anxiety, as well as muscle tension. Stress can in fact deactivate the functioning of the left hemisphere. It is only with the integration of the two hemispheres, that we are able to optimally function and maintain our attachment relationships (Siegel, 2003; Taylor, 2006; Schore & Schore, 2008; McGilchrist, 2009; Schore, 2009; Hill, 2015; Baylin & Hughes, 2016; Cozolino, 2016).

How both hemispheres relate to attachment

As noted before, there has been a shift in focus in our understanding of what creates therapeutic change. Up until the decade of the brain, therapists favored approaches that utilized the skills of the left hemisphere, such as insight-oriented, talk therapy, and cognitive therapy. In his landmark book *The Master and His Emissary*, Iain McGilchrist (2009), a psychiatrist and writer, proposes that up until recently, society as a whole emphasized left hemisphere values. In a search for certainty in a fragmented world, people clung to rational, detailed reasoning and with this, tended to discount unconscious, intuitive, holistic ways of being. McGilchrist (2009) writes that this focus has made us lose "access to the world beyond words, the world 'beyond' our selves" (p. 399), and argues for the inclusion of the experiential right hemisphere into our beings. With the increased understanding of the role the functions of the right hemisphere play in our emotional development, attachment theorists and therapists are in line with McGilchrist's thinking. They have become more inclusive in their approaches, understanding that emotion and nonverbal communication factor into therapeutic change as well. Schore (2009) goes as far as proposing that our internal working models are stored mostly in the right brain. Here too is where our implicit memory is housed.

We now understand a secure attachment pattern as being a result of the integration of right and left hemispheric functioning. As an example, if we think back to the Adult Attachment Interview, to produce a coherent narrative, it is the right hemisphere that must access autobiographical material and the left hemisphere must process this material and make sense of it. It is the right hemisphere that is dominant in the first few years of life while primary attachment bonds are forming. This implies that subconscious emotions and attachment schemas are developing before we may have the ability to cognitively understand what we are feeling. It is preverbal. It is only with the development of the left hemisphere that an individual gains the ability to consciously process and understand what was up until this time nonverbal and nonconscious. The development of the self relies on the integration between the two hemispheres. This is critical to forming a secure attachment.

The development of affect regulation and the attachment relationship

At the heart of it, modern attachment theory is a developmental theory of regulation. This begs the question of exactly how do our regulatory abilities develop? And furthermore, how is the attachment relationship involved in this development? Throughout our life cycle, our emotions organize us. They can motivate us and, if all goes well, enable adaptive functioning. But they only do so, if we can regulate them adaptively. As we saw in Chapter 5, it has become clear to attachment theorists that from the very beginning, infants not only experience emotions, but they very rudimentarily regulate them. As we grow and develop, both internal factors, such as our temperaments and our cognitive development, and external factors, such as our attachment relationships, enable us to achieve greater control over our affect regulatory abilities. At first, we are dependent on our caregivers to co-regulate. As our self-capacities, language, cognition, physiology, and neurophysiology develop, we become increasingly capable of soliciting help to achieve regulation or actually regulating ourselves. For instance, an infant cries for help. A toddler, who is now ambulatory, may walk towards his caregiver for a hug. He can tolerate mild levels of frustration and may begin to experience more mature emotions, such as shame, guilt, and pride. A preschooler has increasing verbal skills and can talk about his feelings. He may even be able to describe what he needs. An elementary-school-goer can implement one of three different self-regulatory strategies: entraining the support of others, such as a caregiver or a peer, communicating his needs and feelings, or the beginnings of self-regulation techniques, such as distracting himself. An adolescent is capable of understanding his inner workings and has the beginnings of the capacities for the self-reflection necessary to self-regulation. And, in the best case scenario, an adult is able to understand and integrate his complex needs and emotions and can use this understanding to communicate and express himself, to solicit help if required, and ultimately, to regulate himself (Greenberg & Paivio, 1997; Sroufe, 2000).

Though developmentally we may all have the capacity for self-regulation, we may not always be able to adaptively self-regulate. So much depends on our experiences along the way. And in particular, so much depends on our attachment relationships. Sensitive caregivers contain us, accurately interpret our cues (both verbal and nonverbal), and respond appropriately. What is considered appropriate and adaptive varies according to our stage of development and our needs at the time. Just as children's needs change as they grow, so do the requirements of caregivers. An effective caregiver must maintain a manageable level of arousal for her child across his stages of development. This turns out to be crucial to the maturation of the brain's inhibitory and excitatory systems. Thus, while at first, an infant is able to tolerate low levels of arousal, under the caregiver's careful guidance, he begins to tolerate increasingly longer and more intense periods of emotional arousal. A sensitive caregiver provides just the right amount of stimulation, making sure that stressors are not overwhelming and dysregulating. Think back to the cycles of coordinated/miscoordinated/repair states mentioned in Chapter 5. While coordinated states lead to affective synchrony and resonance, an extremely pleasurable, if aroused state, miscoordination can lead to negative affective states. Though miscoordination between caregiver and child is critical for a child's learning, so too is timely repair, before the level of arousal becomes overwhelming. A little bit of being overwhelmed is the way in which learning takes place. But it needs to be carefully balanced. It must be tolerable for the child. A caregiver evaluates her child's level of arousal, regulates this arousal, and then communicates the regulated emotions back to the child. To do this effectively, a caregiver must negotiate both high and low levels of stimulation. Of note, both members of the dyad are constantly regulating both between and within him or herself (Sroufe, 1996; 2000; Schore, 2009).

An infant can tolerate only small doses of arousal and needs to return to equilibrium soon thereafter. A toddler is eager for more opportunities for mastery, but needs stringent and manageable guidelines so as not to be overwhelmed. A sensitive caregiver provides just this; optimal levels of challenge that a toddler can ultimately master. The caregiver becomes a socialization agent, where she is actively working to inhibit the toddler in order to learn social rules. To do so, she must provide opportunities that allow a child to master situations, and maintain the child's increasingly higher levels of frustration across the life cycle at tolerable levels. A toddler forays out into the world, eager to explore and learn. Oftentimes, he oversteps the boundaries, simply unaware of what is right or wrong. He returns to the caregiver expecting praise, for say drawing on the wall, an exciting activity he has just discovered. Instead, he is met with reproach. His mother is angry. This is a misattunement. The toddler experiences a new emotion; that of shame. He is catapulted into a low arousal state that he is not yet equipped to manage on his own. A sensitive caregiver will gently scold the toddler, teach him what is appropriate (i.e., "we draw on paper and not on walls"), all the while providing love and support. This caregiver will only moderately shame her toddler. The toddler can tolerate the reprimand because he knows that fundamentally, his mother still loves him. It is okay to make mistakes. Misattunement does not mean abandonment. If handled well, this is what gets internalized.

Secure and insecure attachment

Secure attachment

In a secure attachment relationship, distress is resolved more often than not. A child learns from repeated positive experiences that distress is manageable, that he can negotiate even the strongest of emotion, and that he can rely on his caregiver to support him when needed. He comes to see that he is able to flexibly respond to situations and that he can regulate his emotions. He also comes to learn that he can both interactively regulate and ultimately self-regulate as well. In fact, modern attachment theory defines optimal functioning as being able to flexibly alternate between interconnection and autonomous states according to environmental needs. Stable personality organization, our ultimate goal, can be seen as "the ability to maintain flexibly organized behavior in the face of high levels of arousal or tension" (Sroufe, 1996, p. 159). This way of regulating is encoded in an internal working model that operates at the implicit nonconscious level (Schore, 2019; Sroufe, 1996; 2000).

Insecure attachment

What happens when a caregiver is not able to sensitively parent? Or even worse, when a caregiver is the cause of a child's overarousal? What is the effect of experiencing long periods of dysregulation? By now we know that insecure attachments result from frequent bouts of overarousal with little to no interactive repair. Negative affective states overwhelm the child's system too often and the child is unable to adaptively negotiate the ensuing levels of arousal (Schore, 2019). This can occur in several different ways. A caregiver can neglect her child, leaving her child to fend for himself. Alternately, a caregiver can be too intrusive and interfere in a child's attempts at self-regulation. Either way, a child will become dysregulated. Should this occur often enough, his regulatory abilities may become rigid and inflexible and this way of regulating affect becomes encoded as an internal working model. For instance, a toddler is shamed often by his caregiver without repair. His caregiver is punitive and verbally abusive. Minor transgressions take on drastic proportions. The toddler isn't sure what will set his caregiver off and feels that he can do no right. He may come to feel "bad" and unlovable. Shame overwhelms and dysregulates him much of the time. He is easily triggered and finds it difficult to adaptively self-regulate. His caregiver has not provided adequate scaffolding and his ability to both co-regulate and autoregulate is compromised. He may stifle, avoid, or suppress any emotion in order to negotiate his dysregulation. Or he may exaggerate his feelings in the hopes of having his caregiver, just this once, notice him and give him the love he craves.

Window of tolerance

Exactly what does "manageable levels of arousal" mean? When we regulate our emotions, we regulate both what we experience internally and what we express externally. We successfully process the input we perceive and receive. The resulting strength with which we feel the emotion often defines its adaptiveness. Again, emotion can organize, galvanize, and propel us to meet our goals. However, too much emotion can disorganize us and can leave us in disarray. Achieving manageable levels of arousal implies having the ability to reach a balance by regulating our emotional experiences and their expression. Typically, the most adaptive balance seems to be mild to moderate levels of emotion. There are a number of factors that influence our windows of tolerance. Physiological circumstances, such as hunger or fatigue, can affect our degree of tolerance. Our temperaments can as well. And our attachment relationships may shape our windows of tolerance. We learn to attain certain levels of tolerance by implementing the previously described unconscious and conscious processes of affect regulation (Greenberg & Paivio, 1997; Siegel, 1999).

Pat Ogden (2009) and Dan Siegel (1999) have both described the concept of the "window of tolerance" (see Figure 9.2). This window designates the most adaptive levels of arousal. It represents the boundaries of what we can tolerate. At optimal levels of tolerance, we maintain our conscious, verbal, and explicit cognition. We can control our motor activities and our behaviors. We become angry, but not violent. We may feel sad, but are not incapacitated by depression. It is important to note that experiencing the ups and downs of emotion is to be expected. Throughout the day, we are constantly balancing and re-balancing our levels of arousal. High levels come from being excited and low levels occur when we're relaxed. These high and low states are enjoyable when we feel safe. It only becomes problematic when we feel threatened, when our

WINDOW OF TOLERANCE

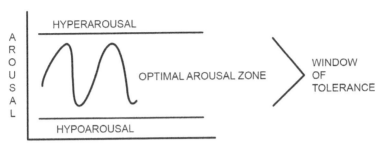

Figure 9.2 Window of tolerance, adapted from Ogden (2015), drawn by Toni Mandelbaum (2020), digitized by Chloe Amen © Toni Mandelbaum

systems are overwhelmed. It is then that we leave our windows of tolerance and become unable to regulate ourselves. Our survival mechanisms activate and we may become hyperaroused or hypoaroused. Our higher cognitive functions may shut down and we may be unable to think rationally. We may be emotionally hijacked (Goleman, 1995). It becomes difficult to be flexibly responsive, to integrate incoming signals, and to process our experiences. We may enter into tumultuous or intransigent states. We become highly dysregulated (Siegel, 1999; Ogden & Fisher, 2015).

Two different processes occur depending on whether we are hyperaroused or hypoaroused. When we are hyperaroused, our sympathetic nervous systems kick into gear. Our heart rate accelerates and we have high energy levels. Our emotions may go from feeling angry to feeling full of rage, from panic to absolute terror, or from excitement to extreme joy. We may feel anxious, irritated, obsessive, uneasy, or distressed. We may want to run, to leave, or to fight. In contrast, when we are hypoaroused, our parasympathetic systems activate. We go into energy-conservation modes. Our energy levels are low. We may disengage or actually dissociate. Our heart rates decelerate and we may feel weak, powerless, passive, apathetic, numb, or unable to move. We may feel extreme shame, disgust, hopelessness, or overwhelming feelings of abandonment (Schore, 2009; Ogden & Fisher, 2015). Recovery involves dampening the strength or intensity of the arousal. It may require the activation of more complex cognition and thought. It may be a physiological process, such as reinstating regulated breathing. Overall, it means regulating and organizing the dysregulated affect (Siegel, 1999).

Attachment and window of tolerance

Porges' (2017) model, described in Chapter 7, explains the relationship between attachment and our windows of tolerance (see Figure 9.2). When we feel safe, or use our neuroception and appraise safety, we can enjoy our feelings of arousal. We can use our social engagement system. We connect with others and we can regulate our emotions. However, when we don't feel safe, and we neurocept a threat, we may not be able to access our social engagement system. Our sympathetic nervous systems respond and we may become hyperaroused. If this fails, our parasympathetic nervous system, or the dorsal vagal system, activates and we may become hypoaroused. To be clear, hyperactivating and deactivating strategies can occur within the window of tolerance. We can still use these strategies while being adaptively regulated. However, those who are insecurely attached are more likely to become so dysregulated that they experience emotion outside of the window of tolerance. For instance, a child who neurocepts danger because his mother is rejecting may feel elevated arousal, or even hyperarousal. This elevated arousal can motivate the child to please his mother and thereby avoid her rejection. Should this be a pattern of response, this child with an insecure attachment gains less experience with flexibly integrating emotions into his window of tolerance. His learning is stunted. Patterns get reinforced and his window of tolerance stagnates (Ogden & Fisher, 2015). Insecurely attached individuals tend to be rigid and inflexible when dealing with different levels of emotional arousal and their windows of tolerance are smaller than those who are securely attached.

Attachment clinicians aim to expand clients' windows of tolerance using the therapeutic relationship to do so. They work with the idea that while a limited window of tolerance may have been adaptive at the time, it is not currently adaptive. With moment-by-moment tracking, an attachment therapist mimics the dance a caregiver does, cycling from attunement to misattunement and then repairing the misattunement. While Chapter 12 will address this more fully, a brief case example will show how an attachment therapist may work with a client. Diane rarely asked for help. She could do it alone, she felt. Why rely on others when they'd just let her down? Growing up, her parents had both ridiculed her every time she needed help with anything. A school project, practicing a cartwheel. Any and all of this became fodder for teasing. Diane handled this by turning off her needs. She became completely self-reliant, almost obsessively so. This worked at the time. She was able to grow up in this rejecting household and left home as soon as she was able. The only problem was that she was lonely. She functioned well, made a good living, and managed her own household. But she had no one to share any of this with. Not only was she lonely but she became dysregulated any time she felt anything at all. She had to stick to her routine, to the familiar, and never venture out of that comfort zone. To tackle this, I, as her therapist, needed to work at the edge of the boundaries of windows to increase both negative and positive affect tolerance (Schore, 2009; Ogden & Fisher, 2015). The goal was for Diane to experience new levels of arousal within the confines of a safe relational space. In order to grow, she needed to be supportively pushed beyond her comfort zones. As Bromberg (2006) states, our clients must be "safe but not too safe" for their windows of tolerance to expand. I gently complimented Diane on her ability to take care of herself. She was so proficient at it, I said. But then I pointed to the conflict she had. It was so tiring always being in control, always having to manage alone. And it was so very lonely. As I talked, Diane began to tear up. I knew this was difficult for her, that showing emotion to me was hard, so I switched tacks. I stopped and asked her what was happening for her in her body. By doing that, I was regulating her. I was taking her out of a painful moment and allowing her to focus on her body, not her feelings. She had gone beyond her window of tolerance, but I had contained that. Had I asked her to tell me more about feeling lonely, feeling afraid, or feeling vulnerable, it may have been too much for her. By focusing on her body, I was shifting her out of the state she was in. When she was visibly calmer, having recovered her level of tolerance, I kept talking in a soothing voice, reminding her that I was there, that together we would work through this, and that it was safe for her guard down just a little bit. What I hoped was that she felt understood, attuned to, and that this would also expand her window of tolerance by increasing her positive feelings too. She smiled weakly and I felt a rush of warmth - that of connection.

Persistent dysregulation

What happens to us if we are under chronic stress? If we are traumatized? We can be hyperaroused or hypoaroused for short periods of time, but what if we don't re-balance? If we remain outside our window of tolerance for extended time periods? According to attachment theory, initially, an alarmed child turns to a caregiver for safety and security. The child expects to be re-regulated. If it is the caregiver herself who is a source of threat, the child has a dilemma. He continues to be alarmed and his sympathetic system kicks in. He may become hyperaroused. Should this continue, another reaction may occur in response to this "relational trauma" and the child may dissociate. Importantly, this parasympathetic response is actually a way to regulate overwhelming affect. It is adaptive at the time as it allows the child to conserve energy so that the ensuing detachment isn't catastrophic. Using this defense mechanism, the child tries to avoid being noticed as that could bring on more rejection or instill more fear (Schore, 2009). This is the dorsal vagal response Porges (2017) describes. It is akin to feigning death.

Experiencing prolonged hyperarousal can result in feeling panicky, anxious, or alarmed much of the time. It can cause a deficit in being able to effectively regulate these intense emotions. Adults who have experienced excessive periods of hyperarousal may have dramatic or rapid shifts in emotions. They may quickly cycle from fear, anger, and even extreme joy to hopelessness, shame, or just feeling flat. Those who experience prolonged periods of hypoarousal may mostly feel parasympathetic emotions (Ogden, 2009). Think back to Tronick's (2007) still-face paradigm mentioned in Chapter 5. Should a child repeatedly experience disruptions in connection, like those experienced during the still-face, he may cycle into hypoarousal often. In fact, this may become his mode of being so that he can preserve his energy and himself. Shame and disgust often occur in this heightened parasympathetic state as do hopeless and helpless thoughts. And the child's implicit memory may encode this defense in an effort to avoid the recurrence of the relational trauma (Schore, 2019). All of this may contribute to developing "faulty neuroception" where an individual has difficulty appraising the safety or danger of a situation. Everything can come to feel unsafe (Ogden & Fisher, 2015).

Summary

We learn to regulate our affect within our attachment relationships. This regulation occurs both consciously and nonconsciously, often happening outside of our awareness. The making sense of our emotions is within our awareness. We now understand a secure attachment pattern as being a result of the integration of right and left hemispheric functioning. We connect right-brain to right-brain, mind-to-mind, and body-to-body. All of us function best within our window of tolerance, but we only grow when our boundaries are gently expanded. We can handle this pushing only within the confines of a safe and secure relationship, when we are experiencing a mind, body, and emotional connection. And it is through this full connection, this intersubjective understanding, that change occurs in the therapy room.

Chapter 10

Mentalization

Since the advent of psychotherapy, talking has been touted as one of the most important mechanisms of change. In fact, it is well-known that Sigmund Freud used the term "the talking cure" to describe the fundamental curative agent in psychoanalysis. We go to therapists to "talk" about our feelings and this helps enormously. And that is not the only place we talk. Our partners serve as sounding boards. They listen to us talk. We talk to our friends when we have problems. We encourage children to "use words" to express themselves. And somehow, through this use of words, we often feel better. Cognitively framing what we feel seems to decrease stress. It seems to aid in emotion regulation. As Dan Siegel (Siegel & Bryson, 2012) says, when our emotions are hijacked or they overwhelm us, it is helpful to "name it to tame it." It has been shown that simply giving an emotion a name helps an individual regulate himself. The left brain is engaged in a way that is calming to the right brain. It seems that though researchers have shown the importance of accessing our emotions and giving credence to the right brain, particularly in the first few years of life, the left brain's capacities are still deemed essential to our regulating our emotions. Attachment theorists have moved more and more towards the notion that it is the *integration* of the right and left brains' functioning that is critical to adults' abilities to regulate ourselves and ultimately, to our optimal functioning.

Over the years, researchers, theorists, and philosophers alike have grappled with understanding the interaction between feelings and rational thought. How much do our emotions rule us? How much power does our cognition have to influence our emotions? And when it comes to emotion regulation, what part is emotionally driven and what part is rationally driven? Though most often it is understood that both the right and left brain are involved in emotion regulation, the extent of involvement has been in question. Thus, while Schore was exploring regulation theory (Schore, 1994; Schore & Schore, 2008; Schore, 2019), other attachment theorists, such as British psychoanalyst Peter Fonagy, were focusing on another theory: mentalization theory (Fonagy Gergely, Jurist, & Target, 2002; Hill, 2015). In contrast to regulation theory, which emphasizes the role of primary affect in our regulation, mentalization theory stresses the role of our secondary affect. Recall the concepts of primary and secondary emotions

(Chapter 8), where primary emotions are our body's first response to a stimuli. It is physiological, as most of the time the autonomic nervous system is activated. It is experienced in the right brain and is nonverbal. On the other hand, secondary emotion, or categorical emotion, consists of our primary emotions that have been cognitively assessed and evaluated. According to this theory, the cognitive, verbal, and representational processing in our left brains is deemed critical to our ability to regulate ourselves. Primary affect regulation is seen as a precursor of mentalization, which can be briefly defined as the reading and making sense of one's own or another's mental states. It entails understanding one's own or another's feelings, thoughts, wishes, or intentions (to be explored later in this chapter). Developmentally, at first, we regulate ourselves via interaction with caregivers who help us achieve regulation or calm. With optimal growth we come to automatically regulate ourselves, without much conscious awareness that we are doing so. As we mature over time, especially after the development of productive language, our conscious cognitions come more into play, giving meaning to our feeling states. We are able to tell ourselves stories about how we felt or what we thought. Words lend complexity to our emotional experiences, allowing us to adjust our emotions, either upward or downward, in the service of our unfolding sense of self. With mentalization, which depends crucially on language, comes the capacity for self-understanding and for perceiving where another person may be coming from. It enables us to comprehend and potentially predict the behavior of others, all of which encourages and creates social connection. And much like emotion regulation in and of itself, the capacity to mentalize is seen as developing within the context of the infant–caregiver attachment relationship (Fonagy et al., 2002; Slade, 2005).

History

Metacognitive monitoring

The construct of mentalization was born out of Mary Main's research on the Adult Attachment Interview (see Chapter 3). Main had noticed that many individuals with a secure state of mind with respect to attachment demonstrated "metacognitive monitoring," or actively monitoring what one is saying and thinking in the moment. These were the speakers who noticed any contradictions in what they were saying while they were doing the interview. They showed an appearance–reality distinction, where they understood that the same situation can be experienced differently at different times. For instance, a study was performed where children were asked if a man wearing a mask was still a man. Because this is a developmental construct, many 3-year-olds were not able to distinguish between the appearance of the mask and the man behind the mask. A man wearing a Batman mask was seen as really being Batman. In an adult, a lack of being able to use the appearance-reality distinction could manifest in a speaker's saying something like, "he always spoke loudly and that meant he was always angry with me". In contrast, someone who is able to make the appearance-reality distinction would say "my father spoke very loudly. Some would say he screamed. It came across as anger, but actually, he was hard of hearing." Another ability these speakers may also demonstrate, and a subcategory of the appearance-reality distinction, is that of representational diversity. For instance, a man says that his brother sees their childhood very differently to how he sees it and, he supposes, they were treated very differently by their mother when they were younger. Yet another subcategory of the appearance-reality distinction and another manifestation of metacognitive monitoring is demonstrating representational change. Here, a speaker acknowledges that something that is true at present may not have been the case when he was growing up. These were the interviewees who may have said that they now realize that what they had believed to be true at the time may actually not have been true. For instance, a speaker may use the adjectives "lazy" and "stupid" to describe his father, but as he begins to give evidence for what he is saying, he says something like:

> As I am sitting here talking, I realize that I am repeating what my mom told me about my dad. If I think about it more, my dad wasn't lazy or stupid. It's just that he was in a car accident and broke both legs, which meant he couldn't work anymore. He was a manager of a construction site. It's strange as I never really thought about it before, but my mom was so angry that he lost his job. Even though it really wasn't his fault.

In speaking this way, the subject demonstrates his awareness of changes in his own thoughts and also shows that he recognizes that he is talking to someone else. Overall, those with secure states of mind with respect to attachment often utilized metacognitive monitoring during their interviews (Main & Goldwyn, 1998).

In a seminal chapter, Main (1991) expanded on metacognitive monitoring, describing the ability to monitor oneself and further detailing Bowlby's (1973) original concept of single versus multiple models of attachment figures. Think back to Bowlby's concept of an internal working model, the encoded general paradigm of relating that a child develops based on his experiences with his primary caregiver. Those who have a single model of their attachment figure tend to be securely attached. They are likely to operate in a unified, cohesive manner in times of distress as well as during times of feeling safe. However, it is possible, according to Bowlby, to operate from multiple working models developed based on the same attachment figure. Should this be the case, those with multiple models may have different and even contradictory ways of operating in their attachment relationships. Main suggested that metacognitive monitoring may not develop for those with multiple models, as having these multiple models negatively impacts the formation of a cohesive and coherent sense of self.

It was this idea that led Main to examine the notion of coherence. She proposed, and later research supported, that the overall *coherence* of a narrative was the strongest correlate of a secure state of mind with respect to attachment, while incoherence was related to insecure states of mind. Coherence, as noted in Chapter 3, manifests itself in consistent, truthful, and logical discourse. Recall that Hesse (2016) stated that the "central task the [AAI] interview presents to participants is that of (1) producing and reflecting on memories related to attachment, while simultaneously (2) maintaining coherent, collaborative discourse with the interviewer" (p. 556). To maintain coherence, a speaker must integrate his attachment-related experiences into a single model and those with a single model of attachment tend to present more coherently than those with multiple models of attachment-related experiences. Coherence denotes an individual's ability to be flexible in thought and to deploy attention constructively. Incoherence signals inflexible and often disjointed, unintegrated thinking, usually as a result of multiple models of attachment (Slade, Grienenberger, Bernbach, Levy, & Locker, 2005). In this way, Main proposed that coherence and metacognition were inter-related.

In order to better understand the coherence of discourse, in the mid-1980s, Peter Fonagy, Miriam Steele, and Howard Steele, initiated the London Parent-Child Study. They set out to replicate Main's findings, that of the intergenerational transmission of attachment. Based on her original sample, Main (Main et al., 1985) had noted that there was a strong correlation between a mother's state of mind with respect to attachment and her child's attachment classification. In their study, Fonagy and the Steeles conducted the AAI (Adult Attachment Interview) with 100 mothers and 100 fathers and, with an interesting twist, they did the interviews before the men and women (couples) had given birth to their first children. Following the birth, at one year of age (with the mothers) and then at 18 months (with the fathers), the babies' attachment classifications were measured using the Strange Situation. What they found was startling. The mother's representation of attachment was strongly associated with her child's attachment pattern 75% of the time. Mothers with dismissing states of mind were more likely to have children with avoidant attachment patterns, while mothers with preoccupied states of mind tended to have children with ambivalent attachment patterns. A mother's unresolved state of mind during their AAI was associated with her child's disorganized attachment patterns. And this was true when the mother's representation was evaluated *before* the birth of her child (Fonagy, Steele, & Steele, 1991). Independently, these same cross-generational patterns were observed for fathers' AAIs and their first-born children's attachments to them at 18 months of age (Steele, Steele & Fonagy, 1996). In other words, attachment during infancy is relationship specific. We learn what to expect from our mother, how to feel around her and with her, *from our mother*. We learn what to expect from our father, how to feel around him and with him, *from our father*. Some time across development between infancy and the age when we are able to tell a story about our childhood family relationships and thoughts about these relationships in the present, as demanded by the AAI, we come to integrate our diverse relationships with our caregivers into a more-or-less singular pattern of attachment all our own (yet lawfully linked to 4 or 5 major adult patterns of attachment observed around the globe).

Attachment researchers became fascinated with how this could be. *How does a caregiver transmit her attachment state of mind to her child?* Theories abounded, with one in particular taking hold: maternal sensitivity and responsiveness was proposed as the transmission mechanism. As Ainsworth (Ainsworth et al., 1978) had noted, how responsive and available a mother was to her child seemed to directly affect that child's sense of attachment security. However, van IJzendoorn (1995) conducted a meta-analysis and found that while caregiver sensitivity did explain some of the intergenerational transmission of attachment, it only explained a small portion of it. He termed the unexplained variance the "transmission gap" (Van IJzendoorn, 1995, p. 398) to designate the gap in knowledge as to exactly how a caregiver conveys her attachment representation to her child.

Mentalization and the reflective function (RF)

In exploring the intergenerational transmission gap further, another notion surfaced; that of the relational component of metacognition, or thinking about another's thinking. While Fonagy and his study team were corroborating Main's findings that secure subjects were able to utilize metacognition, they also couldn't help but notice another phenomenon taking place. Secure individuals were not only monitoring their own speech and thoughts; they were doing so for the speech and thought of others. Main's original construct was based on an individual's thinking about thinking in that moment, but Fonagy, Steele, Steele, and Target now felt a new construct was in order, one that incorporated thinking about the other's mental state. Thus, the construct of reflective functioning came into being, as an expansion of the concept of metacognitive monitoring of one's behavior to that of the other, as well as all ranges of thought, feelings, wishes, and desires therein (Steele & Steele, 2008). The RF concerns the capacity to verbally represent our wide ranging mentalizations, defined as our reflections on our own *and* on others' mental states. In other words, the RF is the outward manifestation, during discourse, of mentalization. In contrast to introspection, reflective functioning occurs largely outside of awareness (Fonagy, Target, Steele, & Steele, 1998). For example, my client Rita reported to me that she had a fight with her husband the night before therapy. He had come home, yelled at her about dinner not being ready, slammed the door of their bedroom and turned on the TV. She had yelled back, saying she was not his servant, stormed into their bedroom, sat on the far end of their bed, and announced there would be no dinner that night. As she sat there, her stomach rumbling, she suddenly remembered that her husband had met with his boss earlier to discuss a possible raise. She looked up and noticed that her husband's face was white and he was wringing his hands. Realizing that her husband may have had a bad day and that his actions may not have indicated his disdain for her, but in fact may have been more related to his meeting with his boss, Rita moved closer to her husband, and placed her hand on his. She was able to mentalize and understand that her husband was suffering. She then spoke, demonstrating the RF, saying that she sensed that he was in a bad mood and that she was wondering how his meeting had gone. Rita reported that her husband had crumbled at that moment, apologizing for his behavior. He told her that he would not be getting the raise they desperately needed.

Mentalized affectivity

Increasingly, it became clear that mentalization and the reflective function (RF) are not only about metacognitively monitoring speech and thought (Slade, 2005). The constructs also include being able to correctly attribute the emotional states of others, something deemed key to affect regulation (Gergely & Watson, 1996). Those with high RF understand that emotions are not static, that they ebb and flow over the course of time. They grasp the notion that the feeling another displays may not be what he is actually feeling. For instance, in Rita's case, she was able to recognize that the anger her husband displayed at her was not really what he was feeling. Once she understood this, she was able to manage her hurt feelings and have empathy for him. It was not only that he was thinking about his meeting with his boss, but that he was upset about what had happened. This understanding of her husband's emotions enabled Rita to regulate herself. The ability to think about feelings was now a part of the equation. So much so, that Mary Target suggested that mentalizing is actually "the capacity to think about feeling and to feel about thinking" (Slade, 2005, p. 271). More recently, Fonagy and his colleagues (2002) have described the concept of "mentalized affectivity," meaning the ability to consciously understand one's emotional states and to use this to regulate affect. It serves as the key in joining our consciousness with our affective experiences, thereby enabling us to find meaning in our emotions. In fact, full mentalization, they state, requires thinking about feeling *while* feeling an emotion. Recall the concepts of primary and secondary emotions (Chapter 8), where primary emotions are our body's first response to a stimulus. They are physiological as most of the time the autonomic nervous system is activated. They are experienced in the right brain and are nonverbal. On the other hand, secondary emotions, or categorical emotions, consist of our primary emotions that have been cognitively assessed and evaluated. They are predominantly processed in the left brain. Fonagy and his colleagues suggest that it is through mentalized affectivity that we are able to connect our primary and secondary affects to each other in a way that makes sense. Our physiological experiences become defined with language. Our nonconscious processes are made conscious and explicit. In other words, it is through mentalized affectivity that we can merge the activity of our right and left brains. Fonagy and his colleagues propose that it is this capacity that is central to psychotherapy.

Parental reflective function

Ultimately, researchers operationalized the psychological processes that are fundamental to the ability to mentalize. They created a new measure called the reflective function (RF) Scale. This scale analyzes AAI transcripts and focuses on particular questions, such as "why do you think your parents behaved the way they did?" and "what effect do you think the experiences you have been talking about in this interview have had on your adult personality?" These questions push interviewees to think about themselves objectively and also to evaluate their parents' experiences from a different vantage point. In answering these questions, a speaker is forced to evaluate himself and his parents objectively. He must reflect on his experiences and create meaning. The interviewee is assigned a number from an 11-point scale, ranging from −1 (bizarre) to +9 (high RF). Overall, the RF scale measures the awareness of one's own and others' mental states (Fonagy et al., 1998; Slade, 2005).

With the further development of these concepts, researchers began to focus on the parent's ability to reflectively function. This propelled Fonagy and his colleagues to propose that being able to reflectively function was key to a caregiver creating a holding environment for her child, one in which the child comes to feel understood, secure, and safe because his caregiver can contain and give meaning to his experiences. Arietta Slade, a renowned attachment theorist and researcher, took the concept of the RF and developed the Parent Development Interview (PDI), a measure based on the RF scale that examines parental RF, or a caregiver's ability to hold her baby and her baby's mental states in mind (Slade, Aber, Bresgi, Berger, & Kaplan, 2004). The PDI is a measure specifically designed to ascertain a parent's capacity to recognize and reflect on her child's internal experiences. Studies find that there is a relationship between a mother's reflective functioning and her child's attachment pattern (Slade et al., 2005). Based on these findings, researchers hypothesized that perhaps it was reflective functioning that served as the bridge between the parent representation and her child's attachment. They suggest that parental representations of a child are perhaps the mediating link between a parent's attachment representations and her child's attachment behavioral pattern. In other words, they propose that reflective functioning is a critical factor in explaining the transmission of an adult's state of mind with respect to attachment to her child's attachment classification. What is more, they suggest the RF explains the transmission gap.

Mentalization, the reflective function, and attachment

Exactly how are attachment and mentalization connected? Just like the attachment bond itself, researchers propose that there is an evolutionary advantage to mentalization and the RF. As already stated, mentalization concerns the ability to reflect on our mental states, but in particular, our intentional mental states, or our motives, wishes, beliefs, and emotions that may signify action. It enables us to tell pretend modes from what is real, and it allows us to more easily negotiate our emotional experiences. By naming our emotions, we often feel relief. We are able to enhance our understanding of ourselves and it turns out that understanding ourselves is crucial to our optimal functioning. We gain perspective, create structure and organization to our inner world, and we find meaning. Not only is self-knowledge improved upon with mentalization, but we are encouraged to connect with others. By mentalizing, we can better conceptualize another's pretenses, deceits, or plans, and use this to predict future behavior. And if we are able to successfully predict the behavior of others, we are better able to manage our interpersonal interactions. Understanding another's emotions, wishes, or goals enhances our empathy and allows us to better communicate with others. In sum, by mentalizing and reflectively functioning, we can regulate our emotions more effectively, giving meaning and being able to predict our own and others' actions. In predicting the behavior of others on our own, we become less dependent on others to do so for us. It is part of learning to auto-regulate.

Because of the capacities enabled by the RF, some say it is fundamental to our being able to form secure attachment relationships and in fact, research bears this out. Not only are securely attached individuals more inclined to mentalize than their insecurely attached counterparts, but caregivers who are more able to mentalize tend to have children who are securely attached (Fonagy et al., 1998; Hill, 2015). We can suppose that a secure child feels safe to explore his mental states. He has a caregiver who contains his distress, all the while communicating to him that though he is a separate being, he is not alone. In this way, the caregiver conveys to her child that he can cope. We can think of this from a neurobiological perspective, when the reward system is online because of an attachment figure's availability, even when the amygdala is triggered, the securely attached individual can maintain high activation in the prefrontal cortex areas. Conversely, studies have found that in comparison to securely attached children, insecurely attached children do worse on mentalizing tasks (Fonagy, Luyten, Allison, & Campbell, 2016). It is proposed that a caregiver who has difficulty understanding the mind of her child will tend to have an insecurely attached child. A dismissing caregiver will have trouble mirroring her child's negative feelings because it is too overwhelming for her. At the same time, she will struggle to put together a coherent picture of her child's mental state. She will simply shut her child out, leaving him without the necessary scaffolding to form his own sense of a coping self. Thus, this child will internalize that he is on his own, but is overwhelmed much of the time. He will tend to also dismiss the mental states of others. A preoccupied caregiver may be unable to disentangle her own feelings from the feelings she imagines her child to have. In these instances, a child will feel uncontained and instead, may internalize the caregiver's difficulties managing emotion. The child will lack a sense of self, instead merging with his caregiver at a cost. He will tend to focus only on the mental states of others and not on himself. In both these cases, the child maintains proximity to his caregiver at the expense of developing reflective functioning. He cannot maintain effective levels of prefrontal cortex functioning during times of stress. Lastly, a caregiver who is unresolved in her attachment states of mind often has a child with a disorganized attachment classification. These disorganized children may be hypervigilant, intently observing a caregiver who may be threatening to him. He lacks the sense of safety to explore and effectively develop his own mental states (Fonagy, 2001; Fonagy et al., 2002).

The development of RF

Given the connection between attachment and RF, theorists understand RF as a developmental ability. Furthermore, they see the growth of RF as being largely dependent on the caregiver's ability to accurately read her infant's mental states, meaning it develops within the context of the attachment relationship. The question becomes how does a child learn that his mind is his own? And how does he learn that others have their own separate minds? Furthermore, how does he come to understand that what occurs in his mind, his feelings and thoughts, are different to actual reality; that they are only representations of what is real? And, importantly, how is the attachment relationship involved in this learning process?

A confluence of factors influence the development of reflective functioning. Heredity, biology, and the environment, and in particular our social interactions, all effect its evolution. While all children are born with the capacity for a theory of mind, or being able to interpret one's own and others' mental and emotional states, not everyone develops this capacity to the same extent. Our environment very much influences its trajectory. At first, infants experience primary emotions and are very much dependent on their caregivers to regulate and reflect on these. With time, they develop the capacity to gain secondary control over their primary emotions. They can effect change in their emotional responses, inhibiting or changing certain reactions in order to attain a cognitive goal. Primary emotions become categorical emotions. They are organized and more accessible. Not only do children understand their own emotions better, but they grow to understand the emotions of others.

According to mentalization theory, under the best of circumstances (i.e., having a secure attachment relationship), four facets of mentalizing may develop chronologically: the teleological, psychic equivalence, and pretend modes which all culminate in full mentalization.

Teleological mode

At this stage, a child cannot understand that something may represent something else. Intent merges with action. For instance, if you accidentally bump into a child, the child perceives it as a direct attack. He cannot evaluate the intention behind the action. The capacity to understand the representational nature of behaviors only comes into play during the second year of life.

Psychic equivalence mode

During this stage, the child has some awareness of things being representational, but cannot tease apart what is real from what is represented. The internal world merges with external reality. An example of this is magical thinking. If you wish someone dead and she dies, you killed her.

Case example

Goldie began attending therapy because she was having panic attacks at work. The panic attacks began when she was passed over for a promotion. As a nurse, she did her best to take care of her patients. She was attentive to details, kind, and compassionate. She would often forgo her own needs for those of others around her. When her supervisor promoted her friend and not her, Goldie began to feel she couldn't do her job properly. She always had been filled with doubt and had tried her hardest to be the best nurse she could. But with this disappointment, her worst fears appeared to be true. She was useless and worthless, she reported. Goldie's family history shed some light on the origin of her negative feelings.

Goldie and her sister were raised by a single mother who worked two jobs and wasn't home much of the time. By the age of seven, Goldie had taken over the parenting role of her sister. She was making their meals, doing their laundry, and walking her sister to and from school and then getting herself to school after that. Her mother would come home from her first job, sit on the couch, drink, and watch TV. She would then prepare to go to her next job, leaving the house late at night and returning in the early hours of the morning. When her mother was home, Goldie did her best to stay out of her way, but that was not always possible. When she did interact with her mother, her mother would criticize her, telling her she couldn't do laundry right. The food she cooked was terrible. She was no good, just like her good-for-nothing father. She was stuck in the mode of "psychic equivalence," where her mother's words had become her reality. She was no good. She was someone who had to work extra hard just to do what most could do without trying. When she was passed over for a promotion, this was further validated.

Pretend mode

Overcompensation occurs during this mode. A child's internal world is seen as being unrelated to his external world. In other words, the internal world is completely decoupled from external reality and representations are seen as completely separate entities that are unrelated to any part of reality. What exists is only what is in our mind. What we don't see, we ignore. Reality may be viewed as threatening. Examples of this are dissociation, grandiosity, or denial.

Case example

Anton was in his thirties. Despite being an extremely successful businessman, one of the best in his field, he seemed unable to maintain a relationship with a significant other. He had had a string of relationships, all with women who were younger and less educated. While he had attended Yale, he tended to date those who had either not gone to college or who were attending no-name colleges, a fact he announced many times during our initial session. And once he finished college, he continued this pattern. Why couldn't he meet someone who was his equal, he bemoaned.

It quickly became clear that Anton needed to be the best at everything. He picked "weak" partners and alternated between trying to better them and denigrating them constantly. Meanwhile, he was unable to acknowledge any weakness in himself. He was stuck in the "pretend" mode. If he just projected out any feelings of vulnerability, he no longer had to feel them. He unconsciously was picking partners who were the objects of his projections and in this way, he could maintain his view that he was the best.

Full mentalization

Full mentalization occurs with the integration of all of the above modes. There is an understanding that representations are just that – representations. They are separate from the reality to which they refer. Internal worlds are seen as distinct from the outside realities. With full mentalization, children grasp that what they perceive may not be the truth. They understand that another person may view things differently and, what is more, may have different notions or ideas about the same things. Suddenly different viewpoints exist. The capacity to mentalize only develops by the fourth or fifth year (Fonagy et al., 2002; Wallin, 2007; Hill, 2015).

Fonagy and his colleagues (2002) make it clear that they believe it is a secure attachment relationship that enables the optimal development of these modes and ultimately of full mentalization.

Caregiver sensitivity

How exactly does an attachment relationship facilitate the development of mentalization? Fonagy and his colleagues propose that the answer is found in sensitive caregiving. They suggest that a sensitive caregiver provides more than just responsivity and availability, as Ainsworth (Ainsworth et al., 1978) had initially purported. A sensitive caregiver also reflects on a child's experiences in a way that enables the child to understand the representational nature of feelings. The child comes to "feel felt" (Siegel, 1999), or to feel known, accepted, and understood. During times of distress, a sensitive caregiver is tasked with both providing a safe haven to a child to reregulate his dysregulation as well as to serve as a secure base from which to explore the environment when the child is regulated. She must contain her feelings, recognize her child as a separate entity and accurately "read" her child's mental state, and then respond with her child's well-being in mind. The sensitive caregiver reflects on her child's experiences both to soothe and to encourage coping. The initial reflection mirrors the child's feelings. It is comforting, providing the much needed intimacy to the child. For instance, a mother mirrors her child's sadness to her child and he feels contained. He now understands his feelings and this is calming. Once the child is soothed, a sensitive caregiver then may not mirror the child exactly. She may reflect on the child's behavior in a manner that suggests they aren't aligned. But then she will always realign. Think back to the dance caregiver–child dyads do where they cycle from attunement to misattunement to repair and then back to attunement, and to the notion of the window of tolerance. The sensitive caregiver pushes her child to expand his window of tolerance by empathizing and joining with her child's mental state and then breaking from this empathy in a constructive way. Thus, the parent's reflection is at first the same and then different from the contents of her child's mind (Fonagy et al., 1998). This promotes coping and the learning of self-regulation.

At first, the mirroring is nonverbal. Then, once language develops, a caregiver's reflections become verbal. Again, it is crucial that a caregiver is able to most-of-the time accurately reflect her child's mental state back to her child. A toddler is just learning to walk. He haltingly walks across a patch of grass and all of a sudden, falls down. He looks at his mother, on the verge of tears. She says to him in a soothing voice "Ouch, you fell down. But you're okay," and smiles. The toddler gets up again and continues to walk. It is through this process of vacillating between sameness and difference that a child comes to understand that reflections can be both the same and different. Had the mother yelled "Oh no, you klutz, you fell down. Stay where you are," the toddler would not have felt soothed or encouraged. He would have felt his physical hurt more intensely. His feelings would not be separated from those of his mother's. He would not feel "felt" and nor would he learn from the experience. Ultimately, it is the sensitivity of a caregiver that allows the child to start organizing his experiences in a way that enables him to pair words with specific emotions, and then to develop a secure attachment.

Social biofeedback theory

The social biofeedback theory of parental affect-mirroring (Gergely & Watson, 1996) proposes a way to understand just how this more comprehensive view of parental sensitivity aids a child in learning that internal emotions and mental states can be represented externally. The theorists build on the supposition that infants are born with an innate tendency for social referencing. When they find themselves in confusing situations, they are wired to look to their caregivers for guidance. According to Gergely and Watson (1996), it is the caregiver's vocal and facial responses to her child's expressions of emotion that aid in the child's learning to reflect. They propose that a caregiver repeatedly externally displays her child's expressions back to him and through this repetition the child learns about the dispositional nature of mental states. Two mechanisms are used by sensitive caregivers to mirror their children's affect and "teach" them about representation: contingency and markedness.

Contingency (highlighting sameness)

In contingent mirroring, a parent represents her child's emotion accurately. The mirrored affect is the same, but not completely the same. It is the same in that the child feels understood, but different enough that the child recognizes the emotion as not his own. Through this process, a child comes to recognize the connection between his own expressions and his parent's mirroring displays. A mental link is formed where he connects his emotion to his parent's emotion. But he also can differentiate one from the other. He comes to realize that his internal world is not the same as his external world; they are decoupled and are not one and the same. A child cries when his playmate touches his toy during a playdate at his house. A mother makes a sad face and says "Oh, you're feeling sad. It's hard to share," giving words to the child's feelings in a contingent manner. Additionally, in these interactions, a child feels a sense of agency when he realizes that he impacts his caregiver and that he can induce change in his caregiver's and in his own mental state. The child feels better. Ultimately, this contingency between parent and child forms the foundation for being able to regulate affect (Fonagy et al., 2002).

Markedness (highlighting difference)

Somehow, the caregiver must convey to her child that her mirrored expressions are not her own expressions. They must feel understood, but the reflected emotion must be different in a way that is not too different. During an intersubjective moment, the feelings a sensitive caregiver displays are a representation of her child's feelings; not her own. The child needs to understand this in order to develop the capacity to mentalize. Gergely and Watson (1996) propose that the "referential decoupling" of a child's feelings from his parent's feelings occurs through something called "markedness," a term coined to describe the way a caregiver mirrors her child's feelings to her child so that the child understands it as a representation and not as real. Through marking, a child comes to understand that a parent's reflected emotion belongs to him and not to his parent. A mother opens her mouth, widens her eyes and then exclaims "How frustrating!" when a five-year-old bursts into tears because he can't tie his shoe laces on his own. If the mother marks her comment appropriately, the child will recognize the mother's emotion is meant for his situation, not for hers. She must effectively communicate that she is not frustrated with him, but is helping him to label his emotion, to understand that he is feeling frustrated. Saying "It's frustrating to try hard to tie those laces and still have trouble tying them!" helps mark the experience as the child's own. Marking usually occurs when a caregiver exaggerates an emotional expression. It is related to playfulness and being able to pretend, having an "as-if" quality to it. The parent's response must be sufficiently playful, so as not to overwhelm the infant with "real" emotion. For instance, a mother could say with a smile, "Those laces are so wiggly. They just jump out of your hands like bunny rabbits!" But to be effective, a caregiver's as-if response must also retain a similarity to the marked expression so that it is still recognizable to the child. It is proposed that this "referential anchoring" occurs with highly contingent responsivity, where the mother accurately matches her child's affect display enough to tell her child what he is feeling. Overall, relevant cues are highlighted, telling the child what to notice in his caregiver's response so that he can figure out what he himself feels. Thus, children will experience both realistic expressions of emotion and marked emotions. They come to learn the difference between the two.

Disrupted affect mirroring

Affect expressions that are not effectively mirrored back to the child may be detrimental to his ability to mentalize. Though just one pathway amongst many, such as biological vulnerabilities and genetic predispositions, caregiving that fails to effectively mirror a child's emotions leads to deficiencies in mentalizing and can result in pathology. Disrupted affect mirroring can occur in a number of ways. Firstly, a caregiver can mirror an emotion to her child so that the child feels the emotion actually belongs to the caregiver. The caregiver's affect-mirroring may be congruent, but may not mark a child's emotional display. For example, a caregiver mirroring unmarked anger to her child can instill fear. A caregiver exclaims loudly "Wow, you're terrible at tying laces. You don't seem to be able to do it!" Instead of soothing him, it may appear she is angry with him, which becomes even more dysregulating. Those who are preoccupied in their state of mind with respect to attachment (E) are likely to produce unmarked affective responses like this. In these cases, caregivers tend to respond to their children's affect with unmarked, realistic displays of emotion. Thus, the child may be unable to decouple his internal world from his caregiver's reaction. He will feel her emotion is too real. Too, his unmarked emotion, a primary emotion, may not be secondarily represented in the child's mind. The child may be unable to own his emotion as his. Furthermore, his dysregulated affect may escalate in intensity, instead of deescalating (Fonagy et al., 2002).

A lack of category congruence defines the second way disrupted affect mirroring can occur. Here, a caregiver mirrors an emotion in a way that is disconnected from what her child is actually feeling. She may mark the emotion, but miss the boat and misrepresent her child's emotion. For instance, if a father calls his four-year-old son a liar when he proudly proclaims to his father that he is stronger than the Hulk. The child is small for his age and is simply trying to feel powerful. The father misunderstands this need and reacts from his own fear that he is raising an immoral child. Thus, his response is incongruent with the child's primary emotion and will induce a distorted secondary representation in his son. The boy will perhaps mislabel his very natural desire to feel strong as "bad." It can be proposed that those who are dismissing in their state of mind with respect to attachment (Ds) are likely to produce marked affect that lacks congruence. Should this type of interaction occur often, the child will lose out on opportunities to learn to organize and understand his feelings, which may compromise his ability to mentalize.

Case example

Gloria began therapy in order to leave Lorraine, her partner of ten years. She was unhappy, though she couldn't pinpoint why. Gloria was a daycare worker. She had been working at the same place since she graduated high school. At various points in time, she had contemplated changing jobs. But she always talked herself out of that, reminding herself that her work was steady and that she could support herself and Lorraine on her income. She and Lorraine began dating at the same time that Gloria began working at the daycare center. Lorraine was 16 years her senior, and had seemed calm to Gloria. This was a big draw as Gloria had grown up in a chaotic household. Though her parents were still married, their relationship had been filled with conflict. Her mother had withdrawn to her room for most of Gloria's childhood, sleeping the day away while Gloria was left to her own devices. When her father came home from work, he often yelled at Gloria for not getting dinner ready for him or for leaving clothing strewn around the house. He would then yell at Gloria's mother who would slam the door and sleep some more. There was an unspoken expectation that she would assume the household responsibilities while her mother retreated more and more. Though Gloria didn't remember much of her childhood, she did report that she had been "very sensitive" and would often cry "for no reason." At least, this is what her parents told her. Gloria tried to rebel in high school. She began failing school. No one noticed. She became promiscuous. Still no one noticed. She didn't care really, she said. While she talked, her facial expressions remained placid, almost lifeless. She droned on and often, I had trouble keeping myself focused. Her emotions were so far from her conscious awareness. Eventually, when Gloria was a senior in high school, her father left her mother for another woman and her mother fell apart even more. Gloria lived at home for five years after high school to take care of her mother. She eventually moved in with Lorraine, though to an apartment only around the corner from her mother.

When Gloria began therapy, she wasn't able to mentalize. Because her mother was depressed, it is very likely that she was not able to effectively attune to Gloria. Gloria grew up pushing her emotions away. She had to manage on her own, without leaning on anyone as there was no one there to help her. Her memories of childhood were few and far between and her emotions were dampened. It worked for her when she was growing up. It helped her to survive. But it wasn't working now. She felt distant from others and, if really pushed, she acknowledged she was lonely. She also felt trapped in a relationship, but saw no other way. She felt she couldn't leave.

Once I had established a connection with Gloria, I tried to empathize with her situation. I attempted to maintain congruence with what she was expressing. That must be really hard to live with Lorraine when you don't want to be with her. It was, she nodded, without expression. You must have been in pain while your parents fought. Yes, she said, though she couldn't really remember what she felt. My efforts at conveying compassion seemed to fail miserably and I wasn't sure why. No matter how hard I tried, I could not break into Gloria's inner world. Week after week, she complained about Lorraine. Lorraine didn't do any housework. Gloria came home after a long day spent with little kids, and still had to make dinner. Lorraine slept a lot of the time, Gloria complained. Lorraine was in between jobs and seemed perfectly happy to sit on the couch and watch soap operas. But when I asked why she stayed with Lorraine, Gloria said she just couldn't leave her. What kind of person does that, she said with anger bristling just beneath the surface. I asked her what she was feeling as she said that and she said she felt fine. It just was what it was. Maybe it was just her lot in life to be unhappy.

As empathizing was not working, my next strategy was to confront Gloria, trying to mark my responses as different. I suggested that she was being loyal to her mother in staying with Lorraine. Gloria vapidly disagreed. I then said that perhaps she was expressing anger at her father for his leaving her mother by staying with Lorraine and remaining unhappy. Gloria shook her head, saying that didn't feel accurate. In an attempt to get a rise from her, I proposed to Gloria that she would never leave, that she was going to remain unfulfilled for her whole life. Much to my chagrin, she agreed with me. My attempt at marking my reaction as different to hers wasn't working. It was too far from what Gloria was feeling. There was no anchor she could grab onto.

As therapy progressed, I began to both empathize and then elaborate in a way that was slightly different to what Gloria was saying. When she complained that Lorraine was lazy, I responded by saying that must be so hard to have to do it all, to never get a break, and to continually be expected to do everything on your own. But, I added, it also must be hard to feel paralyzed, to feel unable to protect yourself, just like you felt during childhood. Slowly, I introduced the notion that she may have some agency, that she wasn't as helpless as she had felt most of her life. I vacillated between empathy and very small confrontations. When I empathized, I made sure to lean forward, to maintain eye contact with Gloria, if only for a bit. I would then pull back, but only slightly, saying how perhaps she had more control than she felt she had. I would lean forward once more, rejoining with her, labeling what she may feel.

I said that I understood how overwhelming it may be to feel trapped (congruence), but that she was strong, that she had taken care of herself in a very positive way (marking my response, making sure she knew it was about her). The more I empathized and then highlighted her strength, the more Gloria seemed to feel empowered. She began coming into session reporting that she recognized that she had felt weak and powerless for a lot of her life, but said she was beginning to realize that this was how she felt then, and not now (appearance-reality distinction). Her father had made her feel trapped and because of this, she had felt responsible for her mother in a way that was crippling. She now recognized the similarities between her relationship with her mother and her relationship with Lorraine (mentalizing). As she talked of her loneliness over the years, tears welled up for her, something that had never happened before. She was beginning to allow her emotions to surface. She soothed herself, acknowledging that her staying with Lorraine was something she was choosing to do. She felt a sense of agency, understanding that she did not have to remain in an unhappy relationship. This reflection enabled her to regulate her emotions. She began feeling more and more capable of leaving. Therapy took years. One day, Gloria arrived and announced she had done it; she had asked Lorraine to leave. She couldn't have felt prouder of herself.

Summary

We can safely conclude that mentalizing is crucial to our being able to regulate ourselves. It develops in the context of a secure attachment relationship and also enables secure attachment relationships to form. Over the years, researchers have continually tried to explain the transmission gap in the intergenerational transmission of attachment. One promising avenue that has been investigated is how RF is related to this transmission. However, though there is evidence to suggest that this gap is partially explained by RF, it is becoming increasingly clear that this is not the full story. In a recent meta-analysis, mentalization and caregiver sensitivity was shown to explain only part of the variance in attachment security. In fact, a transmission gap of 89% was ascertained (Van IJzendoorn & Bakersmans-Kranenburg, 2019). Thus, the intergenerational transmission of attachment seems to be explained by multiple pathways, including caregiver sensitivity and the RF, but also neurobiological, ecological, and attachment relationship factors. One factor that is almost certainly involved in this transmission is affect regulation. Affect regulation is shaped by and also shapes our attachment relationships.

In sum, it is clear that affect regulation involves the right and the left brain. Accessing primary emotions is critical, but so is gaining a cognitive understanding of these primary emotions. It is the integration of emotion with cognition that is critical to optimal affect regulation. When the reptilian brain joins forces with the limbic system and the neocortex, we become a well-functioning whole. We experience our emotions. We label them and give words to that experience. In so doing, our world becomes filled with meaning.

Chapter 11

Attachment and therapy
The client

Something clicked for me one day while I was supervising Raya. She was 24 years old and fresh out of graduate school and was working with Murray, a veteran therapy-goer, having been in therapy with new social workers for over ten years. He would begin working with one therapist and then move on to the next, when each therapist inevitably left the community health center for her next job. Murray was in his fifties. He was morbidly obese and had been for most of his life. He lived alone, dined alone, and spent most of his time on his own. He had no male friends and had had only a handful of relationships with women, all of which had ended after a month or two. He was unable to say why. Therapy was his one social connection, but even with that, he struggled to truly connect. He looked at the floor for most of his sessions, spoke softly, and seemed to want to hide himself, despite his very visible presence. Raya spent most of her first few sessions with him gathering data. He was an only child, the son of two teachers. His father had been incredibly strict and his mother had been overly subservient. Murray caved in to whatever his father asked, while his mother stood by and watched silently. Occasionally, he would be beaten for any small transgression, such as forgetting to bring his plate to the sink. Raya reported that she had begun to sense that Murray had conflicted feelings about his mother. Raya described that though he spoke about loving her, his mouth pursed as he talked. He was furious with her, she said. One day, she knocked on my door. A lightbulb had gone off for her, she said. She had the answer as to how to help him. He was clearly stuck in anger at his mother and she could encourage him to see that. He would then be able to move forward. She announced her hypothesis about his difficulty with women. He was stuck in the oedipal phase, she said proudly. I looked at her for a few seconds, thinking of how to respond. While this could be true and Murray's issues with women could stem from unresolved Oedipal issues with his mother, it wouldn't help Raya know what to do in therapy. I couldn't help it, but "so?" slipped out of my mouth. She looked at me, stunned. I explained my reaction, realizing it had been unsuperviserly. "That may be true," I said, "but what will you do with it?" Over the next week, I mulled over my response. It reinforced what I had known for a while; that understanding Murray's difficulties, or any client's difficulties, no matter what the cause, was only part of the story. To effect change was more than insight alone. Raya's job was not only to help Murray understand his oedipal conflict. It was something more, a way of doing therapy that could help Murray feel different. It would involve a mind-body-emotion connection. Attachment theory held the answers for me to help Raya inspire change in her client.

Change from an attachment perspective

Attachment theory and change

Though Bowlby was a trained psychoanalyst, during his time, his theory was divorced from practice and remained as just that − a theory. While his empirical observations and research sparked a theoretical revolution, allowing psychology to merge with science, there was little implementation of attachment theory in clinical work. For whatever reason, clinicians were not drawn to Bowlby's work. However, over the years, this has changed. Beginning with Mary Main's work in the 1980s, psychoanalysts, and soon other psychotherapists, began reclaiming the theory (Slade, 2016). The more clinicians have tried to ascertain the essence of what promotes change in the therapy room, the more the healing power of relationships has come into focus. As has been already noted, there is now strong neurobiological evidence to show that our relationships both shape and change us. We are born with certain predispositions, such as our temperament and our inherited traits. But science has demonstrated that it is our environment, and in particular, our attachment bonds that seem to have an enormous effect on our developmental trajectory. Therefore, it now seems critical that clinicians use the attachment relationship to inform clinical practice.

But how exactly do we use the theory in practice? Throughout this book, we've examined the developmental pathway of the attachment relationship, exploring the dynamic of the caregiver–child dyad. We've seen how relationships may impact our neurobiology as well as our psychophysiology. In particular, our ability to negotiate stress seems very much impacted by the security of our attachment relationships. Our body encodes our experiences. And emotions serve a purpose. They are our ways of communicating within relationships. They help engender relationships. And they aid us in adapting to our environment. We've looked at how the effective regulation of these emotions is a crucial aspect of our well-being. Yet, we haven't explicitly delineated how attachment theory can be used to highlight goals of therapy, to formulate cases, to guide our clinical work, and ultimately to encourage change in our clients. This chapter will address these questions. We will explore how therapy is not only a science; it is an art, but one that can be studied. We will examine human connections and attachment theory in clinical practice. It should be noted that this discussion is far from exhaustive and, because of the scope of the book, only skims the surface of practicing therapy from an attachment perspective.

As explored in Chapter 1, Bowlby (1973) talked of the importance of attachment from "cradle to grave." He hypothesized that with extensive repetition, attachment bonds are ultimately encoded as "internal working models," or mental representations of our expectations for interactions in future relationships. These models are viewed as resistant to change. Research has shown that barring trauma or a significantly different relational experience, there is substantial continuity of attachment organizations across the life span (Waters, Weinfield, & Hamilton, 2000; Main, Hesse, & Kaplan, 2005). It is critical to note that disconfirming experiences, both negative AND positive, can effect changes to attachment. Change is possible, which is good news for clinicians. The question becomes, how can we achieve disconfirming experiences? In other words, how do we help our clients change?

Emotion, cognition, behaviors and change

Attachment theorists suggest that change involves both emotions and cognitions. It is not about only feeling new emotions. Nor is it about having insight into old patterns. And nor is it simply about altering behaviors. It is a combination of all three. A client undergoes disconfirming experiences in the here-and-now. Feelings and emotions, both those stored in nonverbal memory as well as explicit emotions and memories, are processed anew. However, as Tronick (2007) states, change is not only about experiencing something new, or about behaving differently. It is also about the meaning that one assigns to these novel experiences. Bringing emotions to light allows for them to be modified. With modification and new creations of meaning, a client gains a different perspective on his emotions. This process of emotion-feeling and meaning-making enables a client to integrate his experiences into new ways of being.

Emotion regulation and change

To be able to experience something new, a client must first be regulated. If a client is either hyperaroused or hypoaroused, he is unable to process anything new. Affect regulation is key to change. When a client is regulated, he is able to notice what is happening in himself. He can maintain objectivity during discourse. He is flexible and creative, feeling free to explore new ideas and experiences. His window of tolerance is wide and he can accept changes. In attachment terms, he feels safe and secure. He is able to process overwhelming feelings in more manageable doses. Thus, change necessitates a client to develop the capacity to self-regulate even when distressed. It requires clients to tolerate stress (Greenberg & Paivio, 1997; Stark, 2017).

Therapeutic relationship and change

According to attachment theory, it is only when feeling safe and secure that a client can better tolerate distress. A secure therapeutic relationship is one where a client feels safe. He feels able to be vulnerable, to let down his guard. So much of therapy is about a client's being able to open up to another human being in ways that he has never felt safe enough to do before (Greenberg & Johnson, 1988). So much of this relationship occurs outside of our awareness. A secure therapeutic relationship is a relationship that involves inter-subjectivity (Schore, 2009), or right-brain to right-brain connections. It is a connection not only between minds, but between bodies as well. It is a connection where the client "feels felt" (Siegel, 1999). Change occurs within this connection. Ultimately, it is about processing emotions and cognitions *with* another. As Diana Fosha (2002), the founder of accelerated experiential-dynamic psychotherapy (AEDP) writes, "[t]he ability to process experience, together with an understanding other, is mutative; it transforms the experi-ence, the self, and most likely the other" (p. 21). Change happens when one no longer feels unbearably alone.

Goal of attachment therapy: integration

When working from an attachment perspective, our goal for our clients is integration. Dan Siegel (2012) has written extensively about the concept of integration, particularly as it relates to attachment theory. In the late 1970s, Siegel began his career as a medical student, eager even then to integrate ideas. He was fascinated by the intersection between science and subjectivity. Following a year of travel and self-exploration, he realized that psychiatry may hold the answers he sought. However, he found his training fell short. There was little discussion of what facilitated mental well-being or even of what that was. What is more, there was not much collaboration between the many different fields of thought. This fueled him on. He sought to under-stand what promoted healing. Siegel continued his studies, doing a research training fellowship. He used this time to try to merge and synthesize the many disparate camps concerning the human condition. He arranged a study group of 40 scientists from various academic departments to examine the relationship between the mind and the brain. A definition of the brain proved to be no problem at all. But there was a complete lack of agreement when it came to defining the mind. Something that was seemingly simple proved to be not simple at all. What is a mind? Siegel set to work to explore this fur-ther. He stated that "[a] core aspect of the mind can be defined as an embo-died and relational process that regulates the flow of energy and information" (Siegel, 2012, p. xxvi). Our thoughts, emotions, and other mental activities are generated by this flow of energy. It was a definition that most of Siegel's colleagues agreed upon, despite their varying backgrounds. And thus, the field of interpersonal neurobiology came into being, a field that created a unified approach to understanding the mind and optimal mental well-being. A healthy mind was determined to be a mind that was integrated (Siegel, 2010a; Siegel, 2012).

The definition of integration

Integration, a key principle of interpersonal neurobiology, is defined as the linking of different parts of a system. It is the joining, and not the merging, of separate, differentiated areas. Thus, the goal in therapy is to support differentiation of our different parts of ourselves and to enable these differentiated parts to interact and link together. With integration comes adaptiveness, emotional balance, a sense of coherence, and relational health and well-being. In fact, integration is viewed as the underlying mechanism of emotion regulation. It is seen as scaffolding both self- and interactive regulation. According to attachment theorists, the capacity for integration is developed within relationships. A developmental phenomenon, it involves an interaction between our internal neurophysiological activities and our external environment, and in particular, our relationships. In fact, the purpose of the attachment bond can be seen as enabling the adaptive regulation of stress and fear and the internalization of these regulatory processes leads to integration.

Vertical integration

Vertical integration involves the integration of the neocortex, the limbic system, and the brain stem (see Figure 11.1). Our thoughts, emotions, gut reactions, and instinctual responses work together to form a cohesive and

THE TRIUNE BRAIN

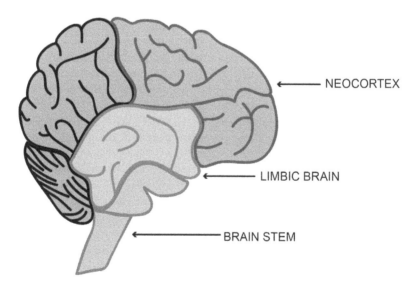

— NEOCORTEX

— LIMBIC BRAIN

— BRAIN STEM

Figure 11.1 Triune brain, drawn by Toni Mandelbaum (2020), digitized by Chloe Amen
© Toni Mandelbaum

coherent self-state. A "cortical override" process may occur where our neocortex monitors our limbic system and our brain stem, thereby inhibiting impulses, calming strong reactions, and promoting effective self-regulation. When operating from a fully integrated state, we are unlikely to act before thinking, except in cases when acting without thinking is necessary to survival. Not only does our neocortex oversee our limbic system and brain stem, but the activities in these "lower" areas influence our neocortical functioning. With vertical integration, emotions that have remained outside of our consciousness are brought into our awareness. Our physiological reactions come to the forefront as well. In noticing a bodily felt sensation and symbolizing it, we gain more access to our emotional and bodily feelings. We work towards identifying triggers and understanding our perceptions and bodily felt senses. This enables us to synthesize and integrate our emotions and cognitions, thereby creating new meanings. Our brain is better coordinated and we regulate ourselves, functioning as a whole (Siegel, 2012).

Studies support that vertical integration helps with effective self-regulation. For instance, researchers have found that when individuals verbally label their affect while viewing an image there is less amygdala activity in comparison to when these individuals perceptually process that image. What is more, there is more activity in the right ventrolateral prefrontal cortex (RVLPFC) while individuals are linguistically, and not perceptually processing the image. The RVLPFC is an area of the brain that is involved with representative processing of emotions as well as with top-down inhibition. Lastly, researchers found an inverse relationship between RVLPFC activity and amygdala activity during affect labeling. These results suggest that in naming our emotions, we are "taming" them. Our amygdalae activity seems to be inhibited by the activity of our right ventrolateral prefrontal cortices. It seems that putting feelings into words may help regulate our affect (Lieberman et al., 2007).

In therapy, helping a client achieve vertical integration can involve a top-down or a bottom-up approach. In fact, it seems most effective for therapists to work with a combination of approaches, using the brain, emotions, and bodily reactions. Clinicians aid clients to become more aware of their input from their bodies, their limbic areas, and their brainstems. Therapists encourage clients to "name and tame" their emotions. They also facilitate a client's capacity to have a deep, visceral experience, one where emotions and psychophysiological reactions are brought into the therapy room. For instance, practicing mindful breathing while expressing feelings helps a client better regulate himself. Creating awareness of moment-to-moment experiences aid us in moving towards integration.

Horizontal integration

Horizontal integration involves integration between the right and left hemispheres of the brain. Recall (Chapter 10), the right brain is dominant in conveying and accepting nonverbal signals. It is also more involved with the bodily stress response, in the keeping of autobiographical memories, and in implicit, emotional processes. In other words, the right hemisphere is dominant in somatic,

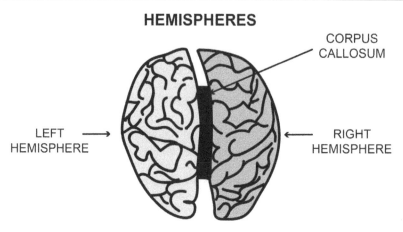

Figure 11.2 Hemispheres, drawn by Toni Mandelbaum (2020), digitized by Chloe Amen © Toni Mandelbaum

autobiographical, and emotional activities. The left hemisphere processes more linearly and more literally than the right hemisphere. It tends to favor logic and is linguistically focused. As opposed to the autobiographical memory bent of the right hemisphere, the left hemisphere aids more in factual memories. With horizontal integration comes holistic feelings, memories, reasoning, imaginings, and mental activities. A horizontally integrated individual feels what his body is communicating and has a logical perspective on his surroundings. Someone with bilateral integration can flexibly alternate between the two hemispheres, depending on what is needed in the moment. For instance, should a situation demand analytic reasoning, a horizontally integrated individual can lean more heavily on his left hemispheric functioning to adapt to this environmental need. Alternatively, should a situation require holistic processing or creative, intuitive feelings to be more present, a horizontally integrated individual can favor his right hemispheric functioning. In terms of attachment, it should be noted that horizontal integration enables an individual to produce coherent narratives. This, as the Adult Attachment Interview (Chapter 3) indicates, is the telltale sign of attachment security. Thus, bilateral integration can help reach attachment security.

Impaired integration

If integration involves the achieving of an adaptive, self-regulatory state, impairments to integration cause the opposite. With impaired integration, compromised abilities to regulate the self ensue and chaos and/or rigidity may result. To understand this better, it is helpful to explore integration in the context of windows of tolerance. In general, integration can only occur when we are within our window of tolerance (see Chapter 10).

WINDOW OF TOLERANCE

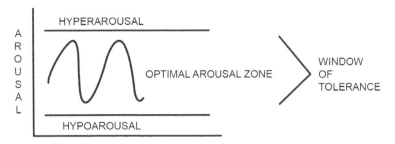

Figure 11.3 Window of tolerance, adapted from Ogden (2015), drawn by Toni Mandelbaum (2020), digitized by Chloe Amen © Toni Mandelbaum

Think back to Porges' polyvagal theory (Chapter 7). When we feel safe, our social engagement system is activated. Our ventral vagal allows us to inhibit, regulate, or calm our sympathetic nervous system. We can engage others and we are within our window of tolerance. However, when we are too activated to engage our social engagement system, our sympathetic nervous system may kick in and we enter fight-or-flight mode. We are outside our window of tolerance in that we are hyperaroused and we cannot focus on integrating ourselves. An alternate reaction occurs when we are so overwhelmed by stress or trauma that we do a "dorsal dive," activating the dorsal vagal complex. We become hypoaroused. Our blood pressure drops, our hearts slow, and we are rendered immobile.

When we are outside of our window of tolerance, and we are either hypo- or hyperaroused, we have difficulty maintaining a sense of coherence. When we are hyperaroused, we can become reactive or disorganized. We may easily fly into a rage or become overwhelmed with fear. Our amygdalas go into overdrive, and we may be "emotionally hijacked" (Goleman, 1995). We are likely to act irrationally and are unable to use our thoughts to contain our emotions. Our Broca's area, the area of the brain responsible for speech, can become inhibited and we have difficulty expressing ourselves (Cozolino, 2016). In other words, there is chaos. On the other hand, when we are hypoaroused, we may become rigid or defensive. We may be inflexible in our thinking. We are not free to adaptively respond to stressful situations.

It should be noted that we may have different windows of tolerance for different states of mind. For instance, Paul had a narrow window of tolerance for anger because during his childhood, anger was hardly ever expressed. When it was expressed, it was sudden and explosive. There was no repair process to speak of; anger felt dangerous. Paul began attending therapy because he was conflict avoidant and it was causing trouble in his relationship with his partner Penny. Paul would stonewall Penny whenever they had a slight disagreement.

Penny was very comfortable with anger. However, her window of tolerance was narrow for perceived rejection. The two were constantly triggering each other. When Paul would stonewall Penny, she would feel rejected. She would express anger at being rejected and Paul would withdraw even more. Therapy involved helping Paul to widen his window of tolerance for anger and aiding Penny to widen her window of tolerance for feeling rejected. Encouraging fluid integration between the two involved them both being able to flexibly shift between anger and the sadness associated with rejection and to maintain an empathic connection while doing so. This interpersonal integration promoted the effective self-regulation of both partners.

Attachment and integration

A confluence of factors may impact an individual's ability to attain integration. Genetic causes and environmental factors may undermine the process. From an interpersonal neurobiological perspective, the attachment relationship is viewed as essential to the activation and growth of integration in the brain as well as to emotion regulation. In other words, neurobiological and emotion regulatory integration is nurtured when differentiated individuals are linked with one another in compassionate and caring secure attachment relationships. As Siegel (2012) writes, "[i]ntegrative relationships cultivate integrative brains" (pp. 27-4). And integrative brains promote secure attachment relationships.

It follows that ruptures in relationships can lead to impaired integration. In fact, each insecure attachment strategy can be seen as a degree of integrative failure, with mild failure at one end of the spectrum and profound integrative failure at the other end, as with disorganized/unresolved attachment. Those with dismissing states of mind with respect to attachment[1] tend to be excessively differentiated, or "compulsively self-reliant" (Bowlby, 1969/1982). As discussed in Chapter 3, these individuals have difficulty integrating themselves within relationships. They tend to become rigid in their strategies for negotiating stressors. In contrast, those who are preoccupied in their attachment states of mind may become overly linked with others and may develop impaired differentiation. Their strategies for negotiating stressors may appear chaotic, where their attachment systems become excessively activated and they seem overly aroused. These individuals can also become rigid, where they become stuck in the chaos. Those with unresolved states of mind tend to utilize both chaotic and rigid strategies, as they are unable to formulate an organized strategy of response. Oftentimes, this can lead to dissociation which can be viewed as a severe lack of integration (Siegel, 2012; Ogden & Fisher, 2015).

The main goal of therapy from an attachment perspective is to promote integration (Siegel, 2012). Attuning to our clients encourages emotion regulation and with this, a flexible flow of energy results. Response flexibility is engendered, bounding the chaos and moving away from rigidity. Clients are helped to respond to situations appropriately. They create structure for their emotions in overwhelming situations, and deepen emotional experiences when it behooves them to do so. They respond flexibly. In scaffolding these varying responses, we widen our clients' windows of tolerance. Enabling "being" with an experience before "doing" is fostered within a secure therapeutic relationship. In this way, a client moves towards an integrated, healthy, and whole self.

Phases of therapy from an attachment perspective

How do we work towards integration? How do we target our interventions? If we are to do so, it is helpful to first assess a client for impaired integration and then to "diagnose" where a client may have impaired integration. What are the client's attachment strategies? Where is a client rigid in his responses to distress? Where is he chaotic in his strategies to negotiate stressors? Is he undifferentiated or does he seem to have his own sense of identity, as an individual with a secure state of mind with respect to attachment would have? Is he able to connect with others in meaningful ways? These are all questions that should be asked in order to ascertain a client's level of integration.

Therapy occurs in phases. Initially, there is an engagement phase, which involves gathering data about and assessing a client and then formulating a case to figure out where to intervene. At the same time, the clinician and client are forming a relationship. The clinician tailors her interactions to sensitively meet the specific needs of each client. A dismissing client will require different boundaries to a preoccupied client. A secure client will be able to tolerate much more initially in comparison to an unresolved client. The engagement phase leads into a "working" phase, during which clinical interventions occur. The last phase is the termination phase, where treatment winds down (Daly & Mallinckrodt, 2009). In this chapter, we'll focus on the initial phase of therapy, including data gathering and case formulation. The next chapter will explore the "working" phase from the perspective of the clinician. Additionally, the termination phase will be briefly covered.

Assessment

Engagement phase

We start by getting to know who our client is. Attachment theorists have always viewed the environment as playing a critical role in development. Think back to Chapter 1 where Bowlby's theory differed from the prevailing psychoanalytic theory at the time in many ways, including his belief that "real-life experiences – the way parents treat a child – is of key importance in determining development" (Karen, 1994, p. 46). He wholly believed that context mattered. From the beginning, attachment theory was a systemic theory, where an individual's inner experiences were seen as being organized by dynamic transactions and where the individual was seen as continually growing and adapting within his context. This view carries through until today. As we have seen, attachment strategies emerge from early dyadic experiences. But that is not the full picture. In fact, an individual's attachment strategies are affected by the interaction of a confluence of factors, such as genetic make-up, neurobiological profile, temperament, the external environment and in particular the stressors of the external environment, culture, gender, socioeconomic status, and relationship status. Changes in relationships in an individual's environment or experiencing trauma or loss will also likely have an impact on an individual's attachment strategy. As Bowlby suggested, though internal working models of attachment tend to remain stable, they can be revised and updated with changes in major life circumstances.

As a social worker by training, I have been schooled in looking at the person-in-environment. Thus, in assessing a client, I feel that both intrapsychic factors and extrapsychic factors are at play. The brain, the mind, the body, and the environment all factor into the development of our regulatory abilities, our attachment strategies, and our general well-being. In the social work field, assessment can be understood as a "form of logical analysis, where a practitioner comes to know his or her case through acknowledgment of the client's own story, interpreted through the screen of an available knowledge base that is relevant to the case situation" (Meyer, 1993, p. 17). We can only know a client's whole story by taking his intrapsychic functioning, his attachment history, and his unique context into account.

Data gathering from an attachment perspective

1 Client in context: balancing the unique with the general

A. CULTURE

Is attachment a purely Western construct? Can we apply attachment classifications to other cultures? These questions have been debated since attachment theory's inception. There are those theorists who ascribe to the universality hypothesis, which states that all infants will form attachment bonds to one or more particular caregivers. They argue that Ainsworth herself formulated the concept of maternal sensitivity and attachment classifications while studying infants in Uganda and that these constructs held true through ample repetitions of the Strange Situation study (Mesman, Van IJzendoorn, & Sagi-Schwartz, 2016). On the other hand, there are others who vehemently disagree with this, viewing attachment security and insecurity as a purely Western concept that is not applicable to other cultures. They point out that most attachment research has been conducted in Western cultures and furthermore, the notions of attachment security itself is deeply intertwined with Western values (Wei, Russell, Mallinckrodt, & Zakalik, 2004; Wang & Mallinckrodt, 2006; Mesman et al., 2016).

To date, the limited cross-cultural attachment research has supported the universality of attachment (Mesman et al., 2016). However, as clinicians, it is critical that we are aware that though the attachment bond may be a universal phenomenon, there are many different cultural values at play. Just as with our emotions (see Chapter 8), the little research that exists seems to support the universality of attachment bonds, but with different cultural displays. For instance, in Japan, emotional constraint is encouraged, and thus, may not be a sign of an avoidant attachment. Collectivist values are lauded and dependency is fostered, resulting in what could be construed as ambivalent attachment. The same is true in Taiwan, where identity is very much associated with belonging to a group or being part of a relationship and direct expression of feelings and emotions is discouraged, viewed as being immature. These ways of being may appear to be manifestations of insecure attachments, but within context, are very normative ways of being. It is critical that we assess our clients' attachments from a culturally-specific standpoint (Wang & Mallinckrodt, 2006).

Not only is it important to be aware of the context of our clients' attachments, but we must also acknowledge that not all cultures are subject to the same experiences in the same environments. For instance, in Wei's study (Wei et al., 2004), different ethnic groups reported different levels of attachment anxiety and avoidance. African Americans and Asian Americans reported more attachment avoidance in comparison to the Caucasian subjects, while Asian Americans and Hispanic Americans reported greater attachment anxiety in comparison to the Caucasian subjects. As we cannot assume that all ethnic groups share similar experiences of the world, we must do as the old social work adage suggests: start where the client is. Research supports that therapeutic interventions that hone in on specific cultural groups are four times more likely to succeed than interventions that group cultures together (Griner & Smith, 2006). It seems evident that we must get to know our clients within their cultural contexts.

B. GENDER

Though males and females may have different communication styles, attachment researchers note that neither gender falls disproportionately into any attachment category (Mikulincer & Shaver, 2007). In terms of brain development, studies show that boys develop white matter more rapidly than girls do. Furthermore, adolescent girls tend to have better language abilities in comparison to adolescent boys. Females' amygdalae generally develop 18 months earlier than those of their male counterparts. This is true of the hippocampus as well. Thus, in terms of fostering attachment relationships with teenage boys, it is important to take into account that boys may physiologically experience emotion differently to girls and often it may be more difficult for them to express themselves compared to teenage girls simply because of their neurophysiology (Jensen & Nutt, 2015). Though little research thus far has focused on attachment and transgender or gender-nonconforming people, there is evidence to suggest that attachment security is associated with positive transgender identity, whereas attachment insecurity is related to shame with regard to gender identity (Amodeo, Vitelli, Scandura, Picariello, & Valerio, 2015). Clinicians should note that attachment security can serve as a protective mechanism in negotiating gender identity.

C. SEXUALITY

Research suggests that attachment processes in same-sex couples largely correspond with heterosexual couples, where attachment insecurity in both partners is associated with less positive relationship experiences (Mohr, Selterman, & Fassinger, 2013). In western society, though attachment processes may be similar for stigmatized groups, including gay and lesbian individuals, environmental factors often differ. There is societal pressure to suppress certain identities, values, or beliefs. Shame and feelings of unworthiness can accompany this external stress and lack of acceptance. Studies find that attachment security can serve to buffer an individual against external pressures. For instance, it has been found that attachment security is linked with feeling comfortable with the disclosure of sexual orientation (Mikulincer & Shaver, 2007). Thus, as always, clinicians should strive to provide the safety and security necessary to form secure relationships.

D. TEMPERAMENT

There has been an ongoing debate between the two most oft accepted developmental frameworks explaining individual differences in socioemotional functioning and personality development: attachment and temperament. Temperament is defined as "stable patterns of and predispositions toward emotional and behavioral responses that are assumed to be at least partially influenced by genetic mechanisms" (Compas, Connor, Saltzman, Thomsen, & Wadsworth, 1999, p. 238). In contrast to attachment theorists, temperament researchers believe that our traits are the result of neurophysiological mechanisms, and not the result of relational interactions. It should be noted that they do believe some neurophysiological mechanisms can be modified by environmental factors. Because temperament theorists purport that responsivity and reactivity to stimuli is shaped by our temperaments, those in the temperament camp believe that it is mostly an infant's temperament that explains his reactions in Ainsworth's Strange Situation; not his attachment style. For instance, they purport that infants who are avoidantly attached may have inhibited temperaments, exhibiting higher levels of arousal in response to novel and/or stressful stimuli which leads to withdrawal behaviors. Because of this, they tend to be more reactive. Therefore, they state, the infants' behaviors are not necessarily due to attachment insecurity. Their temperaments must be factored into the equation. While attachment theorists disagree with the notion that attachment security or insecurity is only a matter of a child's temperament, they don't disagree with the idea that temperament may influence and affect a caregiver's sensitivity to her child, which can then impact attachment security. In fact, research supports that usually there is an interaction between temperament and attachment style. In one study, it was found that inhibited toddlers had elevated levels of cortisol (stress hormone) when approached by a clown only when in insecure attachment relationships. Inhibited toddlers in secure relationships did not have increased levels of cortisol when approached by a clown. As clinicians, it is critical that we factor in our clients' temperaments and acknowledge that this can play a part in our clients' reactivity. It is also critical that we understand just how much difference a secure relationship makes in enabling our clients to better regulate themselves (Nachmias et al., 1996; Bradley, 2000; Mikulincer & Shaver, 2007; Vaughn & Bost, 2016).

E. SOCIO-ECONOMIC STATUS

Poverty is rampant, with close to 22 percent of American children living with material deprivation (Tough, 2012). This deprivation, whether lack of adequate nutrition, lack of suitable learning materials in the home, or lack of adequate housing, presents significant obstacles to positive outcomes for many children. Beyond the material deprivation is the often damaging effect of the chronic stress that can occur with poverty. Researchers such as Evans and Kim (2012) document that the overwhelming stress caused by poverty is the mediating link between early-life socioeconomic status (SES) and the negative impact on later functioning. In fact, those growing up in poverty are much more likely to suffer physical and psychological disorders (Tough, 2012). For instance, Isaacs (2012) found, in terms of school readiness, that children from low-income families, in comparison to those from moderate or high income families, do worse on measures of non-cognitive skills such as learning-related behaviors (i.e., paying attention) and externalizing behaviors (i.e., disrupting others). Reeves and colleagues (Reeves, Venator, & Howard, 2014) reported that levels of persistence and self-control correlate with family income, where the more family income there is, the greater the level of persistence and of self-control. This is largely related to the stress of living in poverty. Experiencing chronic stress has been shown to negatively affect attention, speed of information processing, working memory, episodic memory, and executive functioning. As has been stated (Chapter 7), attachment security can serve to buffer against the devastating effects of stress. As clinicians, we must see our clients in context and then work towards creating a buffer against the environmental stressors they face.

F. PSYCHOPATHOLOGY AND ATTACHMENT STYLES

What is psychopathology? Psychopathology can be seen as a consequence of deficits in affect regulatory abilities (Bradley, 2000). Though we all feel emotions, a distinguishing feature for those who have mental disorders is difficulty with regulating certain emotions. Not only do individuals with mental disorders have trouble down-regulating negative emotions, but they tend to have difficulty with up-regulating, sustaining, or simply responding to positive emotions. Because of this, a person can get stuck outside his window of tolerance and experience prolonged periods of what may feel like unbearable negative emotions. For instance, there is neurobiological evidence that individuals with anxiety disorders exhibit deficits in not only paying attention to threatening stimuli, but in disengaging from that threatening stimuli when necessary. Studies found reduced activation in the dorsolateral prefrontal cortexes of those diagnosed with anxiety disorders. This can lead to less effective regulation of attention and, together with increased sensitivity in the brain stem and limbic system, can result in hyper-focusing on distressing stimuli (Johnstone & Walter, 2014; Joormann & Siemer, 2014).

Research has shown that there are many converging processes that can lead to psychopathology, including genetic predispositional vulnerabilities, neurobiology, and surrounding environmental factors (Sroufe, 2005). Where does attachment fit in? Fosha (2009) "understands psychopathology as resulting from the individual's unwilled and unwanted aloneness in the face of overwhelming emotions" (p. 182). Experiencing prolonged distress without the safety of a secure attachment relationship can be devastating. Research bears this out. Though there is no direct correlation between any specific psychopathology and patterns of attachment, insecure attachment styles are seen as risk factors for mental disorders (Mikulincer & Shaver, 2007). As mentioned in Chapter 7, the attachment system itself has been viewed as a distress regulatory system. Recall that researchers suggest that insecure attachment patterns may simply be "failed coping," or responses to stress, while secure attachment patterns may represent adaptive coping responses to stress (Spangler and Grossman, 1993; Gunnar et al., 1996). Failed coping often leads to dysregulated affect, while adaptive coping tends to lead to regulated affect. Because of this link between attachment strategies and affect regulation, attachment theorists view unavailable, inconsistent, or rejecting caregiving and attachment insecurity as one of the potential vulnerabilities leading to developing psychopathology, or prolonged "failed" affect regulation. An insecurely attached individual's negative expectations of self and others as well as his maladaptive coping strategies often preclude him from effectively managing his affective experiences. He is vulnerable to experiencing overwhelming stress which can lead to mental disorder. In contrast, attachment security has been shown to serve as a buffer against developing psychopathology. A secure individual's positive views of self and others as well as his more flexible regulatory abilities serve as protective factors. Thus, as clinicians, we can strive to form secure relationships to help our clients who struggle with psychopathology.

Part of our assessments as clinicians can involve diagnosing psychopathology. It is helpful to understand that the attachment literature has noted a connection between attachment strategies and psychopathology in four different categories of mental disorders: affective disorders, posttraumatic stress disorder (PTSD), eating disorders, and personality disorders. Though this is far from exhaustive, as a complete list would be beyond the scope of this book, this section will focus on these four areas.

Affective disorders   Within the adult attachment literature, the most extensively researched affective disorders are anxiety and depression. Very briefly, anxiety disorders refer to feelings of excessive fear or anxiety. Thirty percent of adults will suffer from an anxiety disorder at some point in their lives. Depression results in sadness and/or loss of interest in once pleasurable activities (American Psychiatric Association, 2013; see DSM-V for a more in-depth definition). Overall, research supports a consistent link between attachment anxiety, including preoccupied attachment, and both anxiety disorders and depression. In general, increased attachment anxiety is associated with more symptoms of anxiety and depression. The linkage is not quite as clear with attachment avoidance, but half the available studies suggest that avoidant individuals are more likely to experience depression and anxiety than are those who are securely attached. Fearful attachment, in comparison to avoidant attachment, is more clearly associated with depression and anxiety disorders. While attachment insecurity is a risk factor, attachment security has been shown to be a protective factor against experiencing these affective disorders (Mikulincer & Shaver, 2007; Gillath, Karantzas, & Fraley, 2016).

Posttraumatic stress disorder (PTSD)   PTSD is a disorder occurring in individuals who have witnessed or experienced traumatic events, including accidents, natural disasters, war, rape, abuse, or terroristic acts. It is characterized by repeated reliving of the event with unwanted flashbacks or nightmares (intrusion). The individual can feel detached or dissociated from others (avoidance). He may be easily triggered and react strongly to minor occurrences (American Psychiatric Association, 2013; see DSM-V for a more in-depth definition). Research into attachment in adults and PTSD has gained much momentum within the past few years. By definition, a traumatic experience shakes the foundations of an individual's perceived security and safety, thereby affecting the attachment system. Attachment security has been found to serve as a buffer against the devastating impact of traumatic experiences, while attachment insecurity serves as a risk factor to those undergoing trauma and developing PTSD. Research shows that anxious attachment is linked to intrusive responses, while avoidant attachment has been related to denying trauma and general avoidance responses (Mikulincer & Shaver, 2007; Gillath et al., 2016). Disorganized attachment in infancy is a further risk factor to developing later dissociation and disturbance (Sroufe, 2005).

Eating disorders   Individuals with eating disorders have disturbed eating behaviors and thoughts and emotions related to eating. They tend to be overly focused on food and their weight. Anorexia nervosa is diagnosed when individuals are at least 15% less than what is considered a healthy body weight. They fear being overweight, severely limit their food intake, and have body dysmorphia. Bulimia nervosa is diagnosed when clients binge eat often, consuming vast quantities of food in short amounts of time. They then often will purge, self-inducing vomiting. This cycle occurs frequently. Often, they maintain a normal weight and may even be overweight. Binge eating disorder occurs when individuals binge, eating large amounts of food in short periods of time, and lack control during the binge period. Unlike with bulimia nervosa, those with binge eating disorder do not try to rid themselves of the food (American Psychiatric Association, 2013; see DSM-V for more comprehensive definitions). In general, studies have found that attachment insecurity is positively associated with eating disorders. In particular, those with anorexia nervosa tend to be more avoidantly attached, while those with bulimic behaviors tend to be more anxiously attached (Mikulincer & Shaver, 2007; Gillath et al., 2016).

Personality disorders   Personality disorders are characterized by ways of thinking, feeling, and behaving that deviates from the cultural norm, causes distress and problems in interpersonal relationships, and are persistent and pervasive from the age of 18 years onwards. Importantly, personality disorders involve difficulties with emotional regulation.

There are different types of personality disorders. A great deal of research has found associations between attachment anxiety, including preoccupied states of mind, and the Cluster B personality disorders, such as borderline personality disorder (characterized by a pervasive pattern of instability in close relationships, self-image, and affects, as well as impulsivity), histrionic personality disorders (characterized by patterns of attention seeking behavior and excessive emotion), and narcissistic personality disorders (characterized by a pattern of needing admiration from others coupled with a lack of empathy for others). Additionally, attachment anxiety, including preoccupied states of mind, are correlated with Cluster C personality disorders, including dependent personality disorders (characterized by needing to be taken care of and compliant, clingy behavior), avoidant personality disorders (characterized by patterns of excessive shyness, low self-esteem, and intense sensitivity to criticism), and obsessive-compulsive personality disorders (characterized by patterns of intense focus on orderliness, control, and perfection). Attachment avoidance, including dismissing states of mind, have been associated with the Cluster A personality disorders, including schizoid personality disorder (characterized by detachment in interpersonal relationships and little emotional expression, as well as less investment in how others perceive them), paranoid personality disorder (characterized by patterns of suspicion of others and avoidance of closeness because of this), and schizotypal personality disorder (characterized by discomfort with close relationships and having distorted thinking and odd behavior) (Mikulincer & Shaver, 2007; American Psychiatric Association, 2013; Gillath et al., 2016).

2 Measures of attachment

Brief Adult Attachment Interview (mentioned in Chapter 3), Who-To, and the ECR-S (mentioned in Chapter 4) or any of these measures are not diagnostic tools. They are research instruments that can be used as assessments of attachment styles. They are not and should not be used as a substitute in diag-nosing using the Diagnostic and Statistical Manual of Mental Disorders (DSM) (Berant & Obegi, 2009). However, they can be used to gather information about our clients for the purposes of assessment.

Case formulation from an attachment perspective

Emotions and strategies serve a purpose

In thinking about a client and formulating an appropriate intervention, it is helpful to examine the purpose emotions and strategies may be serving. Most times, there is a purpose that the impaired integration is serving. For instance, secondary emotions are hiding primary emotions as it has been safer to express the secondary emotion as opposed to the primary emotion (see Chapter 8 for definitions of primary and secondary emotions). A partner expresses anger to hide his enormous feelings of shame. Anger is more acceptable to him, whereas the expression of shame would render him overwhelmingly vulnerable. Thus, his secondary emotion of anger serves to protect him from having to face his shame. However, his secondary emotion is also getting him into trouble. He continually alienates his partner because he gets angry so much of the time.

Emotions and strategies may have been adaptive at one time

Shame (see Chapter 8) is an example of a strategy that may be serving a pur-pose. Though it may be maladaptive at present, it may have been adaptive during childhood. Core shame often leads to impaired integration. While there is appropriate shame that helps a child be socialized (i.e., a mother saying "don't pick your nose in public" when she catches her two-year-old sticking her finger up her nose), there is also core shame, where a caregiver breaks the attunement with her child without fostering appropriate repair. In these cases, a child's sympathetic exploration system is activated and he feels excited to dis-cover the world. His wonder at drawing on the wall with a bright orange crayon quickly turns to shame when his mother yells at him and tells him he is bad. His parasympathetic system is activated. Without the necessary repair, he may come to internalize this rapid shift between sympathetic and para-sympathetic systems as his being unlovable and worthless in general. According to attachment theory, his survival depends on being unconditionally loved, but in that moment he may instead feel shunned, rejected, and perhaps acute pain. To continue to flout his caregiver's wishes is dangerous. Thus, internalizing and experiencing shame may actually help the child to maintain proximity to his parent and therefore, may serve a purpose at the time. "I am bad" is a safer conclusion than "My mom may reject me at any moment" or "I am angry at my mom for making me feel bad." In this way, the child internalizes his experiences and refrains from challenging a caregiver who likely can't handle it and who may react to challenge with further rejection. It is therefore better for the child to internalize shame and not to externally react, thus ensuring the caregiver will stay involved in his care. Over time, negative experiences like this may be encoded as visceral, emotional memories and the child may come to expect negative reactions like this in other relational encounters. In fact, this negative feeling may ironically feel safe and any attempts at feeling better may be destabilizing. Holding onto this self-negation may be a way to hold onto the hope that at some point in time, if he just feels bad for long enough, his caregiver will actually begin to love and accept him. This dynamic may transfer to future relationships, and partners either are viewed as potential rejecters or as duped if they actually love the individual. "He doesn't see the real me," is a conclusion often reached in those with intense shame. In the meantime, the feelings of being unlovable can lead to insecure attachment patterns. Again, these can be viewed as adaptive strategies at the time. They protect the individual from rejection and ensure survival. However, shame that lasts through a lifetime may become maladaptive if not adequately addressed. Emotion regulation becomes compromised and integration is impaired (Beebe & Lachmann, 2002; Slade, 2004; Siegel, 2012; Cozolino & Davis, 2017; Stark, 2017).

Case formulation based on maladaptive strategies

In the late 1990s, Mardi Horowitz (1997) proposed a way of formulating cases from a psychodynamic perspective. I have found that his formulation, with some modification, can be utilized when doing therapy from an attachment perspective. Horowitz wrote of the defensive compromises individuals develop to shield themselves from their unconscious conflicts and fears. He presented the following format (p. 39):

Presenting symptoms *"Problematic compromise"*	*"Quasi-adaptive compromise"*
"Dreaded state"	"Desired state"

We can adapt this to an attachment perspective. By viewing attachment strategies as adaptive for a time and as serving a purpose, we can understand a case with the following format:

Quadrant of case formulation

Presenting symptoms (problematic behavior preventing connection)	Insecure attachment strategy (adaptive strategy during childhood, but now maladaptive)
Dreaded attachment state (i.e. rejection, isolation)	Desired attachment state (i.e. connection)

The upper right-hand corner displays the presenting problems a client may be having. For example, Lucy is a 39-year-old, single woman who is desperately trying to date. She keeps dating men who lie to her or cheat on her. She is consequently very anxious about the dating process, almost to the point of being unable to get herself to date for fear of repeating her pattern, which she inevitably does. The upper left-hand corner of the quadrant is for the maladaptive strategy, or in attachment terms, the insecure attachment strategy. Lucy is insecurely attached and presents with a preoccupied state of mind with respect to attachment. She is chaotic in her attempts to manage her distress, is easily overwhelmed, and senses rejection at the slightest hint of anything negative. When she senses this rejection, she becomes smothering to her partner of the moment. She unwittingly chooses men who are unavailable and rejecting. This perpetuates her maladaptive strategy, a strategy that worked well with her rejecting mother when she was a child. Her mother demanded complete adulation and Lucy provided that by suppressing her own attachment needs. Lucy's dreaded state of rejection belongs in the lower left-hand corner of the quadrant. Ultimately, what she truly fears is that she is unlovable. This is not in her conscious awareness, but it propels her to date men who don't love her, thereby confirming her worst fear. Lucy's desired attachment state belongs in the lower right-hand corner. She is craving love and connection, though it eludes her in every relationship.

The dreaded state can be understood as a dissociated or disowned emotional experience. These emotions simply have been too overwhelming to experience and thus, the client has developed defensive adaptations to keep these feelings, such as helplessness, hurt, and intense sadness, at bay. Growing up, it may have been easier to blame the self and disown any anger at a parent in order to preserve the attachment relationship. A therapist can use the quadrant to assess for disowned states and to formulate a plan to allow for integration.

Client's tasks in therapy from an attachment perspective

A client comes into therapy because she is in pain. Her strategies for negotiating distress are no longer working. She needs to improve her emotion-regulation strategies so that she can more adaptively respond to stressors. She needs to be vulnerable, to accept fallibility, and to re-own her uncomfortable, dissociated emotions and experiences. She needs to be strong in order to be vulnerable. Strength comes from feeling secure and feeling loved. Self-acceptance is a byproduct of attachment security and a huge part of therapy is promoting the acceptance of oneself using the therapeutic relationship to do so. A central tenet of Gestalt therapy is as Beisser (1970) writes, "change occurs when one becomes what he is, not when he tries to become what he is not." Therapy from an attachment perspective embraces this concept. A client can only explore, examine, and accept herself if she feels safe and is operating within her window of tolerance. Only when she feels secure enough can she let go of the maladaptive, compromised strategies. Thus, it is from this secure base that exploration and change can occur.

Part of a client's feeling safe involves recognizing her triggers. She may come to realize that she is neurocepting danger when there isn't any in the present. Her perception may be based on past experiences, which have been encoded and because of this, may have become an automatic reaction. Recall that our brains have two different processing speeds. Our primitive, nonverbal, implicit processing occurs quickly. Our more conscious, slower systems responsible for language and abstract thought are processed more slowly. In fact, there may be as much as a half a second difference between the two. This difference may explain why a client may repeat unhelpful patterns again and again. She has learned and oftentimes unconsciously encoded implicit ways of being that belie rational thought. It has been shown that 90% of input to the neocortex is from internal processing and not from the external world. Thus, a client may be acting before even realizing why she is acting. Her actions may be solely based on patterns developed in the past (Cozolino, 2016). Attachment strategies in particular fall into this pattern, where internal working models often dictate how a client acts and reacts in relationships. This can be in direct opposition to the stimuli encountered in the present. In order to achieve integration, essentially, a client needs to "unlearn" her maladaptive strategies and learn new ways of being. Psychotherapy is just that: it provides the opportunity to "unlearn" old patterns and to "restory" existing narratives based on new experiences. Recall the adage "neurons that fire together, wire together." With practice in therapy, the pathways in brains increasingly "fire together" and therefore "rewire together." This promotes change.

Client's obstacles to change from an attachment perspective

"Unlearning" can be difficult and scary. Though we all have a push towards health and integration, we also have a tendency to hold on to the safety and security of what is familiar, even if it is maladaptive, dysfunctional, or self-destructive. A client's resistance to change is often due to fear. Additionally, the notion of change is filled with the loss of what may have been if change had occurred sooner. A client must accept and grieve what has been lost if she is to move forward. Additionally, a lot of reactions occur outside of our awareness. For instance, the amygdala is processing information so quickly, often way before it is consciously registered. Attachment patterns kick in based on past experience and not always based on what is happening in the here and now. Thus, the wish to change may conflict with patterns of interaction that have been in operation for close to a lifetime. Thinking of the quadrant of case formulation, the maladaptive strategies are often firmly in place, outside of conscious awareness. Not only are they entrenched, but they are serving a purpose. These strategies have been developed in an attempt to negotiate stressors that feel unmanageable as well as to maintain proximity to an unreliable caregiver. A client may hold on to maladaptive strategies because she worries that her worst fears will happen if she lets go of these strategies. Opting to change and use an unproven strategy may seem overwhelmingly risky and therefore, a client will often stubbornly cling to a way of being that is clearly making her unhappy. Ultimately, she must come to understand that the risk is worth the pain. She must realize that, though the maladaptive strategies were once upon a time adaptive, they aren't adaptive now. For example, in the past, shutting down and stifling any emotion worked to stay close to a rejecting mother. However, now shutting down is in fact shutting out anyone who attempts to be close to the client. The client is ensuring that she will be safe, but so very lonely. Thus, there is a huge cost to clinging to these strategies. Though it will be difficult to change, it is possible, and in fact worthwhile to take the plunge.

Note

1 When talking about secure and insecure attachments, I use the terms coined by developmental psychologists; "dismissing," "preoccupied," and "unresolved." These terms connote states of mind with respect to attachment and speak to the various strategies an individual utilizes when distressed. I have chosen these terms over the terms used by social psychologists, "attachment-related anxiety," "attachment-related avoidance," and "fearful attachment," all of which connote patterns of attachment usually measured by self-report instruments.

Chapter 12

Attachment and therapy

The therapist and intervention

Even more recently, Schore (2019) has talked of another paradigm shift in the study of attachment and psychotherapy. Because of innovations in neurobiological research, the study of brain-to-brain connections has begun. No longer are scientists limited to the study of just one brain; they can now conduct neuroimaging between brains! We now have scientific proof that cerebral signals are not limited to occurring within one discrete brain, but can travel across multiple anatomically separated, but communicating brains (Ray, Roy, Sindhu, Sharon, & Banerjee, 2017). This research lends itself to the notion that we truly are relational creatures, influenced by and influencing others all the time. Therapy therefore involves this interaction, this "I–thou" (Buber, 1958) experience, that often happens outside our awareness. Interactive regulation leads to self-regulation. We are wired to connect and it is through this interactive experience, both in terms of expression and receiving, that change occurs. What does this mean for us as clinicians? If our selves are integral to the change process, how do we use ourselves to facilitate change?

Clinician's stance in therapy from an attachment perspective: facilitating horizontal integration

Surrogate attachment figure

Though Bowlby's work did not lead to a new way of doing therapy, he did have ideas about the role of a therapist in therapy from an attachment perspective. He stated that "The therapist's role is analogous to that of a mother who provides her child with a secure base from which to explore the world" (Bowlby, 1988, p. 140). Bowlby suggested that the therapist can use her relationship with her client to explore a client's internal working models through his transference with the therapist. This continues to be the role assumed by attachment therapists. Like in the caregiver–child dyad, the therapist at first co-regulates with a client and works towards the goal of enabling auto-regulation in order to achieve integration.

Safety

Not much can be accomplished in therapy if a client does not feel safe. Our right brains need to feel safe before our left brains can be engaged. Therefore, a clinician's first aim is to foster safety and security within the therapeutic relationship so that the client can involve the social engagement system (Porges, 2017). Safety occurs during the engagement phase and is psychological as well as physiological. We balance distance with closeness, depending on the needs of the client. Therapeutic distance can be defined as our level of transparency within the therapeutic relationship and involves level of emotional intimacy, intensity, and presence in the here-and-now (Daly and Mallinckrodt, 2009). Thus, our secure presence is conveyed in the moment, both verbally and nonverbally. Our intonations, our facial expressions, our gaze, our gestures, and our body movements should all communicate that we are a secure base for our clients. We are not neutral beings. We are attuned, sensitive and responsive to our client's affects and cues.

Safety with clients with dismissing state of mind

Creating safety for a client with a dismissing attachment strategy involves treading gently and leading with more therapeutic distance than may be needed with other clients. As the client will tend to easily shut down and use deactivating strategies, a clinician must approach him with caution. This is a client who has firm, rigid, inflexible boundaries. He will shy away from connection, for example, needing to sit further away from his therapist. He'll struggle to talk about his feelings and he'll be easily scared off from doing so. He is someone who is used to going it alone and may view attempts to empathize with his struggles as intrusive. Thus, at first, the clinician should be careful not to be effusive. She must convey compassion, but must respect the boundaries a dismissing client puts in place. Only with time can the clinician slowly bring feelings into the room.

Safety with clients with preoccupied state of mind

Creating safety for a client with a preoccupied attachment strategy involves setting fewer boundaries and creating less therapeutic distance at first. This is a client who will feel easily rejected. He is fearful of being on his own, scared that he will disintegrate without the acceptance of others. The clinician must allow the client to join with her, sensitively accepting any overtures the client makes in session. For example, whether the client pulls his chair closer to the therapist or attempts to joke with the therapist, the therapist must make a pointed effort to be warm and welcoming of any and all joining efforts. Only later in the treatment process can the therapist begin to set the boundaries that a preoccupied client needs and in so doing, render the client's hyperactivating strategies unnecessary.

Safety with clients with unresolved state of mind

Creating safety for a client with an unresolved attachment strategy involves conveying acceptance. Using a bottom–up approach is extremely helpful (see later in this chapter). This is a client who either hyperactivated or hypoactivated. He is easily triggered and may be physiologically on edge or physiologically numb. At first, the clinician must tread gently, primarily using techniques to engage the client's bodily sensations. Only once the client feels safe, can any work begin.

Acceptance

Therapy from an attachment perspective involves true acceptance. A therapist strives to create a nonjudgmental environment where a client feels free to express all affect, including those of differing types, ranges, and strengths. Part of acceptance involves encouraging the client to practice self-acceptance. Oftentimes change can only occur if a client has accepted where he is at. We strive to allow acceptance. We communicate that we can tolerate negative as well as positive emotion. In so doing, we give permission to the client to explore troubling old and challenging new emotions.

Attunement

The therapist strives for a state of resonance, or attunement with her clients. Attunement occurs when our nervous systems are synchronized with others. It is a deep emotional connection that is conveyed both explicitly and implicitly, right-brain to right-brain as well as left-brain to left-brain. To create this attunement, therapists are warm and unconditionally accepting, as Carl Rogers (1961) advocated all those years ago. We enable our clients to be heard and to "feel felt" (Siegel, 1999). It feels good physiologically and thus encourages more attunement. This becomes the foundation of a secure attachment bond. Ultimately, connecting in this way leads to a sense of integration.

Empathy

We do our best to experience empathy for our clients. Empathy can be defined as imagining and truly understanding the inner world of another being while, at the same time, maintaining our own objectivity (Cozolino, 2014). We put aside our feelings and place ourselves in the other's shoes. We do this while staying firmly rooted in ourselves. We are able to regulate ourselves and, because we are regulated, we can focus our attention on another. In other words, we don't lose ourselves, but we connect with the other in a meaningful way. A therapist's empathy enables the client to view himself differently. He gains self-compassion as well as the confidence to believe he is worthy of connection. In this way, empathy facilitates the formation of secure attachments.

Co-constructed relationship

The attachment relationship is a fluid and dynamic relationship. It is authentic, where each enters into a real relationship. The therapist is not a blank slate, but a being who engages with another being. The attachment therapeutic relationship is co-constructed (Fogel, 1993) where each individual's affect modifies and is modified by the other, just like within the mother–child dyad.

Clinician's tasks in therapy from an attachment perspective: the "working" phase

Same and different

Bromberg (2006) notes that a therapeutic relationship should feel "safe but not too safe." According to attachment therapists, growth occurs at the boundaries of a client's window of tolerance. Once safety is established, a clinician becomes accepting and empathic, but, at the same time, not too accepting. Too much sameness is unhelpful as is too much difference. An attachment-based therapist encourages a client to step outside of maladaptive, but comfortable zones, providing supportive scaffolding all the while. The clinician oscillates between challenge and support and then support and challenge.

From an attachment perspective, it should be noted that co-regulation does not involve synchronicity, or pure mirroring, alone. Individuals within a dyad alternate between times of complete matching of another's state and times of experiencing complementary or even discordant emotions from the other. Recall (Chapter 5) that Beebe and Lachmann (2002) found that it was optimal for a caregiver–infant interaction to have mid-range vocal coordination, a level that predicted secure attachment. Indeed, scores outside of midrange predicted insecure attachment. As clinicians, we can understand that a mid-range level of coordination is most beneficial to a client's becoming better able to self-regulate. We should not be always in complete synchrony with our clients and neither should we always be misaligned. There should be a balance and we and our clients should flexibly maneuver between interactive and self-regulation in a balanced fashion. Our reflections should be both the same and different, as mentioned in Chapter 10 when discussing the development of mentalization. This is how we engender affect regulation. We accept. And then we challenge (such as speaking to the price the client is paying by using maladaptive strategies) and, immediately, we provide empathic support (such as empathizing with how hard it is to change and how comfortable and familiar the maladaptive coping strategies are). Through this repetitive challenge, a client becomes aware of both the cost of his defensive strategies and also how desperately he has held on to them and has been afraid to change. What was once ego-syntonic will hopefully become ego-dystonic (Stark, 2017). Recognizing this tension is stressful, but a secure attachment with the therapist allows the client to adaptively negotiate this stress. Additionally, change evokes feelings of regret and loss. Throughout the process, the therapist provides support, acceptance, and empathic attunement. Growth occurs through this delicate dyadic dance.

Same and different with clients with dismissing state of mind

A dismissing client will have a narrow, rigid window of tolerance. He tends not to experience a wide range of emotions and, in fact, is easily overwhelmed by most emotions. He often has a preoccupation with self-regulation at the expense of being able to interactively regulate himself. Once safety is established, a clinician validates and then challenges the client's deactivating strategies.

EXAMPLE

Ben had been coming regularly to therapy for two years. In general, he was stoic, hardly smiling. He had few memories of his childhood. He remembered that his mother lay in bed much of the time. He couldn't say why. He also remembered that he often took care of himself and his little brother. He was an average student, trying to go through school unnoticed, figuring it was the easiest way to go. He was college educated and currently, worked in a book-store. After therapy began, Ben decided to take a creative writing course, something he had wanted to do for a while. One day, he came to our session and told me, with no expression on his face, that one of his stories had been accepted into a creative writing journal. I matched his state (the same) and said congratulations without much emotion. I then paused and waited for him to look up from the floor. I pushed a bit further, knowing that he in general felt safe with me. I wondered what he may be feeling at that moment. He said nothing really. I knew it would push him beyond his window of tolerance to say that I was proud of him at that moment, so I gently asked if perhaps he felt proud of himself. He shook his head, indicating he didn't. I then pushed a bit further, all the while taking note of his nonverbal cues. I asked him to imagine feeling proud and fur-ther asked what that might feel like. His bottom lip started to quiver. I kept going, saying that it was an accomplishment, one that others may feel proud of and sug-gested that I could imagine that he at least felt happy for his achievement because I was impressed (different). Ever so slowly, he nodded yes. We sat together with me feeling so proud of him and him tolerating this feeling quietly.

Same and different with clients with preoccupied state of mind

A preoccupied client will have a chaotic but rigid window of tolerance. He tends to be overwhelmed by emotions and has difficulty creating cognitive structures around his experiences. He often excessively monitors others at the expense of his ability to regulate his own affect. Once safety is established, a clinician can challenge his hyperactivating strategies.

EXAMPLE

Jeanine was unhappily married to a man that tried hard to please her. He was not emotional and was "boring." Worse, when she cried, he left her alone and retreated to the bedroom to watch TV. Session after session, she complained that her husband was the worst husband and cried as she spoke of her bad luck in landing up in a lifeless marriage. She often cried in session. As she seemed to feel safe in our relationship, I began to gently confront her. When she cried, I empathized with her, saying how hard it must be to be married to someone who was unresponsive to her. I imagined how lonely she must feel when he watched TV. As I talked, she teared up more. She began to sob. At that point, I knew that I had to help her create structures to the chaos she was feeling. My empathizing with her was in fact overwhelming to her. I started to pull back slightly. I shifted focus, asking her what she was feeling in her body. I asked about her stomach, her heart, and her head. I was drawing her out of her hyperactivating state. Her sobbing had stopped. "I just wish he would be there for me like he was when we were first married." I then shifted her out of her emotional state and asked for her cognitive understanding of why things may have changed. As she talked, I matched her sadness once again, empathizing with her about how sad she felt. By cycling between matching and mismatching, I allowed her to regulate her intense emotions.

Same and different with clients with unresolved state of mind

An unresolved client will be operating outside of his window of tolerance much of the time. He will have no coherent strategy for negotiating stressors. It is not possible to intervene before safety is established and establishing safety may become the sole focus of therapy. Therefore, it is not advisable to intervene or challenge boundaries until the client feels safe.

Attunement, misattunement, and repair

Often, our work as therapists is not only about being the same and different to our clients. It is about negotiating the repair process that follows misattunement. This is akin to a caregiver–child dyad where the repair process is vital to enabling a secure relationship to form. Recall (Chapter 5) that Ed Tronick noted that coordinated states between caregivers and infants only occur between 30% and 50% of the time (Ammaniti, 2018). And this is not a sign of a negative interaction. In fact, it is necessary to have mismatched states so that an infant has space to recover from stimulation. Following this break in attunement though, it is essential that the misattuned state be repaired. As stated before, Tronick and Cohn's (1989) research found that babies are only in "matching" states with their caregivers for a third of the time. Two thirds of the time, babies and caregivers alternate between matched and non-matched states. As long as the mismatch is adequately repaired in a timely fashion, the relationship becomes secure. In the therapeutic relationship, Tronick (2007) argues that "reparation of messiness rather than synchrony might be a key change-inducing process in therapy and development" (p. 14). With every successive and adaptive cycle of attunement, misattunement, and repair, the client gains an increasing capacity to negotiate ruptures. Essentially, the client learns the art of affect regulation. This leads to a client's sense of integration.

Resistance

A break in synchrony can be viewed in many different ways. For instance, the onus of misattunement in the therapeutic relationship can either be ascribed to the client or to the therapist. How it is seen will change the nature of the therapeutic intervention. If the onus is on the client, a break in synchrony may be understood as a client's resistance to change. When this perspective is engaged, a therapist may confront a client's lack of attunement with the therapist. This may have the unintended consequence of further shaming the client. It also doesn't facilitate the much needed repair. If however, the therapist assumes more responsibility for the break and then for the repair, just like in the caregiver–child dyad, shame is experienced in tolerable amounts and the client is scaffolded towards achieving repair.

Example

Cassy began attending therapy to address her difficulties in relationships. She had never had a relationship for longer than two months and she had no explanation as to why this was the case. She would fall rapidly in love but inevitably, her partner would quickly fall rapidly out of love with her. Shortly into her therapy, she met Steve. He was the love of her life, representing everything she had ever wanted in a partner. Soon though, she began reporting that he wasn't returning her phone calls. He stood her up on several occasions. She expressed confusion and a great deal of sadness. A month into our working together, she mistakenly called Steve "Barry." She stuttered, saying I mean Steve, and then was silent for a while. She coughed after about five minutes of silence and then sheepishly acknowledged that actually she had been seeing Steve and Barry at the same time, but hadn't wanted to tell me because she was embarrassed. I suddenly felt angry. I also felt duped. We had been struggling together to figure out why things weren't working out with Steve and all the while, she had been carrying on with another man. Luckily the session ended at that moment and I had time to process how to respond. At the start of the next session, I thanked Cassy for telling me about Barry. I acknowledged her courage at what must have been difficult to expose in therapy and I applauded her strength in being honest about something about which she was ashamed. Cassy's posture softened. She had been bracing herself, almost expecting me to be angry with her. She started talking about her difficulties in staying faithful to her partners. Later, at the end of therapy, we discussed this moment. She relayed that because her honesty had been validated, she felt less shame and more of an ability to expose her vulnerabilities in a fruitful way.

Clinician techniques in therapy from an attachment perspective

Facilitating bottom-up regulation and integration

Focus on breathing

Breath work is a "bottom-up" approach, allowing us to gain control over our bodily sensations. We engage our brainstems in gaining control over our limbic systems and neocortices. When we inhale, our sympathetic nervous systems are stimulated, resulting in an increased heart rate. In contrast, when we exhale, our parasympathetic nervous systems activate and our heart rates decelerate (Van Der Kolk, 2014). By purposefully controlling our breathing, we can influence our level of stimulation, thereby regulating our bodies. Oftentimes, when we are anxious, we breathe shallowly or we hyperventilate. By paying attention to our breath and shifting it, we regulate ourselves.

Focus on bodily sensations

Delving into physiological sensations enables a client to regulate those sensations. Encouraging a client who is dissociating to notice and feel his feet touching the floor is grounding to the client. Asking a client to put his hand on his heart and rest for a moment helps regulate an anxious client. Suggesting a client manipulate his physical sensations by either tensing or relaxing muscles allows the client to modify the underlying feelings he is experiencing (Greenberg & Paivio, 1997).

Evoking feelings in the room

There are several ways a therapist can bring feelings into the room. One way is by facilitating memories of past emotion episodes or previous situations where similar feelings were felt. Using imagery can be a powerful tool as well. Another way is to ask the client to act as if they are feeling a certain way. For instance, suggesting a client smiles and then teasing apart what it feels like to do so. Additionally, a therapist can be provocative, in a safe way. For instance, a client who stifles anger can be pushed to feel this anger.

EXAMPLE

Betty had been coming to therapy for three years, saying every week how she planned to stand up to her parents who controlled her every move. Yet every week, she would go home and repeat her activities from the previous week. At 32 years old, she continued to live at home. She worked at the local super-market, came home at night, checked Facebook and went to sleep. She reported that her parents controlled her finances and became threatening every time she talked of moving out. She had stopped trying to discuss the matter as she was too afraid of the confrontation that may ensue. After empathizing with her plight, which seemed to do nothing more than enable her to pity herself more, I decided to confront her. I suggested she didn't want to move out and I stated that she wanted her parents to take care of her forever. I said something I knew would get a rise. I told her that she was using her parents as an excuse and was letting herself off the hook. The more I talked, the more Betty became red in the face. Now, I thought, our work can begin. Her anger had risen to the surface. By bringing emotions into the room, the therapist and client can elaborate on these feelings. Together, the therapist and client can understand the purpose the emotions are serving. They can allow a cognitive overlay to occur, thus enabling the regulation of these emotions. In this way, they can work towards integration.

Facilitating top-down regulation and integration

Name and tame emotions

Therapy involves naming and re-organizing emotions. Our primary and secondary emotions (as mentioned in Chapter 8) are brought into cognitive awareness. Putting feelings into words allows the client to develop a reflective objectivity to what he is feeling. This enables the neocortex to regulate the limbic system and the brain stem's activities. A clinician oscillates between helping the client expand on his inner experience and reflecting on this inner experience. In this way, a client gains top-down awareness of his emotional experiences.

Mindful awareness

Mindfulness can be seen as the paying attention to and noticing the present moment. It involves being open and accepting and having no judgment or expectations of the moment. It is a form of "top-down" attentional control, where we engage our neocortex in containing our emotional and physiological experiences. We notice the five "building blocks" or our experiences, including our thoughts, our emotions, our perceptions and sensations, our physical move-ments, and our bodily feelings. Mindful practices calm the sympathetic nervous system. Therapists use "directed mindfulness" to focus a client on particular internal experiences. The process itself encourages a client's curiosity about himself. It also helps a client learn to begin to auto-regulate. Essentially, it begins to move the client towards integration (Siegel, 2012; Ogden & Fisher, 2015).

Tracking

A therapist working from an attachment perspective will track and process a client's physical, emotional, and cognitive moment-by-moment experiences. We "stay" with them throughout the process. Clients are asked to expand on their sensations in each of these domains, flexibly cycling between them. Primary emotions are separated from categorical responses. Clients are asked to notice their breathing, their heart rates, and their movements. They talk about their feelings, both negative and positive, and their thoughts are tracked in relation to these feelings. Unpacking physiological sensations, linking them to emotions, and linking emotions to thoughts is regulating to the client. It is also imparting how to self-regulate. It is helping the brain develop new pathways and reinforcing new synaptic connections. Tracking is part of what ultimately leads a client toward integration.

Intensification

A therapist purposefully intensifies an emotion in session by focusing on all physiological sensations and cognitions in order to heighten the experience. For example, Rachel announced that her mother had been abusive. She said it with a smile and then nervously laughed, saying that because she survived the abuse, she could survive anything. She was about to move on to a different topic when her therapist stopped her. He said to her that he noticed that when she talked about something as painful as being abused, she had a smile on her face. He asked her if she noticed this. She started to smile more, appearing uncomfortable. Her therapist pointed out that she was smiling again. Rachel squirmed in her seat and said she was feeling a bit hot and asked if they could open a window. The therapist pressed on, suggesting that Rachel was hot because perhaps she was feeling something that she wasn't comfortable feeling. This continued with Rachel trying to distract and the therapist commenting on Rachel's trying to distract from what she may be feeling. This technique is utilized only when a client feels safe enough to tolerate increased experiencing of an emotion or cognition he may have been avoiding.

Reframing

Reframing can be used in many instances. It is often utilized when confronting maladaptive strategies that are not serving the client well. A therapist can change the meaning given to maladaptive strategies by showing the client that they were adaptive at the time. A rejecting mother would not have handled anger well, so it was critical to the client's survival to suppress his anger. Framing suppression as adaptive removes the shame associated with this coping strategy and enables the client to confront the present strategy that isn't working for him and to begin the process of letting go. Reframing is also used with emotions. Once primary emotions have been accessed, they can be framed as attachment strategies that have been used to protect the individual, but are now no longer helpful. For instance, uncovering the primary emotion of fear that has been covered with secondary anger and then framing the anger as protective can be very helpful to the client. In this case, it is very helpful to the client to understand that his anger had been serving a purpose, but that it is now pushing others away. With this, the client may begin to see that his anger is costing him more than helping him. Reframing it in this way helps the client to begin to let go of his anger and to claim his fear. Then true work can begin.

The termination phase

Attachment theory began with Bowlby's investigations into the effects of loss and separation and in some sense, in a successful course of therapy, this is exactly what termination entails. It is guiding the client through the separation from and the impending loss of an attachment figure. Termination involves managing the dysregulation caused by separation and loss. A client is only ready to manage this loss when he can effectively auto-regulate on his own and can interactively-regulate with others. In other words, when a client can stay within or expertly recalibrate his window of tolerance when he is dysregulated, or when he is able to integrate his mind, body, and emotions, he is ready to terminate therapy.

Termination in attachment therapy involves exploring previous losses as well as the meaning of the current, impending loss. All the while, the therapist sensitively attunes to the client's emotions, allowing both positive and negative feelings into the room. The therapist allows the client to both compliment and voice any criticisms he may have had of the process. During these explorations, the therapist marks differences and highlights the client's individuality, while supporting his free expression. Overall, the therapist conveys to the client that she is confident he can function on her own. She also reassures the client that the "door is always open." In other words, the therapist conveys her willingness to serve as a safe haven in the future should the client ever feel unmanageable distress.

The clinician in therapy

Many years ago, a wise colleague, Rhoda Shralow, said to me "Our clients can only go as far as we've gone." This gave me much pause. While I had always intuitively known that I made an impact on my clients, I often rationalized away my impact, convincing myself that I could hide behind the theories I used. If I conducted therapy that was tried and true and it didn't work, I could relieve myself of responsibility. It was the theory that wasn't working or the client that wasn't "ready" to address his issues. Only that wasn't proving to be the case. I felt enormously responsible for how things went. So much seemed in my hands, that it was me influencing the course of therapy, and not just my theories. The same wise colleague also said that in the end, our clients know us better than most others, even if we don't self-disclose. They know how we feel about values, about emotions, about thoughts and ideas. They see how we dress, how we act, and they intuitively know us. I began to realize that it was undeniable. There can be no doubt that we are in the room. We are not blank slates.

The expectations implied by this notion can be overwhelming. We must be empathic, compassionate, attuned, and well-regulated. Not only must we mentalize for ourselves, but we must guide others in the process. We must be able to think on our feet, have perspective on what our clients are exploring, and be able to think coherently in the moment. Much like a sensitive caregiver must simultaneously regulate herself and co-regulate with her child, so must a therapist interactively regulate with a client while at the same time, auto-regulate. What we avoid will become what our clients avoid. We may unconsciously collude, keeping our unintegrated parts out of the therapy room in a way that keeps our clients from fully integrating. The question becomes just how much does a therapist's attachment style impact the therapeutic process? Does it influence the therapist–client relationship? Do our unresolved issues affect our client's trajectory? And the biggest question of all: Do we all have to be securely attached all of the time to be able to effect change?

Bowlby (1988) proposed that effective therapy depended on the therapist's availability to her client and furthermore, that this availability was inextricably linked with the therapist's past attachment history. In general, research supports that the attachment style of the therapist impacts treatment (Berant & Obegi, 2009). In the 1990s, Mary Dozier and her colleagues (Dozier, Cue, & Barnett, 1994) paved the way for research in this area. They examined the attachment styles of 18 case managers and their clients. They found that secure case managers were better able to therapeutically respond to their clients' needs, while insecure case managers tended to intervene more with preoccupied clients than with dismissing clients. Overall, preoccupied case managers intervened much more than did dismissing case managers. In another study, Rubino and colleagues examined clinical psychology graduate student therapists' responses to conflict with role-played clients displaying preoccupied, dismissing, fearful, and secure attachment styles (Rubino, Barker, Roth, & Fearon, 2000). They found that, overall, the therapists with more anxious attachment styles tended to be less empathically responsive, especially with fearful and secure clients. Another study examined attachment and a therapist's countertransference and found that insecurely attached therapists had more negative countertransference, particularly when working with clients of differing patterns of attachment insecurity. For instance, the researchers noted that preoccupied therapists tended to be hostile, rejecting, and critical when working with dismissing clients, and dismissing therapists tended to exhibit this type of countertransference behavior with preoccupied clients. From an attachment perspective, this can be interpreted as the client having a style of relating that actually challenges the therapist's regulatory strategies. Thus, a preoccupied client may overwhelm a dismissing therapist with his emotional intensity, creating anxiety in the therapist. The therapist may become rejecting due to her own anxiety (Mohr, Gelso, & Hill, 2005).

It seems clear that we play a part in what happens in the therapy room. What if we aren't securely attached? David Wallin (2007) has a comforting answer to this somewhat troubling question. He writes that during the course of therapy, we may inhabit different states of mind with respect to attachment. The categories are not discrete; they are dynamic and change according to context. A clinician can vacillate between secure, preoccupied, dismissing, or unresolved states of mind, depending on what is triggered by the client. As the therapeutic relationship is co-created, so much of what occurs in therapy is because of the interaction between the therapist and client. Thus, when we are in a secure state of mind, we are flexible and free to explore. Recall the qualities of a secure state of mind with respect to attachment mentioned in Chapter 3. We are coherent and have perspective. We can regulate ourselves and at the same time, focus on co-regulating with our client. When operating from a dismissing state of mind, we shut down our own emotional experiences as well as those of our clients. We use deactivating strategies and tend to be rigid, lacking flexibility in our responses to our clients. In this state, we use our left brains, relying more on cognitively focused interventions. This means we are cut off from the emotional content in the room. When operating from a preoccupied state of mind, we are immersed in our emotions, often having difficulty with maintaining our perspective. We may merge with our clients' experiences, losing sight of our boundaries. In this state, we lean on our right-brains. Our limbic system may be reactive and our neocortex may not activate as readily as we need it to. We may feel helpless and unsure of our abilities to help. We are overwhelmed, just like our clients may be. Lastly, we may operate from an unresolved state of mind. When previous losses or traumatic experiences are activated, we can be triggered. We may lapse in the monitoring of our reasoning and then become overly controlling. We may feel flooded, lacking a coherent state of mind, or we may temporarily dissociate. Because we can become rigidly stuck in our own trauma, we may be unable to be present for our clients.

It is worth noting that when therapists operate from insecure attachment states of mind, it is not always a liability for clients. For instance, when we are in a dismissing state of mind, we are better able to set firm boundaries, while when we are in a preoccupied state, we may be able to truly resonate with our clients' experiences. In an unresolved state, we understand the enormous impact of trauma and loss. In fact, research supports that often clients require us to use non-complementary strategies to theirs. In a meta-analysis of therapist–client matching in therapeutic relationships, Bernier and Dozier (2002) concluded that early in treatment, complementarity was critical for engagement, but that as treatment progressed, non-complementarity in attachment styles produced better outcomes. In Dozier's original study, results showed that secure case managers were better able to "read" their clients' needs and responded to underlying needs, while insecure case managers tended to respond to their clients based simply on what their clients said they needed. In other words, secure case managers were able to provide disconfirming experiences that challenged clients and pushed them to grow, while insecure case managers simply gave their clients what they expected. For instance, preoccupied clients expect others to treat them as fragile and needy, and insecure case managers treated them as such, while dismissing clients expect others to be unavailable to them and found that insecure therapists intervened very superficially and in so doing, were not emotionally available. In yet another study, researchers found that dismissing clients had better alliances with case managers who used less deactivating strategies, while clients who were less deactivating had better alliances with case managers who were more deactivating. Non-complementarity in attachment styles was better for the therapeutic relationship (Tyrrell, Dozier, Teague, & Fallot, 1999).

In sum, our insecure states of mind can either be harmful or helpful. In treatment, Bowlby (1988) suggests that intervening flexibly is critical to a successful therapeutic outcome. He recommends initially joining with the client, thereby creating a secure base. Once there is a sense of security, a therapist can challenge a client's maladaptive strategies. In other words, a therapist can use non-complementary strategies to provoke a client to reexamine and adapt his current strategies. Timing is everything. Challenging too soon can alienate a client, while always soothing and agreeing with the client can halt any chance of change. As stated before, co-regulating affect requires us to be the same and different to our clients. We must soothe and challenge, providing the safety and security necessary for our clients to tolerate the challenge. Again, the road to integration is paved with expanding windows of tolerance in a manageable way. The key for us is to maintain flexibility in our responses so that we are sensitively reacting to the changing needs of our clients in the moment. We must maintain awareness of our internal processes, no matter what they are, whether we are operating from a secure or an insecure state of mind. What we feel often gives us information about our clients. We can wonder to ourselves what we may be avoiding, what our clients may need to avoid as well, or what we may be colluding on, or over-involved with. We should be constantly evaluating our objectives and whether they are based on our clients' needs or our own. Additionally, we should examine our motivations. All the while, we must pay attention to our bodies, to what we are feeling physically as well as emotionally. Overall, we need to regulate ourselves so that we can interactively regulate with our clients. To enable our clients to fully integrate, we need to be integrated ourselves.

Epilogue

When I think about it, there have been two other pivotal moments, other than the three mentioned in the prologue, along my journey towards writing this book. Several years ago, I attended a conference where Jude Cassidy spoke. She had been a student of Mary Ainsworth many years before and she concluded the conference with a story about a moment she'd shared with her advisor. Together, they sat on the porch one night. Cassidy asked Ainsworth what she supposed security may look like in a six-year-old. Ainsworth thought for a while and then said "feeling understood." After another pause, she added, "I think that is what security is at any age; feeling understood." I suddenly felt a rush of warmth. It was so simple really. To foster security meant to make someone feel understood. But then the warmth I felt dissipated. Exactly how could I convey to my clients that I understood them? Was it by empathizing with them? Accepting them completely? Resonating with them in the moment? I have realized through the process of writing this book that understanding my clients involves all of the above and something else, something critical. It involves truly listening, and I've realized that this book has been a journey towards understanding how to do so.

The book begins in the here and now, journeys back to the origins of attachment theory and then travels back to the present. To recap, in this day and age, when loneliness prevails, it seems people may be losing the capacity to listen. With digital usage on the rise and the decline of face-to-face social interactions, people are becoming accustomed to being on their own. However, there is a huge cost. As stated in the book's introduction, social isolation and loneliness are hazardous to our physical and psychological health. Attachment theory offers an antidote to this growing problem in Western society. According to the theory and to research that supports it, we are wired to be in relation to and with other human beings.

The "what." John Bowlby founded the theory, expanding it to explain the bond and whether or not it was secure. Mary Ainsworth built on this, observing three different attachment styles in infants during her laboratory Strange Situation that she devised. The classifications were as follows: secure, anxious, and avoidant. Mary Main added a fourth, that of disorganized attachment and with this, researchers had a way to observe, classify, and understand attachment behaviors. In 1985, Main and her colleagues moved the study of attachment from infant behaviors to adults' mental representations when they devised the Adult Attachment Interview. This instrument became a window into individuals' internal working models and with it, researchers and theorists were well on their way to understanding the intricacies of an individual's state of mind with respect to attachment. The social psychologists added more to the field with the study of attachment romantic bonds in adulthood. They also provided researchers with valid and reliable self-report measures that ascertained attachment along two dimensions: attachment-related anxiety and attachment-related avoidance. By this point, there was a large literature on attachment theory, but next to nothing on using this theory in practice.

The "how." The infant attachment researchers began examining the moment-to-moment interactions of an infant with his caregiver. This began the beginnings of understanding how attachment relationships form and how attachment develops over time. The Decade of the Brain in the 1990s added new layers to the "how" of attachment bonds. It became clear that our brains are malleable and that environment plays a part in shaping the development of our brains. In particular, the attachment bond is now seen as influencing our development, both physiologically and psychologically. Attachment patterns and strategies are clearly dynamic, transactional interactions that both influence and are influenced by our relationships. With all the growing research, it was now understood that a secure attachment bond involved the integration of mind, body, and emotion. All played a part.

The "why." As researchers and theorists and then therapists delved further into understanding the attachment bond, it became obvious just how essential this bond is to our well-being. The answer to why it is so critical lies in its role in our learning to regulate ourselves and also to interactively regulate with others. We learn to auto- and co-regulate within the attachment bond. It is a bond that helps us to manage our emotions, our cognitions, and our physiological reactions, in particular in response to stress. Without a safe space, we flounder. We become overwhelmed. And we have trouble remaining within our windows of tolerance. Our overall functioning is affected.

This brings me to my final pivotal moment that led to the writing of this book. A few years ago, I was on a tour of Soweto, in South Africa. The tour guide relayed how members of the Zulu tribe typically used to greet each other. They would say "Sawubona," which literally means "I see you, you are important to me and I value you." People used to respond with "Shiboka," or "I exist for you" (retrieved from https://exploringyourmind.com/sawubona -african-tribe-greeting/). The tour guide continued, saying that in the past, when someone said "Sawubona" to another person, he wanted to hear how that person was, what that person was thinking about, and what the person may have been feeling. It was not a flippant remark. It was an invitation to be heard. "Imagine," he said, "sitting on a park bench and talking for hours. That is what used to happen in the old days." "Now," he shook his head sadly, "no one really wants to hear how another person is. There is no time. We've lost so much. We've stopped feeling like we exist." I felt a cold chill. It was true. Without truly being heard, we cease to exist. I have thought about the notion of Sawubona many times since then. And in writing this book, I now see that attachment theory is a map for clinicians. In knowing it, it allows us to know others. It enables us to truly listen.

References

Ainsworth, M. D. S. (1973). The development of infant–mother attachment. In B. Caldwell & H. Ricciuti (Eds.), *Review of child development research* (Vol. 3). Chicago, IL: University of Chicago Press.

Ainsworth, M. D. S., Blehar, M. C., Waters, E., & Wall, S. (1978). *Patterns of attachment: A psychological study of the strange situation.* Hillsdale, NJ: Lawrence Erlbaum Associates.

Ainsworth, M. S., & Bowlby, J. (1991). An ethological approach to personality development. *American Psychologist*, 46 (4), 333–341.

Allen, J. P. (2008). The attachment system in adolescence. In J. Cassidy & P. R. Shaver (Eds.), *Handbook of attachment, Second edition: Theory, research, and clinical applications* (pp. 419–435). New York: The Guilford Press.

American Psychiatric Association. (2013). *Diagnostic and statistical manual of mental disorders* (5th ed). Washington, DC: Author.

Ammaniti, M. (2018). Implicit knowledge from infancy to the psychotherapeutic relationship: The contribution of Daniel Stern. *Psychoanalytic Inquiry*, 38 (2), 138–147. doi:10.1080/07351690.2018.1405670.

Amodeo, A. L., Vitelli, R., Scandurra, C., Picariello, S., & Valerio, P. (2015). Adult attachment and transgender identity in the Italian context: Clinical implications and suggestions for further research. *International Journal of Transgenderism*, 16, 49–61. doi:10.1080/15532739.2015.1022680.

Anacker, C., O'Donnell, K. J., & Meaney, M. J. (2014). Early life adversity and the epigenetic programming of hypothalamic-pituitary-adrenal function. *Dialogues in Clinical Neuroscience*, 16 (3), 321–333. PMCID: PMC4214175

Anderson, G. O. (2010). Loneliness among older adults: A national survey of adults 45 +. Washington, DC: AARP Research. https://doi.org/10.26419/res.00064.001.

Austrian, S. G., & Mandelbaum, T. (2008). Attachment theory. In S. G. Austrian (Ed.), *Developmental theories through the life cycle* (pp. 365–414). New York: Columbia University Press.

Bakwin, H. (1942). Loneliness in infants. *American Journal of Diseases of Children*, 63 (1), 30–40. doi:10.1001/archpedi.1942.02010010031003.

Banks, A., & Hirschman, L. (2015). *Wired to connect: The surprising link between brain science and strong, healthy relationships.* New York: Penguin Random House.

Barkley, R. A. (2012). *Executive functions: What they are, how they work, and why they evolved.* New York: The Guilford Press.

Bartholomew, K., & Horowitz, L. M. (1991). Attachment styles among young adults: A test of a four-category model. *Journal of Personality and Social Psychology*, 61 (2), 226–244. doi:10.1037/0022-3514.61.2.226.

Baylin, J., & Hughes, D. A. (2016). *The neurobiology of attachment-focused therapy: Enhancing connection & trust in the treatment of children & adolescents*. New York: W. W. Norton.

Beebe, B., & Lachmann, F. M. (2002). *Infant research and adult treatment: Co-constructing interactions*. New York: The Analytic Press.

Beebe, B., & Steele, M. (2013). How does microanalysis of mother-infant communication inform maternal sensitivity and infant attachment? *Attachment & Human Development*, 15 (5–6),583–602. https://doi.org/10.1080/14616734.2013.841050.

Beebe, B., & Stern, D. (1977). Engagement-disengagement and early object experiences. In N. Freedman & S. Grand (Eds.), *Communicative structures and psychic structures* (pp. 35–55). New York: Plenum.

Beisser, A. (1970). The paradoxical theory of change. In J. Fagan, & I. L. Shepherd (Eds.), *Gestalt therapy now* (pp. 77–80). New York: Harper & Row.

Benson, E. (2002). The synaptic self: Without synaptic plasticity, learning- and the self- would be impossible. *Monitor on Psychology*, 33 (10), 40.

Berant, E., & Obegi, J. H. (2009). Attachment-informed psychotherapy research with adults. In J. H. Obegi, & E. Berant (Eds.), *Attachment theory and research in clinical work with adults* (pp. 461–489). New York: Guilford Press.

Bernier, A., & Dozier, M. (2002). The client–counselor match and the corrective emotional experience: Evidence from interpersonal and attachment research. *Psychotherapy: Theory, Research, Practice, Training*, 39 (1), 32–43. doi:10.1037/0033-3204.39.1.32.

Blair, C. (2010). Stress and the development of self-regulation in context. *Child Development Perspectives*, 4 (3), 181–188. http://dx.doi.org/10.1111/j.1750-8606.2010.00145.x.

Bowlby, J. (1944). Forty-four juvenile thieves: Their characters and home-life. *International Journal of Psycho-Analysis*, 25, 19–53.

Bowlby, J. (1951). Maternal Care and Mental Health: A Report Prepared on Behalf of the World Health Organization as a Contribution to the United Nations Programme for the Welfare of Homeless Children. Geneva: WHO.

Bowlby, J. (1953). *Child care and the growth of love*. London: Penguin Books.

Bowlby, J. (1958). The nature of the child's tie to his mother. *International Journal of Psycho-Analysis*, 39, 350–373.

Bowlby, J. (1960a). Separation anxiety. *International Journal of Psycho-Analysis*, 41, 89–113.

Bowlby, J. (1960b). Grief and mourning in infancy and early childhood. *International Journal of Psycho-Analysis*, 15, 9–52.

Bowlby, J. (1961a). Separation anxiety: A critical review of the literature. *International Journal of Psycho-Analysis*, 1, 251–269.

Bowlby, J. (1961b). Processes of mourning. *International Journal of Psycho-Analysis*, 42, 317–340.

Bowlby, J. (1969, 1982). *Attachment and loss: Volume 1: Attachment*. New York: Basic Books.

Bowlby, J. (1973). *Attachment and loss: Volume II: Separation and anger*. New York: Basic Books.

Bowlby, J. (1980). *Attachment and loss: Volume III: Loss, sadness and depression*. New York: Basic Books.

Bowlby, J. (1988). *A secure base*. London: Routledge.

Bradley, S. J. (2000). *Affect regulation and the development of psychopathology*. New York: The Guilford Press.

Brennan, K. A., Clark, C. L., & Shaver, P. R. (1998). Self-report measurement of adult attachment: An integrative overview. In J. A. Simpson & W. S. Rholes (Eds.), *Attachment theory and close relationships* (pp. 46–76). New York: The Guilford Press.

Bretherton, I. (2003). Mary Ainsworth: Insightful observer and courageous theoretician. In G. Kimble & M. Wertheimer (Eds.), *Portraits of pioneers in psychology, Vol. V* (pp. 317–331), Hillsdale, NJ: Lawrence Erlbaum Associates.

British Medical Journal. Editorial (1942). Loneliness in infancy. *British Medical Journal*, 2, 345, September 19.

Bromberg, P. M. (2006). *Awakening the dreamer: Clinical journeys*. Mahwah, NJ: Analytic Press.

Buber, M. (1958). *I and thou*. New York: Charles Scribner's Sons.

Buss, C., Davis, E. P., Shahbaba, B., Pruessner, J.C., Head, K., & Sandman, C. A. (2012). Maternal cortisol over the course of pregnancy and subsequent child amygdala and hippocampus volumes and affective problems. *Proceedings of the National Academy of Sciences of the United States of America*, 109 (20), E1312–E1319. http://dx.doi.org/10.1073/pnas.1201295109.

Cacioppo, J. T., Hughes, M. E., Waite, L. J., Hawkley, L. C., & Thisted, R. A. (2006). Loneliness as a specific risk factor for depressive symptoms: Cross-sectional and longitudinal analyses. *Psychology and Aging*, 21 (1), 140–151. https://doi.org/10.1037/0882-7974.21.1.140.

Cacioppo, S., Capitanio, J. P., & Cacioppo, J. T. (2014). Toward a neurology of loneliness. *Psychological Bulletin*, 140 (6), 1464–1504. https://doi.org/10.1037/a0037618.

Carr, E. M., & Nachman, P. (2017). "Just have fun" – Epilogue: Daniel Stern: Contributions to psychoanalysis and developmental psychology, part I. *Psychoanalytic Inquiry*, 37 (4), 270–273. doi:10.1080/07351690.2017.1299506.

Cassidy, J. (1994). Emotion regulation: Influences of attachment relationships. *Monographs of the Society for Research in Child Development*, 59 (2/3), 228–249. http://dx.doi.org/10.1111/j.1540-5834.1994.tb01287.x.

Certain, L., & Kahn, R. (2002). Prevalence, correlates, and trajectory of television viewing among infants and toddlers. *Pediatrics*, 109 (4), 634–642. https://doi.org/10.1542/peds.109.4.634.

Chan, S., & Debono, M. (2010). Replication of cortisol circadian rhythm: New advances in hydrocortisone replacement therapy. *Therapeutic Advances in Endocrinology and Metabolism*, 1 (3), 129–138. doi:10.1177/2042018810380214.

Coan, J., Schaefer, H., & Davidson, R. J. (2007). Lending a hand: Social regulation of the neural response to threat. *Psychological Science*, 17, 1032–1039. doi:10.1111/j.1467-9280.2006.01832.x.

Coan, J. A. (2016). Toward a neuroscience of attachment. In J. Cassidy & P. R. Shaver (Eds.), *Handbook of attachment: Theory, research, and clinical applications* (pp. 242–272). New York: The Guilford Press.

Compas, B. E., Connor, J. K., Saltzman, H., Thomsen, A. H., & Wadsworth, M. (1999). Getting specific about coping: Effortful and involuntary responses to stress in development. In M. Lewis & D. Ramsay (Eds.), *Soothing and stress* (pp. 229–256). Hillsdale, NJ: Lawrence Erlbaum Associates.

Compas, B. E., Connor, J. K., Saltzman, H., Thomsen, A. H., & Wadsworth, M. E. (2001). Coping with stress during childhood and adolescence: Progress, problems, and potential in theory and research. *Psychological Bulletin*, 127 (1), 87–127. http://dx.doi.org/10.1037//0033-2909.127.1.87.

Coppola, G., Vaughn, B. E., Cassibba, R., & Constantini, A. (2006). The attachment script representation procedure in an Italian sample: Associations with Adult Attachment Interview scales and with maternal sensitivity. *Attachment & Human Development*, 8 (3), 209–219. http://dx.doi.org/10.1080/14616730600856065.

Cozolino, L. (2014). *The neuroscience of human relationships: Attachment and the developing social brain* (2nd ed.). New York: W. W. Norton & Company.

Cozolino, L. (2016). *Why therapy works: Using our minds to change our brains.* New York: W. W. Norton & Company.

Cozolino, L., & Davis, V. (2017). How people change. In M. Solomon & D. J. Siegel (Eds.), *How people change: Relationships and neuroplasticity in psychotherapy* (pp. 53–72). New York: W. W. Norton & Company.

Crowell, J. A., & Hauser, S. T. (2008). AAIs in a high-risk sample: Stability and relation to functioning from adolescence to 39 years. In H. Steele & M. Steele (Eds.), *Clinical applications of the Adult Attachment Interview* (pp. 341–370). New York: The Guilford Press.

Crowell, J. A., Treboux, D., & Waters, E. (2002). Stability of attachment representations: The transition to marriage. *Developmental Psychology*, 38, 467–479. http://dx.doi.org/10.1037/0012-1649.38.4.467.

Crowell, J., & Waters, E. (2005). Attachment representations, secure-base behavior, and the evolution of adult relationships: The Stony Brook Adult Relationship project. In K. E. Grossmann, K. Grossmann, & E. Waters (Eds.), *Attachment from infancy to adulthood: The major longitudinal studies* (pp. 223–244). New York: The Guilford Press.

Daniel, S. I. F. (2015). *Adult attachment patterns in a treatment context: Relationship and narrative.* New York: Routledge.

Darwin, C. (1872). *The expression of the emotions in man and animals.* London: John Murray.

Daly, K. D., & Mallinckrodt, B. (2009). Experienced therapists' approach to psychotherapy for adults with attachment avoidance or attachment anxiety. *Journal of Counseling Psychology*, 56 (4), 549–563. doi:10.1037/a0016695.

De Bellis, M. D. (2001). Developmental traumatology: The psychobiological development of maltreated children and its implications for research, treatment, and policy. *Development and Psychopathology*, 13, 539–564. http://dx.doi.org/10.1017/s0954579401003078.

Diamond, L. M. (2015). The biobehavioral legacy of early attachment relationships for adult emotional and interpersonal functioning. In V. Zayas, & C. Hazan (Eds.), *Bases of adult attachment: Linking brain, mind and behavior* (pp. 79–105). New York: Springer.

Diamond, L. M., & Fagundes, C. P. (2008). Developmental perspectives on links between attachment and affect regulation over the lifespan. In R. V. Kail (Ed.), *Advances in child development and behavior* (Vol. 36, pp. 83–134). San Diego, CA: Elsevier Academic Press.

Dozier, M., Cue, K. L., & Barnett, L. (1994). Clinicians as caregivers: Role of attachment organization in treatment. *Journal of Consulting and Clinical Psychology*, 62 (4), 793–800. doi:10.1037/0022-006X.62.4.793.

Dozier, M., & Kobak, R. R. (1992). Psychophysiology in attachment interviews: Converging evidence for deactivating strategies. *Child Development*, 63 (6), 1473–1480. doi:10.2307/1131569.

Dykas, M. J., Woodhouse, S. S., Cassidy, J., & Waters, H.S. (2006). Narrative assessment of attachment representations: Links between secure base scripts and adolescent attachment. *Attachment and Human Development*, 8 (3), 221–240. http://dx.doi.org/10. 1080/14616730600856099.

Eisenberger, N. I., Master, S. L., Inagaki, T. K., Taylor, S. E., Shirinyan, D., Lieberman, M. D., & Naliboff, B. D. (2011). Attachment figures activate a safety signal-related neural region and reduce pain experience. *National Academy of Sciences*, 108 (28), 11721–11726. doi:10.1073/pnas.1108239108.

Ekman, P. (2003). *Emotions revealed: recognizing faces and feelings to improve communication and emotional life*. New York: St. Martin's Griffin.

Elliot, R., Watson, J. C., Goldman, R. N., & Greenberg, L. S. (2004). *Learning emotion-focused therapy: The process-experiential approach to change*. Washington, DC: American Psychological Association.

Emde, R. N. (1992). Individual meaning and increasing complexity: Contributions of Sigmund Freud and Rene Spitz to developmental psychology, *Developmental Psychology*, 28 (3), 347–359. http://dx.doi.org/10.1037/0012-1649.28.3.347.

Enlow, M. B., Egeland, B., Carlson, E., Blood, E., & Wright, R. J. (2014). Mother–infant attachment and the intergenerational transmission of posttraumatic stress disorder. *Development and Psychopathology*, 26 (1), 41–65. http://dx.doi.org/10.1017/s0954579413000515.

Evans, G. W. (2003). A multimethodological analysis of cumulative risk and allostatic load among rural children. *Developmental Psychology*, 39 (5), 924–933. http://dx.doi.org/10.1037/0012-1649.39.5.924.

Evans, G. W., & Kim, P. (2012). Childhood poverty and young adults' allostatic load: The mediating role of childhood cumulative risk exposure. *Psychological Science*, 23 (9), 979–983. http://dx.doi.org/10.1177/0956797612441218.

Feeney, B. C., & Kirkpatrick, L. A. (1996). Effects of adult attachment and presence of romantic partners on physiological responses to stress. *Journal of Personality and Social Psychology*, 70 (2), 255–270. doi:10.1037/0022-3514.70.2.255.

Feeney, J. A. (2016). Adult romantic attachment: Developments in the study of couple relationships. In J. Cassidy & P. R. Shaver (Eds.), *Handbook of attachment: Theory, research, and clinical applications* (pp. 435–463). New York: The Guilford Press.

Feldman, R., Singer, M., & Zagoory, O. (2010). Touch attenuates infants' physiological reactivity to stress. *Developmental Science*, 13 (2), 271–278. doi:10.1111/j.1467-7687.2009.00890.x.

Field, T. M. (1981). Infant gaze aversion and heart rate during face-to-face interactions. *Infant Behavior and Development* 4, 307–315. https://doi.org/10.1016/s0163-6383(81)80032-x.

Flinn, M. V., & England, B. G. (1995). Childhood stress and family environment. *Current Anthropology*, 36 (5), 854–866. http://dx.doi.org/10.1086/204444.

Fogel, A. (1993). *Developing through relationships: Origins of communication, self, and culture*. Chicago, IL: University of Chicago Press.

Fonagy, P. (2001). *Attachment theory and psychoanalysis*. New York: Other Press.

Fonagy, P., Gergely, G., Jurist, E., & Target, M. (2002). *Affect regulation, mentalization, and the development of the self*. New York: Other Press.

Fonagy, P., Luyten, P., Allison, E., & Campbell, C. (2016). Reconciling psychoanalytic ideas with attachment theory. In J. Cassidy & P. R. Shaver (Eds.), *Handbook of attachment: Theory, research, and clinical applications* (pp. 780–804). New York: The Guilford Press.

Fonagy, P., Steele, H., & Steele, M. (1991). Maternal representations of attachment during pregnancy predict the organization of infant-mother attachment at one year of age. *Child Development*, 62 (5), 891–905. doi:10.2307/1131141.

Fonagy, P., Target, M., Steele, H., & Steele, M. (1998). *Reflective Functioning Manual, Version 5.0, for Application to Adult Attachment Interviews*. London: University College London.

Fosha, D. (2002). The activation of affective change processes in Accelerated Experiential-Dynamic Psychotherapy. In J. J. Magnavita (Ed.), *The comprehensive handbook of psychotherapy. Volume 1: Psychodynamic and object relations psychotherapies* (pp. 309–344). New York: John Wiley & Sons.

Fosha, D. (2009). Emotion and recognition at work: Energy, vitality, pleasure, truth, desire & the emergent phenomenology of transformational experience. In D. Fosha, D. J. Siegel, & M. F. Solomon (Eds.), *The healing power of emotion: Affective neuroscience, development & clinical practice* (pp. 172–203). New York: W. W. Norton & Company.

Fosha, D., Siegel, D. J., & Solomon, M. (2009). Introduction. In D. Fosha, D. J. Siegel, & M. F. Solomon (Eds.), *The healing power of emotion: Affective neuroscience, development & clinical practice* (pp. vii–xiii). New York: W. W. Norton & Company.

Fraley, R. C., & Waller, N. G. (1998). Adult attachment patterns: A test of the typological model. In J. A. Simpson & W. S. Rholes (Eds.), *Attachment theory and close relationships* (pp. 77–114). New York: The Guilford Press.

Fraley, R. C., & Shaver, P. R. (2000). Adult romantic attachment: Theoretical developments, emerging controversies, and unanswered questions. *Review of General Psychology*, 4 (2), 132–154. doi:10.1037/1089-2680.4.2.132.

Gee, D. G., Gabard-Durnam, L., Telzer, E. H., Humphreys, B. G., Shapiro, M., Flannery, J., Lumian, D. S., Fareri, D. S., Caldera, C., & Tottenham, N. (2014). Maternal buffering of human amygdala-prefrontal circuitry during childhood but not adolescence. *Psychological Science*, 25 (11), 2067–2078. https://dx.doi.org/10.1177%2F0956797614550878.

Gentzler, A. L., & Kerns, K. A. (2004). Associations between insecure attachment and sexual experiences. *Personal Relationships*, 11 (2), 249–265. doi:10.1111/j.1475-6811.2004.00081.x.

George, C., & Solomon, J. (2008). The caregiving system: A behavioral systems approach to parenting. In J. Cassidy & P. Shaver (Eds.), *Handbook of attachment: Theory, research, and clinical applications*, 2nd ed. (pp. 833–857). New York: Guilford Press.

Gergely, G. (2007). The social construction of the subjective self: the role of affect-mirroring, markedness, and ostensive communication in self-development. In L. Mayes, P. Fonagy, & M. Target (Eds.), *Developmental science and psychoanalysis: Integration and innovation* (pp. 45–88). London: Karnac Books.

Gergely, G., & Watson, J. S. (1996). The social biofeedback theory of parental affect-mirroring: The development of emotional self-awareness and self-control in infancy. *International Journal of Psychoanalysis*, 77, 1181–1212. https://doi.org/10.4324/9780429471643-7.

Gianino, A., & Tronick, E. Z. (1988). The mutual regulation model: The infant's self and interactive regulation, coping, and defensive capacities. In T. Field, P. McCabe, & N. Schneiderman (Eds.), *Stress and coping* (pp. 47–68). Hillsdale, NJ: Erlbaum.

Gillath, O., Karantzas, G. C., & Fraley, C. (2016). *Adult attachment: A concise introduction to theory and research*. New York: Elsevier.

Gilliom, M., Shaw, D. S., Beck, J. E., Schonberg, M. A., & Lukon, J. L. (2002). Anger regulation in disadvantaged preschool boys: Strategies, antecedents, and the development of self-control. *Developmental Psychology*, 38 (2), 222–235. http://dx.doi.org/10.1037/0012-1649.38.2.222.

Goleman, D. (1995). *Emotional intelligence: Why it can matter more than IQ*. New York: Bantam Books.

Goleman, D. (2006). *Social intelligence: The new science of human relationships*. New York: Bantam Books.

Gopnik, A., & Astington, J. W. (1988). Children's understanding of representational change and its relation to the understanding of false belief and the appearance–reality distinction. *Child Development*, 59 (1), 26–37. doi:10.2307/1130386.

Greenberg, L. (2016). Interview Juliette Becking en Les Greenberg over EFT (J. Becking, Interviewer). Retrieved from https://vimeo.com/157982795/2a8c8b3251.

Greenberg, L. S., & Johnson, S. M. (1988). *Emotionally focused therapy for couples*. New York: The Guilford Press.

Greenberg, L. S., & Paivio, S. C. (1997). *Working with emotions in psychotherapy*. New York: The Guilford Press.

Greenough, W., Black, J., & Wallace, C. (1987). Experience and brain development. *Child Development*, 58, 539–559. doi:10.2307/1130197.

Grice, H. P. (1989). *Studies in the way of words*. MA: Harvard University Press.

Griner, D., & Smith, T. B. (2006). Culturally adapted mental health interventions: A meta-analytic review. *Psychotherapy: Theory, Research, Practice, Training*, 43 (4), 531–548. doi:10.1037/0033-3204.43.4.531.

Groh, A. M., Fearon, R. P., Bakermans-Kranenburg, M. J., van IJzendoorn, M. H., Steele, R. D., & Roisman, G. I. (2014). The significance of attachment security for children's social competence with peers: a meta-analytic study. *Attachment & Human Development*, 16 (2), 103–136. https://doi-org.proxy.brynmawr.edu/10.1080/14616734.2014.883636.

Gross, J. J. (2014). Emotion regulation: Conceptual and empirical foundations. In J. J. Gross (Ed.), *Handbook of emotion regulation* (pp. 3–22). New York: The Guilford Press.

Gross, J. J. (2015). Emotion regulation: Current status and future prospects. *Psychological Inquiry*, 26 (1), 1–26. www.tandfonline.com/action/showCitFormats?doi=10.1080/1047840X.2014.940781.

Grossmann, K., Grossmann, K. E., & Kindler, H. (2005). Early care and the roots of attachment and partnership representations: The Bielefeld and Regensburg longitudinal studies. In K. E. Grossmann, K. Grossmann, & E. Waters (Eds.), *Attachment from infancy to adulthood: The major longitudinal studies* (pp. 98–136). New York: The Guilford Press.

Gump, B. B., Polk, D. E., Kamarck, T. W., & Shiffman, S. M. (2001). Partner interactions are associated with reduced blood pressure in the natural environment: Ambulatory monitoring evidence from a healthy, multiethnic adult sample. *Psychosomatic Medicine*, 63 (3), 423–433. https://psycnet.apa.org/doi/10.1097/00006842-200105000-00011.

Gunnar, M. R., Brodersen, L., Nachmias, M., Buss, K., & Rigatuso, J. (1996). Stress reactivity and attachment security. *Developmental Psychobiology*, 29 (3), 191–204. https://doi.org/10.1002/(SICI)1098-2302(199604)29:3%3C191::AID-DEV1%3E3.0.CO;2-M.

Gunnar, M. R., & Barr, R. G. (1998). Stress, early brain development, and behavior. *Infants and Young Children*, 11 (1): 1–14. http://dx.doi.org/10.1097/00001163-19980 7000-00004.

Gunnar, M., & Quevedo, K. (2007). The neurobiology of stress and development. *Annual Review of Clinical Psychology*, 58, 145–173. http://dx.doi.org/10.1146/a nnurev.psych.58.110405.085605.

Gunnar, M. R., & Vazquez, D. (2006). Stress neurobiology and developmental psycho-pathology. In D. Cicchetti, & D. J. Cohen (Eds.), *Developmental psychopathology, Vol 2: Developmental neuroscience* (2nd ed.) (pp. 533–577). Hoboken, NJ: John Wiley & Sons.

Gyurak, A., & Etkin, A. (2014). A neurobiological model of implicit and explicit emotion regulation. In J. J. Gross (Ed.), *Handbook of emotion regulation* (pp. 76–90). New York: The Guilford Press.

Hane, A. A., & Fox, N. A. (2016). Studying the biology of human attachment. In J. Cassidy & P. R. Shaver (Eds.), *Handbook of attachment: Theory, research, and clinical applications* (pp. 223–241). New York: The Guilford Press.

Harlow, H. F., & Zimmermann, R. R. (1959). Affectional responses in the infant monkey. *Science*, 130, 421–432.

Hazan, C., & Shaver, P. (1987). Romantic love conceptualized as an attachment process. *Journal of Personality and Social Psychology*, 52 (3), 511–524. doi:10.1037//0022-3514.52.3.511.

Hazan, C., & Shaver, P. R. (1994). Attachment as an organizational framework for research on close relationships. *Psychological Inquiry*, 5 (1), 1–22. doi:10.1207/s15327965pli0501_1.

Hesse, E. (1996). Discourse, memory, and the Adult Attachment Interview: A note with emphasis on the emerging cannot classify category. *Infant Mental Health Journal*, 17, 4–11. https://doi.org/10.1002/(SICI)1097-0355(199621)17:1%3C4::AID-IMHJ1%3E3.0.CO;2-S.

Hesse, E. (1999). The Adult Attachment Interview: Historical and current perspectives. In J. Cassidy & P. Shaver (Eds.), *Handbook of attachment: Theory, research, and clinical applications* (pp. 395–433). New York: The Guilford Press.

Hesse, E. (2016). The Adult Attachment Interview: Protocol, method of analysis, and selected empirical studies: 1985–2015. In J. Cassidy & P. R. Shaver (Eds.), *Handbook of attachment: Theory, research, and clinical applications* (pp. 553–597). New York: The Guilford Press.

Hill, D. (2015). *Affect regulation theory: A clinical model.* New York: W. W. Norton & Company.

Hinckley, D. (2014, March 5). Average American watches 5 hours of TV per day. Retrieved from www.nydailynews.com/.

Holt-Lunstad, J., Smith, T. B., & Layton, J. B. (2010). Social relationships and mortality risk: a meta-analytic review. *PLoS Medicine*, 7 (7), e1000316. doi:10.1371/journal.pmed.1000316.

Holt-Lunstad, J., Smith, T. B., Baker, M., Harris, T., & Stephenson, D. (2015). Loneliness and social isolation as risk factors for mortality: A meta-analytic review. *Perspectives on Psychological Science*, 10 (2), 227–237. https://doi.org/10.1177/1745691614568352.

Holt-Lunstad, J. (2018). The potential public health relevance of social isolation and loneliness: Prevalence, epidemiology, and risk factors. *Public Policy & Aging Report*, 27 (4), 127–130. https://doi.org/10.1093/ppar/prx030.

Horowitz, M. J. (1997). *Formulation as a basis for planning psychotherapy treatment.* Washington, DC: American Psychiatric Press.

Hutchison, W. D., Davis, K. D., Lozano, A. M., Tasker, R. R., & Dostrovsky, J. O. (1999). Pain-related neurons in the human cingulate cortex. *Nature Neuroscience*, 2, 403–405. doi:10.1038/8065.

Isaacs, J. B. (2012, March). Starting school at a disadvantage: The school readiness of poor children. Retrieved from www.brookings.edu/~/media/research/files/papers/2012/3/19%20school%20disadvantage%20isaacs/0319_school_disadvantage_isaacs.pdf.

Jaffe, J., Beebe, B., Feldstein, S., Crown, C., Jasnow, M., Rochat, P., & Stern, D. N. (2001). Rhythms of dialogue in early infancy. *Monographs of the society for research in child development*, 66 (2) Serial No. 264, 1–132. https://doi.org/10.1111/1540-5834. 00136.

Jancke, L. (2009). Music drives brain plasticity. *F1000 Biology Reports*, 1 (78), 1–6. http s://dx.doi.org/10.3410%2FB1-78.

Jensen, F. E., & Nutt, A. E. (2015). *The teenage brain: A neuroscientist's survival guide to raising adolescents and young adults*. New York: HarperCollins.

Johnson, S. (2008). *Hold me tight: Seven conversations for a lifetime of love*. New York: Little, Brown & Company.

Johnson, S. (2009). Extravagant emotion: Understanding and transforming love relationships in emotionally focused therapy. In D. Fosha, D. J. Siegel, & M. F. Solomon (Eds.), *The healing power of emotion: Affective neuroscience, development & clinical practice* (pp. 257–279). New York: W. W. Norton & Company.

Johnson, S. M. (2019). *Attachment theory in practice: Emotionally focused therapy (EFT) with individuals, couples, and families*. New York: The Guilford Press.

Johnstone, T., & Walter, H. (2014). The neural basis of emotion dysregulation. In J. J. Gross (Ed.), *Handbook of emotion regulation* (pp. 58–75). New York: The Guilford Press.

Joormann, J., & Siemer, M. (2014). Emotion regulation in mood disorders. In J. J. Gross (Ed.), *Handbook of emotion regulation* (pp. 413–427). New York: The Guilford Press.

Kagan, J. (1984). *The nature of the child*. New York: Basic Books.

Karen, R. (1994). *Becoming attached: First relationships and how they shape our capacity to love*. New York: Oxford University Press.

Klohnen, E. C., & Bera, S. (1998). Behavioral and experiential patterns of avoidantly and securely attached women across adulthood: A 31-year longitudinal perspective. *Journal of Personality and Social Psychology*, 74, 211–223. doi:10.1037/0022-3514.74.1.211.

Kobak, R. R., & Sceery, A. (1988). Attachment in late adolescence: Working models, affect regulation, and representations of self and others. *Child Development*, 59 (1), 135–146. http://dx.doi.org/10.2307/1130395.

Kobak, R. (1999). The emotional dynamics of disruptions in attachment relationships: Implications for theory, research, and clinical intervention. In J. Cassidy, & P. R. Shaver (Eds.), *Handbook of attachment: Theory, research, and clinical applications* (pp. 21–43). New York: Guilford Press.

Kobak, R., Cassidy, J., Lyons-Ruth, K., & Ziv, Y. (2006). Attachment, stress, and psychopathology; A developmental pathways model. In D. Cicchetti, & D. J. Cohen (Eds.), *Developmental psychopathology, Vol 1: Theory and method* (pp. 333–369). Hoboken, NJ: John Wiley & Sons.

Kopp, C. B. (1982). Antecedents of self-regulation: A developmental perspective. *Developmental Psychology*, 18 (2), 199–214. https://doi.org/10.1037/0012-1649.18.2.199.

Kosminsky, P. S., & Jordan, J. R. (2016). *Attachment-informed grief therapy: A clinician's guide to foundations and applications*. New York: Routledge.

Lanius, U. F., Paulsen, S. L., & Corrigan, F. M. (2014). Dissociation: Cortical deafferentation and the loss of self. In U. F. Lanius, S. L. Paulsen, & F. M. Corrigan (Eds.), *Neurobiology and treatment of traumatic dissociation: Towards an embodied self* (pp. 5–28). New York: Springer Publishing Company, LLC.

LeDoux, J. (1996). *The emotional brain: The mysterious underpinnings of emotional life*. New York: Simon & Schuster Paperbacks.

LeDoux, J. (2012). Rethinking the emotional brain. *Neuron*, 73 (4), 653–676. doi:10.1016/j.neuron.2012.02.004.

Levenson, R. W., Haase, C. M., Bloch, L., Holley, S. R., & Seider, B. H. (2014). Emotion regulation in couples. In J. J. Gross (Ed.), *Handbook of emotion regulation* (pp. 267–283). New York: The Guilford Press.

Levine, A., & Heller, R. S. (2011). *Attached: The new science of adult attachment and how it can help you find – and keep – love*. New York: Tarcher/Penguin.

Levine, S. (2005). Developmental determinants of sensitivity and resistance to stress. *Psychoneuroendocrinology*, 30, 939–946. http://dx.doi.org/10.1016/j.psyneuen.2005.03.013.

Li, T., & Chan, D. K. (2012). How anxious and avoidant attachment affect romantic relationship quality differently: A meta-analytic review. *European Journal of Social Psychology*, 42, 406–419. doi:10.1002/ejsp.1842.

Lieberman, M. D., Eisenberger, N. I., Crockett, M. J., Tom, S. M., Pfeifer, J. H., & Way, B. M. (2007). Putting feelings into words: Affect labeling disrupts amygdala activity in response to affective stimuli. *Psychological Science*, 18 (5), 421–428. doi:10.1111/j.1467-9280.2007.01916.x.

Lisitsa, E. (2013, May 13). *The four horsemen: Contempt*. Retrieved from www.gottman.com/blog/the-four-horsemen-contempt/.

Losoya, S., Eisenberg, N., & Fabes, R. A. (1998). Developmental issues in the study of coping. *International Journal of Behavioral Development*, 22 (2), 287–313. http://dx.doi.org/10.1080/016502598384388.

McCroy, E. J., De Brito, S. A., Sebastian, C. L., Mechelli, A., Bird, G., Kelly, P. A., & Viding, E. (2011). Heightened neural reactivity to threat in child victims of family violence. *Current Biology*, 21 (23), R947–R948. http://dx.doi.org/10.1016/j.cub.2011.10.015.

McEwen, B. (2000). Stress, definition and concepts of. In G. Fink (Ed.), *Encyclopedia of stress* (Vol. 3, pp. 508–509). San Diego, CA: Academic Press.

McEwen, B. S., & Seeman, T. (1999). Protective and damaging effects of mediators of stress: Elaborating and testing the concepts of allostasis and allostatic load. *Annals of the New York Academy of Sciences*, 896, 30–47.

McGilchrist, I. (2009). *The master and his emissary: The divided brain and the making of the western world*. New Haven, CT: Yale University Press.

McGowan, P. O., Sasaki, A., D'Alessio, A.C., Dymov, S., Labonte, B., Szyf, M., Turecki, G., & Meaney, M. J. (2009). Epigenetic regulation of the glucocorticoid receptor in human brain associates with childhood abuse. *Nature Neuroscience*, 12 (3), 342–348. http://dx.doi.org/10.1038/nn.2270.

MacLean, PD (1985). Brain evolution relating to family, play, and the separation call. *Archives of General Psychiatry*, 42 (4), 405–417. doi:10.1001/archpsyc.1985.01790270095011.

McPherson, M., Smith-Lovin, L., & Brashears, M. E. (2006). Social isolation in America: Changes in core discussion networks over two decades. *American Sociological Review*, 71, 353–375. doi:10.1177/000312240607100301.

Main, M. (1990). Cross-cultural studies of attachment organization: Recent studies, changing methodologies, and the concept of conditional strategies. *Human Development*, 33, 48–61. doi:1159/000276502.

Main, M. (1991). Metacognitive knowledge, metacognitive monitoring, and singular (coherent) vs. multiple (incoherent) model of attachment: findings and directions for future research. In C. M. Parkes, J. Stevenson-Hinde, & P. Marris (Eds.), *Attachment across the life cycle* (pp. 127–159). New York: Routledge.

Main, M. (1995). Recent studies in attachment: overview, with selected implications for clinical work. In S. Goldberg, R. Muir, & J. Kerr (Eds.), *Attachment Theory: Social, developmental, and clinical perspectives* (pp. 407–474). Hillsdale, NJ: The Analytic Press.

Main, M., & Goldwyn, R. (1998). Adult attachment scoring and classification systems, version 6.3. Unpublished manuscripts, University of California, Berkeley.

Main, M., & Hesse, E. (1990). Parents' unresolved traumatic experiences are related to infant disorganized attachment status: Is frightened and/or frightening parental behavior the linking mechanism? In M. T. Greenberg, D. Cicchetti, & E. M. Cummings (Eds.), *Attachment in the preschool years: Theory, research, and intervention* (pp. 161–182). Chicago, IL: The University of Chicago Press.

Main, M., Hesse, E., & Goldwyn, R. (2008). Studying differences in language usage in recounting attachment history: An introduction to the AAI. In H. Steele & M. Steele (Eds.), *Clinical applications of the Adult Attachment Interview* (pp. 31–68). New York: The Guilford Press.

Main, M., Hesse, E., & Kaplan, N. (2005). Predictability of attachment behavior and representational processes at 1, 6, and 19 years of age: The Berkeley longitudinal study. In K. E. Grossman, K. Grossman, & E. Waters (Eds.), *Attachment from infancy to adulthood: The major longitudinal studies* (pp. 245–304). New York: The Guilford Press.

Main, M., Kaplan, N., & Cassidy, J. (1985). Security in infancy, childhood, and adulthood: A move to the level of representation. *Monographs of the Society for Research in Child Development*, 50 (1/2), 66–104. http://dx.doi.org/10.2307/3333827.

Main, M., & Solomon, J. (1990). Procedures for identifying infants as disorganized/disoriented during the Ainsworth Strange Situation. In M. T. Greenberg, D. Ciccetti, & E. M. Cummings (Eds.), *Attachment in the preschool years: theory, research, and intervention* (pp. 121–160). Chicago, IL: The University of Chicago Press.

Matas, L., Arend, R. A., & Sroufe, L. A. (1978). Continuity of adaptation in the second year: The relationship between quality of attachment and later competence. *Child Development*, 49 (3), 547–556. doi:10.2307/1128221.

Matthews, G. A., Nieh, E. H., Vander Weele, C. M., Halbert, S. A., Pradhan, R. V., Yosafat, A. S., Glober, G. F., Izadmeher, E. M., Thomas, R. E., Lacy, G. D., Wildes, C. P., Ungless, M. A., & Tye, K. M. (2016). Dorsal raphe dopamine neurons represent the experience of social isolation. *Cell*, 164, 617–631. http://dx.doi.org/10.1016/j.cell.2015.12.040.

Mesman, J., Van IJzendoorn, M. H., & Sagi-Schwartz, A. (2016). Cross-cultural patterns of attachment: Universal and contextual dimensions. In J. Cassidy & P. R. Shaver (Eds.), *Handbook of attachment: Theory, research, and clinical applications* (pp. 852–877). New York: The Guilford Press.

Meyer, C. H. (1993). *Assessment in social work practice.* New York: Columbia University Press.

Mikulincer, M., & Florian, V. (1997). Are emotional and instrumental supportive interactions beneficial in times of stress? The impact of attachment style. *Anxiety, Stress and Coping: An International Journal*, 10 (2), 109–127. doi:10.1080/10615809708249297.

Mikulincer, M., & Florian, V. (1998). The relationship between adult attachment styles and emotional and cognitive reactions to stressful events. In J. A. Simpson & W. S. Rholes (Eds.), *Attachment theory and close relationships* (pp. 143–165). New York: The Guilford Press.

Mikulincer, M., & Shaver, P. R. (2007). *Attachment in adulthood: Structure, dynamics, and change.* New York: The Guilford Press.

Mikulincer, M., Shaver, P. R., Bar-On, N., & Ein-Dor, T. (2010). The pushes and pulls of close relationships: Attachment insecurities and relational ambivalence. *Journal of Personality and Social Psychology*, 98 (3), 450–468. https://doi.org/10.1037/a0017366.

Mikulincer, M., Shaver, P. R., & Berant, E. (2013). An attachment perspective on therapeutic processes and outcomes. *Journal of Personality*, 1–11. http://dx.doi.org/10.1111/j.1467-6494.2012.00806.x.

Mohr, J. J., Selterman, D., & Fassinger, R. E. (2013). Romantic attachment and relationship functioning in same-sex couples. *Journal of Counseling Psychology*, 60 (1), 72–82. https://doi.org/10.1037/a0030994.

Mohr, J. J., Gelso, C. J., & Hill, C. E. (2005). Client and counselor trainee attachment as predictors of session evaluation and countertransference behavior in first counseling sessions. *Journal of Counseling Psychology*, 52 (3), 298–309. doi:10.1037/0022-0167.52.3.298.

Moutsiana, C., Johnstone, T., Murray, L., Fearon, P., Cooper, P. J., Pliatsikas, C., Goodyer, I., & Halligan, S. (2015). Insecure attachment during infancy predicts greater amygdala volumes in early adulthood. *Journal of Child Psychology and Psychiatry and Allied Disciplines*, 56 (5), 540–548. doi:10.1111/jcpp.12317.

Nachmias, M., Gunnar, M., Mangelsdorf, S., Parritz, R. H., & Buss, K. (1996). Behavioral inhibition and stress reactivity: The moderating role of attachment security. *Child Development*, 67, 508–522. http://dx.doi.org/10.1111/j.1467-8624.1996.tb01748.x.

Nummenmaa, L., Glerean, E., Hari, R., & Hietanen, J. K. (2014). Bodily maps of emotions. *Proceedings of the National Academy of Sciences of the United States of America*, 111 (2), 646–651. https://dx.doi.org/10.1073%2Fpnas.1321664111.

Oitz, M. S., van Haarst, A. D., & de Kloet, E. R. (1997). Behavioral and neuroendocrine responses controlled by the concerted action of central mineralocorticoid (MRS) and glucocorticoid receptors (GRS). *Psychoneuroendocrinology*, 22 (Supplement 1), S87–S93. doi:10.1016/S0306-4530(97)00020-6.

Ogden, P. (2009). Emotion, mindfulness, and movement: Expanding the regulatory boundaries of the window of affect tolerance. In D. Fosha, D. J. Siegel, & M. F. Solomon (Eds.), *The healing power of emotion: Affective neuroscience, development & clinical practice* (pp. 204–231). New York: W. W. Norton & Company.

Ogden, P., & Fisher, J. (2015). *Sensorimotor psychotherapy: Interventions for trauma and attachment*. New York: W. W. Norton & Company.

Ogden, P., Minton, K., & Pain, C. (2006). *Trauma and the body: A sensorimotor approach to psychotherapy*. New York: W. W. Norton & Company.

Panksepp, J., & Biven, L. (2012). *The archeology of mind: Neuroevolutionary origins of human emotions*. New York: W. W. Norton & Company.

Pietromonaco, P. R., & Barrett, L. F. (1997). Working models of attachment and daily social interactions. *Journal of Personality and Social Psychology*, 73, 1409–1423. doi:10.1037/0022-3514.73.6.1409.

Porges, S. W. (1998). Love: An emergent property of the mammalian autonomic nervous system. *Psychoneuroendocrinology*, 23 (8), 837–861. https://doi.org/10.1016/S0306-4530(98)00057-00052.

Porges, S. W. (2017). *The pocket guide to the Polyvagal Theory: The transformative power of feeling safe*. New York: W. W. Norton & Company.

Pressman, S. D., Cohen, S., Barkin, A., Miller, G. E., Rabin, B. S., & Treanor, J. J. (2005). Loneliness, social network size, and immune response to influenza vaccination in college freshmen. *Health Psychology*, 24 (3), 297–306. https://doi.org/10.1037/0278-6133.24.3.297.

Proudfit, G. H., Dunning, J. P., Foti, D., & Weinberg, A. (2014). Temporal dynamics of emotion regulation. In J. J. Gross (Ed.), *Handbook of emotion regulation* (pp. 43–57). New York: The Guilford Press.

Putnam, R. D. (2000). *Bowling alone.* New York: Simon & Schuster.

Quirin, M., Gillath, O., Pruessner, J. C., & Eggert, L. D. (2010). Adult attachment insecurity and hippocampal cell density. *Social Cognitive and Affective Neuroscience,* 5, 39–47. doi:10.1093/scan/nsp042.

Ray, D., Roy, D., Sindhu, B., Sharan, P., & Banerjee, A. (2017). Neural substrate of group mental health: Insights from multi-brain reference frame in functional neuroimaging. *Frontiers in Psychology,* 8, 1–13. doi:10.3389/fpsyg.2017.01627.

Reeves, R. V., Venator, J., & Howard, K. (2014, October 22). The character factor: Measures and impact of drive and prudence. Retrieved from www.brookings.edu/~/media/research/files/papers/2014/10/22-character-factor-opportunity-reeves/the-character-factor.pdf

Rizzolatti, G., & Craighero, L. (2004). The mirror-neuron system. *Annual Review of Neuroscience,* 27, 169–192. doi:10.1146/annurev.neuro.27.070203.144230.

Rizzolatti, G., & Sinigaglia, C. (2006). *Mirrors in the brain: How our minds share actions and emotions.* New York: Oxford University Press.

Robertson, J. (1953). *A two-year-old goes to hospital* [Film]. University Park, PA: Penn State Audio Visual Services.

Robertson, J., & Robertson, J. (1971). Young children in brief separation: a fresh look. *Psychoanalytic Study of the Child,* 26, 264–315. https://doi.org/10.1080/00797308.1971.11822274.

Rogers, C. (1961). *On becoming a person.* Boston, MA: Houghton Mifflin.

Roisman, G. I., Holland, A., Fortuna, K., Fraley, R. C., Clausell, E., & Clarke, A. (2007). The Adult Attachment Interview and self-reports of attachment style: An empirical rapprochement. *Journal of Personality and Social Psychology,* 92 (4), 678–697. http://dx.doi.org/10.1037/0022-3514.92.4.678.

Roisman, G. I., Tsai, J. L., & Kuan-Hiong, S. C. (2004). The emotional integration of childhood experience: physiological, facial expressive, and self-reported emotional response during the Adult Attachment Interview. *Developmental Psychology,* 40 (5), 776–789. doi:10.1037/0012-1649.40.5.776.

Rubino, G., Barker, C., Roth, T., & Fearon, P. (2000). Therapist empathy and depth of interpretation in response to potential alliance ruptures: The role of therapist and patient attachment styles. *Psychotherapy Research,* 10 (4), 408–420. https://doi-org.proxy.brynmawr.edu/10.1093/ptr/10.4.408.

Sander, L. W. (1962). Issues in early mother–child interaction. *Journal of the American Academy of Child Psychiatry,* 1, 141–166. https://doi-org.proxy.brynmawr.edu/10.1016/S0002-7138(09)60013-3.

Sander, L. (1975). Infant and caretaking environment. In E. J. Anthony (Ed.), *Explorations in child psychiatry* (pp. 129–165). New York: Plenum Press.

Sander, L. W. (2000). Where are we going in the field of infant mental health? *Infant Mental Health Journal,* 21 (1–2), 5–20. https://doi.org/10.1002/(sici)1097-0355(200001/04)21:1/2%3C5::aid-imhj2%3E3.0.co;2-s.

Sapolsky, R. M. (2004). *Why zebras don't get ulcers: The acclaimed guide to stress, stress-related diseases, and coping,* 3rd ed. New York: St. Martin's Griffin.

Schore, A. N. (1994). *Affect regulation and the origin of the self: The neurobiology of emotional development.* Hillsdale, NJ: Lawrence Erlbaum Associates.

Schore, A. N. (2003). *Affect dysregulation & disorders of the self*. New York: W. W. Norton & Company.

Schore, A. N. (2009). Right-brain affect regulation: An essential mechanism of development, trauma, dissociation, and psychotherapy. In D. Fosha, D. J. Siegel, & M. F. Solomon (Eds.), *The healing power of emotion: Affective neuroscience, development & clinical practice* (pp. 112–144). New York: W. W. Norton & Company.

Schore, A. (2014, July–September). Integration: An interview with Dr. Allan Schore. Retrieved from www.allanschore.com/pdf/Neuropsychotherapist-6.pdf.

Schore, A. N. (2019). *Right brain psychotherapy*. New York: W. W. Norton & Company.

Schore, J. R., & Schore, A. N. (2008). Modern attachment theory: the central role of affect regulation in development and treatment. *Clinical Social Work Journal*, 36 (1), 9–20. http://dx.doi.org/10.1007/s10615-007-0111-7.

Scott, J. C., Matt, G. E., Wrocklage, K. M., Crnich, C., Jordan, J., Southwick, S. M., Krystal, J. H., & Schweinsburg, B. C. (2015). A quantitative meta-analysis of neurocognitive functioning in posttraumatic stress disorder. *Psychological Bulletin*, 141 (1), 105–140. http://dx.doi.org/10.1037/a0038039.

Seltzer, L. J., Ziegler, T. E., & Pollak, S. D. (2010). Social vocalizations can release oxytocin in humans. *Proceedings of the Royal Society: Series B. Biological Sciences*, 277, 2661–2666. doi:10.1098/rspb.2010.0567.

Shaver, P. R., Belsky, J., & Brennan, K. A. (2000). The Adult Attachment Interview and self-reports of romantic attachment: Associations across domains and methods. *Personal Relationships*, 7, 25–43. https://doi.org/10.1111/j.1475-6811.2000.tb00002.x.

Shaver, P. R., & Mikulincer, M. (2002). Attachment-related psychodynamics. *Attachment & Human Development*, 4 (2), 133–161. http://dx.doi.org/10.1080/14616730210154171.

Shaver, P. R., & Mikulincer, M. (2009). An overview of adult attachment theory. In J. H. Obegi, & E. Berant (Eds.) *Attachment theory and research in clinical work with adults* (pp. 17–45). New York: Guilford Press.

Shaver, P. R., & Mikulincer, M. (2014). Adult attachment and emotion regulation. In J. J. Gross (Ed.), *Handbook of emotion regulation* (pp. 237–250). New York: Guilford Press.

Sherman, L. E., Michikyan, M., & Greenfield, P. M. (2013). The effects of text, audio, video, and in-person communication on bonding between friends. *Cyberpsychology: Journal of Psychosocial Research on Cyberspace*, 7 (2), article 3. http://dx.doi.org/10.5817/CP2013-2-3.

Siegel, D. J. (1999). *The developing mind: Toward a neurobiology of interpersonal experience*. New York: Guilford Press.

Siegel, D. J. (2003). An interpersonal neurobiology of psychotherapy: The developing mind and the resolution of trauma. In M. F. Solomon, & D. J. Siegel (Eds.) *Healing trauma: Attachment, mind, body, and brain* (pp. 1–56). New York: W. W. Norton & Company.

Siegel, D. J. (2010a). *The mindful therapist: A clinician's guide to mindsight and neural integration*. New York: W. W. Norton & Company.

Siegel, D. J. (2010b). *Mindsight: The new science of personal transformation*. New York: Bantam Books.

Siegel, D. J. (2012). *Pocket guide to interpersonal neurobiology*. New York: W. W. Norton & Company.

Siegel, D. J., & Bryson, T. P. (2012). *The whole-brain child: 12 revolutionary strategies to nurture your child's developing mind*. Brunswick, Vic.: Scribe Publications.

Slade, A. (2002). Keeping the baby in mind: a critical factor in perinatal mental health. *Special Issue on Perinatal Mental Health*, Eds. A. Slade, L. Mayes, & N. Epperson, Zero To Three, June/July 2002, pp. 10–16.

Slade, A. (2004). The move from categories to process: Attachment phenomena and clinical evaluation. *Infant Mental Health Journal*, 25 (4), 269–283. doi:10.1002/imhj.20005.

Slade, A. (2005). Parental reflective functioning: An introduction. *Attachment & Human Development*, 7 (3), 269–281. https://doi.org/10.1080/14616730500245906.

Slade, A. (2016). Attachment and adult psychotherapy: Theory, research, and practice. In J. Cassidy, & P. R. Shaver (Eds.), *Handbook of attachment: Theory, research, and clinical applications* (pp. 759–779). New York: The Guilford Press.

Slade, A., Aber, J. L., Bresgi, I., Berger, B., & Kaplan (2004). *The Parent Development Interview-Revised*. Unpublished protocol. The City University of New York.

Slade, A., Grienenberger, J., Bernbach, E., Levy, D., & Locker, A. (2005). Maternal reflective functioning, attachment, and the transmission gap: A preliminary study. *Attachment & Human Development*, 7 (3), 283–298. www.tandfonline.com/action/showCitFormats?doi=10.1080/14616730500245880.

Spangler, G., & Grossman, K. E. (1993). Biobehavioral organization in securely and insecurely attached infants. *Child Development*, 64 (5), 1439–1450. http://dx.doi.org/10.1111/j.1467-8624.1993.tb02962.x.

Spitz, R. A. (1945). Hospitalism: An inquiry into the genesis of psychiatric conditions in early childhood. *The Psychoanalytic Study of the Child*, 1, 53–74. https://doi.org/10.1080/00797308.1945.11823126.

Spitz, R. A. (1946). Hospitalism: A follow-up report. *The Psychoanalytic Study of the Child*, II, 113–118. https://doi.org/10.1080/00797308.1946.11823540.

Sroufe, L. A. (1989). Relationships, self, and individual adaptation. In A. J. Sameroff & R. N. Emde (Eds.), *Relationship disturbances in early childhood: A developmental approach* (pp. 70–94). New York: Basic Books.

Sroufe, L. A. (1996). *Emotional development: The organization of emotional life in the early years*. New York: Cambridge University Press.

Sroufe, L. A. (2000). Early relationships and the development of children. *Infant Mental Health Journal*, 21 (1–2),67–74. https://doi.org/10.1002/(SICI)1097-0355(200001/04)21:1/2%3C67::AID-IMHJ8%3E3.0.CO;2-2.

Sroufe, L. A. (2005). Attachment and development: A prospective, longitudinal study from birth to adulthood. *Attachment & Human Development*, 7 (4), 349–367. https://doi.org/10.1080/14616730500365928.

Sroufe, L. A. (2016). The place of attachment in development. In J. Cassidy & P. R. Shaver (Eds.), *Handbook of attachment: Theory, research, and clinical applications* (pp. 997–1011). New York: The Guilford Press.

Sroufe, L. A., Coffino, B., & Carlson, E. A. (2010). Conceptualizing the role of early experience: Lessons from the Minnesota longitudinal study. *Developmental Review*, 30, 36–51. doi:10.1016/j.dr.2009.12.002.

Sroufe, L.A., Egeland, B., Carlson, E. A., & Collins, W. A. (2005a). *The development of the person: The Minnesota study of risk and adaptation from birth to adulthood*. New York: The Guilford Press.

Sroufe, L. A., Egeland, B., Carlson, E., & Collins, W. A. (2005b). Placing early attachment experiences in developmental context: The Minnesota Longitudinal Study. In

K. E. Grossmann, K. Grossmann, & E. Waters (Eds.), *Attachment from infancy to adulthood: The major longitudinal studies* (pp. 48–70). New York: The Guilford Press.

Sroufe, L. A., & Waters, E. (1977). Attachment as an organizational construct. *Child Development*, 48 (4), 1184–1199. http://dx.doi.org/10.1111/j.1467-8624.1977.tb03922.x.

Stark, M. (2017). The therapeutic use of optimal stress: Precipitating disruption to trigger recovery. In M. Solomon & D. J. Siegel (Eds.), *How people change: Relationships and neuroplasticity in psychotherapy* (pp. 185–219). New York: W. W. Norton & Company.

Steele, H., & Steele, M. (2008). Ten clinical uses of the Adult Attachment Interview. In H. Steele & M. Steele (Eds.), *Clinical applications of the Adult Attachment Interview* (pp. 3–30). New York: The Guilford Press.

Steele, H., Steele, M., & Fonagy, P. (1996). Associations among attachment classifications of mothers, fathers, and their infants. *Child Development*, 67, 541–555. https://doi-org.proxy.brynmawr.edu/10.1111/j.1467-8624.1996.tb01750.x.

Steele, R. D., Waters, T. E. A., Bost, K. K., Vaughn, B. E., Truitt, W., Waters, H. S., Booth-LaForce, C., & Roisman, G. I. (2014). Caregiving antecedents of secure base script knowledge: A comparative analysis of young adult attachment representations. *Developmental Psychology*, 50 (11), 2526–2538. http://dx.doi.org/10.1037/a0037992.

Stern, D. N. (1985). *The interpersonal world of the infant: A view from psychoanalysis and developmental psychology*. New York: Basic Books.

Stern, D. N. (2000). *The interpersonal world of the infant: A view from psychoanalysis and developmental psychology* (6th ed.). New York: Basic Books.

Suchman, N. E., Decoste, C., McMahon, T. J., Rousaville, B., & Mayes, L. (2011). The mothers and toddlers program, an attachment-based parenting intervention for substance-using women: Results at 6-week follow-up in a randomized clinical pilot. *Infant Mental Health Journal*, 32 (4), 427–449. https://doi-org.proxy.brynmawr.edu/10.1002/imhj.20303.

Taylor, J. B. (2006). *My stroke of insight: A brain scientist's personal journey*. New York: Viking.

Thompson, R. A. (2016). Early attachment and later development: Reframing the questions. In J. Cassidy & P. R. Shaver (Eds.), *Handbook of attachment: Theory, research, and clinical applications* (pp. 330–348). New York: The Guilford Press.

Tomkins, S. S. (1962). *Affect, imagery, consciousness: Vol. I. The positive affects*. New York: Springer.

Tottenham, N. (2012). Human amygdala development in the absence of species-expected caregiving. *Developmental Psychobiology*, 54 (6), 598–611. https://DOI-org.proxy.brynmawr.edu/10.1002/dev.20531.

Tottenham, N. (2014). The importance of early experiences for neuro-affective development. *Current Topics in Behavioral Neuroscience*, 16, 109–129. doi:10.1007/978-3-642-54913-7.

Tough, P. (2012). *How children succeed: Grit, curiosity, and the hidden power of character*. New York: Houghton Mifflin Harcourt.

Tromholt, M. (2016). The Facebook experiment: Quitting Facebook leads to higher levels of well-being. *Cyberpsychology, Behavior, and Social Networking*, 19 (11), 661–666. doi:10.1089/cyber.2016.0259.

Tronick, E. Z. (1989). Emotions and emotional communication in infants. *American Psychologist*, 44 (2), 112–119. doi:10.1037/0003-066X.44.2.112.

Tronick, E. (2007). *The neurobehavioral and social-emotional development of infants and children.* New York: W. W. Norton & Company.

Tronick, E. Z., & Cohn, J. F. (1989). Infant–mother face-to-face interaction: Age and gender differences in coordination and the occurrence of miscoordination. *Child Development,* 60 (1), 85–92. doi:10.2307/1131074.

Twenge, J. M. (2017). *iGen: Why today's super-connected kids are growing up less rebellious, more tolerant, less happy – and completely unprepared for adulthood.* New York: Atria books.

Tyrrell, C. L., Dozier, M., Teague, G. B., & Fallot, R. D. (1999). Effective treatment relationships for persons with serious psychiatric disorders: The importance of attachment states of mind. *Journal of Consulting and Clinical Psychology,* 67, 725–733. doi:10.1037/0022-006X.67.5.725.

Ulrich-Lai, Y. M., & Herman, J. P. (2009). Neural regulation of endocrine and automatic stress responses. *Nature Reviews Neuroscience,* 10, 397–409. http://dx.doi.org/10.1038/nrn2647.

Umberson, D., & Montez, J. K. (2010). Social relationships and health: A flashpoint for health policy. *Journal of Health and Social Behavior,* 51 (Suppl): S54–S66. https://dx.doi.org/10.1177%2F0022146510383501.

Van der Horst, F. C. P., & Van der Veer, R. (2008). Loneliness in infancy: Harry Harlow, John Bowlby, and issues of separation. *Integrative Psychological and Behavioral Science,* 42 (4), 325–335. http://dx.doi.org/10.1007/s12124-008-9071-x.

Van der Kolk, B. A. (2003). Posttraumatic stress disorder and the nature of trauma. In M. F. Solomon, & D. J. Siegel (Eds.) *Healing trauma: Attachment, mind, body, and brain* (pp. 168–195). New York: W. W. Norton & Company.

Van der Kolk, B. (2014). *The body keeps the score: Brain, mind, and body in the healing of trauma.* New York: Penguin Books.

Van Dijken, S. (1998). *John Bowlby: His early life.* New York: Free Association Books.

Van IJzendoorn, M. H. (1995). Adult attachment representations, parental responsiveness, and infant attachment: A meta-analysis on the predictive validity of the Adult Attachment Interview. *Psychological Bulletin,* 117, 387–403. http://dx.doi.org/10.1037/0033-2909.117.3.387.

Van IJzendoorn, M. H., & Bakermans-Kranenburg, M. J. (2008). The distribution of adult attachment representations in clinical groups: A meta-analytic search for patterns of attachment in 105 AAI studies. In H. Steele & M. Steele (Eds.), *Clinical applications of the Adult Attachment Interview* (pp. 69–96). New York: Guilford Press.

Van IJzendoorn, M. H., & Bakersmans-Kranenburg, M. J. (2019). Bridges across the intergenerational transmission of attachment gap. *Current Opinion in Psychology,* 25, 31–36. https://doi-org.proxy.brynmawr.edu/10.1016/j.copsyc.2018.02.014.

Vaughn, B. E., & Bost, K. K. (2016). Attachment and temperament as intersecting developmental products and interacting developmental contexts throughout infancy and childhood. In J. Cassidy & P. R. Shaver (Eds.), *Handbook of attachment: Theory, research, and clinical applications* (pp. 202–222). New York: The Guilford Press.

Verhage, M. L., Schuengel, C., Madigan, S., Fearson, R. M. P., Oosterman, M., Cassibba, R., Bakermans-Kranenburg, M. J., & Ijzendoorn, M. H. (2016). Narrowing the transmission gap: A synthesis of three decades of research on intergenerational transmission of attachment. *Psychological Bulletin,* 142 (4), 337–366. http://dx.doi.org/10.1037/bul0000038.

Volkow, N. D. (February, 26, 2010). *A decade after the decade of the brain.* The Dana Foundation. Retrieved from http://dana.org/Cerebrum/2010/A_Decade_after_The_Decade_of_the_Brain__Compilation/.

Walker, E. F., Walder, D. J., & Reynolds, R. (2001). Developmental changes in cortisol secretion in normal and at-risk youth. *Development and Psychopathology*, 13, 721–732. http://dx.doi.org/10.1017/s0954579401003169.

Wallin, D. (2007). *Attachment in psychotherapy.* New York: The Guilford Press.

Wang, C. C. D. C., & Mallinckrodt, B. S. (2006). Differences between Taiwanese and U.S. cultural beliefs about ideal adult attachment. *Journal of Counseling Psychology*, 53, 192–204. doi:10.1037/0022-0167.53.2.192.

Waters, H. S., & Rodrigues-Doolabh, L. (2001, April). *Are attachment scripts the building blocks of attachment representations? Narrative assessment of representations and the AAI.* In H. Waters & E. Waters (Chairs), Narrative measures of attachment for adults. Poster symposium presented at the Biennial Meetings of the Society for Research in Child Development, Minneapolis, MN.

Waters, E. (1978). The reliability and stability of individual differences in infant–mother attachment. *Child Development*, 49 (2), 483–494. doi:10.2307/1128714.

Waters, H. S., & Waters, E. (2006). The attachment working models concept: Among other things, we build script-like representations of secure base experiences. *Attachment and Human Development*, 8 (3), 185–197. http://dx.doi.org/10.1080/14616730600856016.

Waters, E., Weinfield, N. S., & Hamilton, C. E. (2000). The stability of attachment security from infancy to adolescence and early adulthood: General discussion. *Child Development*, 71 (3), 703–706. https://doi.org/10.1111/1467-8624.00179.

Way, B. M., Taylor, S. E., & Eisenberger, N. I. (2009). Variation in the μ-opioid receptor gene (OPRM1) is associated with dispositional and neural sensitivity to social rejection. *Proceedings of the National Academy of Sciences, USA*, 106, 15079–15084. https://doi-org.proxy.brynmawr.edu/10.1073/pnas.0812612106.

Weaver, I. C. G., Cervoni, N., Champagne, F. A., D'Alessio, A. C., Sharma, S., Seckl, J. R., Dymov, S., Szyf, M., & Meaney, M. J. (2004). Epigenetic programming by maternal behavior. *Nature Neuroscience*, 7 (8), 847–854. doi:10.1038/nn1276.

Wei, M., Russell, D. W., Mallinckrodt, B., & Vogel, D. L. (2007). The Experiences in Close Relationship Scale (ECR)-Short form: Reliability, validity and factor structure. *Journal of Personality Assessment*, 88 (2), 187–204. http://dx.doi.org/10.1080/00223890701268041.

Wei, M., Russell, D. W., Mallinckrodt, B., & Zakalik, R. A. (2004). Cultural equivalence of adult attachment across four ethnic groups: Factor structure, structured means, and associations with negative mood. *Journal of Counseling Psychology*, 51 (4), 408–417. http://dx.doi.org/10.1037/0022-0167.51.4.408.

Index

Figures are indexed with italic page numbers

anterior cingulate 90–1, 96, 100
anxiety 3, 13, 49, 56, 99, 105, 122, 125,
  130, 136, 138–9, 141, 145, 189, 208;
  cognitive 148; decreased 139; disorders
  188–9; feelings 137; high 50; low 50;
  maternal 72
apoptosis 83–4, 105
arousal 69, 71, 86, 103, 111, 120, 135,
  139, 145, 150, 152–4; dampening 69;
  elevated 154; emotional 139, 150, 154;
  infant's level of 71–2, 76; levels of 36,
  71, 73–4, 114, 117, 135–6, 150–2,
  186; negative 136; physiological 87,
  110, 135; sympathetic 111
Asian Americans 185
ASQ see Attachment Style Questionnaire
assessments 23, 46, 183–4, 188, 190–1
attached children 22–4, 30, 140, 164
attached individuals 53, 56–7, 59–61, 106,
  110, 154, 164
attachment 49, 51, 96, 185; anxious 51,
  58, 96, 185, 189–90, 216; avoidance
  96, 185, 189–90; behaviors 4, 14–15,
  18, 21, 25, 211; child's 163; clinicians
  154; communication signal 15;
  decreasing overt 66; development of 4,
  12, 25–6, 63–77; disorganized 182;
  dyad 75, 95, 122–3, 139; early 227–8;
  and emotions 4, 116–33; fearful 51, 60,
  189; feelings 35, 43; human 220; infant
  214, 217, 229; infant-mother 21, 28,
  49; insecurity 70, 186, 188–90, 207;
  measuring 4, 53; organizations 16,
  30–1, 176; patterns of 7; perspective 4,
  42, 175, 177, 182–4, 191–4, 196,
  198–9, 203, 205, 207; processes 48–9,
  53, 186; related anxiety 49–51, 57–62,
  211; representations 25, 29–30, 51–2,
  84, 161; research 63, 184–5; researchers
  75, 97, 99, 161, 185; schemas 84,
  95–6, 149; state of mind 161, 192–3,
  208; system 13–14, 18, 20–1, 50, 53–4,
  56, 61, 65, 75, 97, 107, 111, 139–40,
  143, 188–9; and temperament 186;
  theorists 19, 53, 63, 79, 95, 147, 149,
  157, 163, 176, 178, 183, 186, 188;
  therapists 154, 196, 199; and therapy
  174–94, 196–209; therapy 177, 206;
  unresolved 182; value 34–5
attachment bonds 12, 14, 16, 63, 65;
  formed by infants 184; primary 149;

secure 15, 106, 110, 113, 115, 149,
  198, 211
attachment classifications 41, 139, 160, 184;
  caregiver's 41; disorganized 165; parent's
  child's 41; predicted 24; results 70
attachment figures 12–15, 20–1, 37–40,
  49, 52–3, 78, 89, 97–8, 106–9, 122–3,
  126, 133, 139–40, 143, 159; availability
  of 29, 46, 106; secure 113
attachment histories 4, 25, 53, 184;
  insecure 24; known 22; recounting
  223; therapist's past 207
attachment patterns 4, 25, 27, 41, 53–4,
  61, 96–7, 194; adult 51, 53, 216, 218;
  ambivalent 160; anxious 142; child's
  160, 163; insecure 107, 110, 188, 192;
  and strategies 211
attachment-related avoidance 49–51,
  56–7, 60–1, 211; dimension 50, 61;
  downplaying 50, 62; increased 50, 61
attachment-related questions 30
attachment relationships 25–6, 34, 36–7,
  52, 95–7, 99, 108–10, 122, 124,
  126–7, 134–5, 146, 148–50, 165, 175;
  first 146; forming of 211; influencing
  our ability to regulate what we feel
  135; insecure 187; secure 24, 125, 151,
  164–5, 167, 173, 182, 188
attachment security 23, 26–7, 76, 108,
  161, 173, 180, 184, 186–9, 193; early
  24; impacted 25; and insecurity 16, 184
attachment strategies 51, 61, 139, 184,
  188, 192, 194, 206; client's 183;
  individual's 184; primary 140–1;
  secondary 19, 107, 140
Attachment Style Questionnaire 49
attachment styles 18, 43, 51–4, 75, 98,
  186–7, 191, 207, 210; adult 50;
  disorganized 113; endorsed 49; general
  54; insecure 188; measuring 21; non-
  complementarity 208–9; romantic 49
attachment theory 3–17, 21–2, 26, 28, 65,
  77, 80–1, 83, 95, 97, 113, 116, 134–5,
  175–7, 210–12; incorporated 129, 132;
  modern 80, 100, 135, 139, 146, 149,
  151; origins of 17, 210; study of 18
attachments 32, 42, 63, 160; adult 28,
  50–1, 53; secure 16, 54, 70, 108–9,
  123, 149, 151, 168, 198–9
attunement 69–71, 74, 76–7, 79–80, 113,
  154, 168, 191, 198, 201–2; breaks in